P9-DUJ-934

DATE DUE

DEMCO 38-296

The Fruits of Integration

The Fruits of Integration

Black Middle-Class Ideology and Culture,

1960–1990

CHARLES T. BANNER-HALEY

UNIVERSITY PRESS OF MISSISSIPPI

Jackson

Copyright © 1994 by the University Press of Mississippi
All rights reserved
Manufactured in the United States of America

97 96 95 94   4 3 2 1

The paper in this book meets the guidelines for permanence and durability of the
Committee on Production Guidelines for Book Longevity of the Council on Library
Resources.

Library of Congress Cataloging-in-Publication Data

Banner-Haley, Charles Pete T., 1948–
    The fruits of integration : Black middle class ideology and
culture, 1960–1990 / Charles T. Banner-Haley.
        p.   cm.
    Includes bibliographical references and index.
    ISBN 0-87805-647-5. — ISBN 0-87805-648-3 (paper)
    1. Afro-Americans.   2. Middle classes—United States.   3. Afro-
Americans—Intellectual life.   4. Afro-Americans—Civil rights.
I. Title.
E185.615.B285   1994
305.5′5′08996073—dc20   93-30870
                                                                CIP

British Library Cataloging-in-Publication Data available

Dedicated to

A. P.,

R. W., C. K., D. W., J. B., J. L., and C. R. G.

The Talented Tenth of the Negro race must be made leaders of thought and missionaries of culture among their people.

W. E. B. Du Bois (1903)

Contents

PREFACE AND ACKNOWLEDGMENTS

This book was conceived in 1985. How a book is born—where the initial idea comes from—is a mystery I have yet to resolve. In a sense, this book is an extension into the present of a previous study, undertaken as a dissertation project, on African Americans in Philadelphia's middle class during the Depression. However, in many ways the present book arose out simply of a keen desire to explore the revolutionary changes that have taken place within AfroAmerica over the last thirty years. Black America has gone from Jim Crow segregation in the South and near invisibility nationwide to securing civil rights and voting rights—thereby demolishing the most overt features of segregation—and then visibly and proudly producing some of the best cultural contributions that this country has ever seen.

Furthermore, within AfroAmerica there has been an expansion of the middle class. This class not only aided in attaining the civil rights now enjoyed by all African Americans but has also been in the forefront of enlarging the discourse on what America should be. That is to say, the black middle class has grown large enough so that the diversity of AfroAmerica can be seen and heard as it has never been before. That makes for some exciting prospects, as well as some tense ones. The excitement comes from the vitality and richness that newer voices, seldom heard by the nation at large, bring to the question of what America is. The tension arises from two directions. If the black middle class now boasts more members than ever before, they have also increasingly become detached from their sisters and brothers in the inner cities. Concomitant with this is growing concern over identity. Who is authentically black? Those who are immiserated in poverty, victimized by a social system that seems to have relegated them to a perilous existence fraught with crime, drugs, and death at an early age? Or are the authentic voices those who have "gotten over," those who have made it successfully through the system and, while still conscious of their heritage, are more concerned that their families remain secure—that their children get a good education and grow up to be happy, healthy, and proudly black?

The debate over such issues within AfroAmerica continues, and doubtless will preoccupy artists, intellectuals, and students—not to mention ordinary black folks—well into the next century. For if anything can be said about AfroAmerica with certainty it is that black people in America are going through a growing phase that will, as has happened at least several times before in the nation's history, illuminate and enrich the social, political, and cultural landscape. This book is meant as a contribution to that growth and to the ongoing discussion of where America is going. My conviction that integrative cultural diversity exists both within and without AfroAmerica ultimately rests on the perception that the expansion of the black middle class—along with the achievement of civil rights and voting rights—reflects a clear and enduring revolutionary alteration in the social fabric of the nation. As America moves into the twenty-first century there will no doubt be racial tensions. But those tensions will be addressed—indeed, will have to be addressed—on a level of discourse that understands the complexity that integration and cultural diversity have brought to the experiences of black and whites in this society.

Needless to say, this book is by no means the final word on the subject of either the black middle class or the inclusion of new voices in the dialogue over where AfroAmerica is heading. Rather, it should be seen as an historian's attempt to understand the growth, progression, and impact of the expanded black middle class over a thirty-year period. In the end, my hope is that others—particularly students, who will soon become our next leaders—will lend their voices to this discourse, whether through scholarly studies, teaching, or simply conversations with friends and loved ones.

As is the case with any scholarly enterprise, numerous intellectual debts have been incurred. My intellectual debts are particularly deep because I have always assumed a very close fit between scholarship and teaching. Many of the ideas in this book have thus been tried out both on colleagues at various conferences and symposia and on captive audiences of students. As a result, I have not only gotten ample

feedback but my own education has been greatly enhanced. Therefore, I begin with those to whom I am deeply grateful for their help
and faith in what I am about: to students, friends, and colleagues at
SUNY—Cortland in the early to mid-eighties go many thanks. (Portions of chapters 3 and 4 were first delivered as part of a lecture series
entitled "America in the Eighties: A New Agenda.") My thanks to
Ronald Butchart, a good friend, colleague, and comrade, for many
spirited discussions on affirmative action over the last twenty years.
Likewise to John Marciano, not only for some serious conversations
but also for sharing his cottage in Wellfleet, Massachusetts, the summer this book had its genesis. Without the time spent there, I doubt
that this book would have gotten off the ground. Steve Soiffer and
Deborah Pointer also provided comments and encouragement; my
thanks to them.

My students have played a crucial role by reading, commenting on,
and generally supporting my endeavor. Many have gone on to exciting careers in teaching and will certainly have an important impact on
historical studies in the next century. Special thanks and warm appreciation go to Earl Lewis, Eric Tuveson, Christine Remy, Carolyn
Purcell, Kimberley Rhoads, Dayna Wagner, Jamal Swinton, Elizabeth Michel, Karin Raye, Vicki Chun, Jennifer Jopp, Christine Cook,
Simone Nelms, Andres Vasquez, Trinh Dinh, Hans Ottinot, Portia
Cupid, Tracy Frey, Andrew Busser, Jennifer Winkel, Dawn Hamilton, and Kimberley Konrad.

Many thanks must also go to the Frederick Douglass Institute for
African and African American Studies at the University of Rochester.
My tenure there as a postdoctoral fellow in 1986–87 was both intellectually stimulating and extremely enjoyable. Under the direction of
Karen Fields, the atmosphere was one that many scholars can only
yearn for: intelligent people to exchange ideas with, the opportunity
to present one's work in colloquia, and that most precious require-
ment: quiet space to read, reflect, and write. My thanks, therefore, to
Karen Fields for making sure that was the case; to Charlotte Henry,
possibly the world's most indispensable secretary; to Frank "Paco"
Batista for his friendship and gracious hospitality; and to my colleagues at the institute that year, Bosah Ebo, Sang Pang, and Tiffany
Patterson, for their stimulating conversations. Finally, I extend my
deep appreciation to Christopher Lasch, who opened up his depart-

ment's colloquium series so that I could present a portion of this study. That occasion provided for some wonderful exchanges and enabled me to make some needed revisions to my ideas.

I completed this study while in Atlanta, where, as assistant editor on the Martin Luther King, Jr., papers project, I realized that I had to rethink several sections of the manuscript in light of the importance of the southern factor to AfroAmerica. While in Atlanta I built up many debts to people who were genuinely interested in my work, and I also made some deep friendships that will affect me for the rest of my life. Thus, many thanks and warm feelings to Kristie Clements, Carmen Renee Gillespie, John Merriman, Dayna Wagner, and Jon Byrd. Thanks must also go to Clayborne Carson, who as senior editor of the papers project is making a solid contribution to enlightening the nation about the African American experience. Likewise, I extend my gratitude to his staff at Stanford University, especially Pete Halloran and Penny Russell. Working with all these people during my visit in February 1989 was a wonderful and rewarding experience.

Finally, my time in Atlanta cannot go without mention of a close friend, Rick Weaver. Though not a scholar, he nonetheless guided me through the "New South" of the eighties and early nineties as only a southern gentleman can. From him—as with all the others with whom I had close contact with in Atlanta, in particular the many fine people at the Martin Luther King, Jr., Center for Nonviolent Social Change—I learned once again how immensely important the South is to the nation as a whole. Indeed, I saw sincere efforts at integration at work and was stunned by how much has changed since I lived in the South in the early sixties.

My academic debts, some of which have already been mentioned, are extensive. Colleagues have read portions of the manuscript and have given me both words of encouragement and incisive criticism. My thanks go to Larry Greene, Louis Ferleger (who invited me to speak at the Trotter Institute at the University of Massachusetts, Boston), and Robert Paquette, for his insight on this and other projects I am presently engaged in. And my deep thanks to Julius Lester for reading chapter 5 and saving me from some egregious errors.

Possibly my biggest single academic debt, however, is to Eugene D. Genovese and Elizabeth Fox-Genovese. Gene read the entire manuscript with the fine historical eye that has made him one of the premier historians in the nation. Frankly, this book would never had appeared were it not for his serious criticisms and honest concern that I might have totally misread the temper of the times. Betsey was more than generous in listening to my ideas, which may at times have seemed incomprehensible. But she also steered me away from some paths that might have sunk this work. To both of them my deepest appreciation—and absolution from any errors that remain.

That, of course, goes for all who have stood by me on this project. In particular has been the abiding faith and encouragement of associate director Seetha Srinivasan of the University Press of Mississippi. She has been more than patient as I toiled on this manuscript through ups and downs. Pamela MacFarland Holway was a splendid editor who saved me from committing some brutal atrocities on the English language and enabled me to make the book much stronger.

Finally, my family has been most helpful over the course of this project. My sister Shelley, who is engaged in a study of black middle class women, provided valuable insights into the ways in which gender plays an increasingly crucial role in the discourse of the post–civil rights era black middle class. Likewise, I thank my sister Joan for her candid discussions on how to raise emotionally healthy black children in these admittedly difficult (if exciting) times. My brother, Keith, who lives in Tampa, continues to make me acutely aware of the tensions that can come from living in a multicultural world where various racial and ethnic groups struggle for predominance rather than peaceful coexistence. My two aunts, Constance and Gladys, have shown me what historical continuity really means within the context of black history. And last, but certainly not least, the woman who has shared my life, Denise, gets special thanks for putting up with the roller coaster ride that I have put her through. She has been patient, loving, and a friend.

I believe that writing history is a collective enterprise. But in the end the historian alone is responsible for the resulting interpretation. I accept that responsibility.

This book is dedicated to Al Poole, teacher, friend, and mentor, as well as to those who hold a special place in my being.

INTRODUCTION

The Ambiguity of Nomenclature

In 1988, shortly after the presidential election of George Bush, the Reverend Jesse Jackson met with a group of black leaders and heads of various social agencies to set an agenda for AfroAmerica for the coming century. When the meeting was over, the one thing that had received the most attention in the media (and this attention was certainly not discouraged by the conference participants) was the pronouncement that from now on black people would be termed *African Americans*.[1] For those who had been involved in the civil rights–black power movements, however—who had witnessed the struggle to get the nation to change the term from *Negro* to *Black*—the focus on nomenclature was nothing new, nor was the choice of the new term surprising. After all, the designations *Afro-American* and *African American* had been in wide use among black intellectuals, radical black nationalists, and their white followers in academia and literary circles for almost ten years.[2] What was significant about the decision to use the designation was the debate it raised over rationales. On the one hand, no one could really object to the term *African American*, since most black people could, at least in theory, trace their ancestry to Africa. On the other hand, there was the historical necessity for accuracy. It could be argued that, in point of fact, most black Americans probably could not trace their heritage any further than a bill of sale from one slaveowner to another. This is not to deny their Africanness, but it did underscore the troubling question of precisely where in Africa one's origins lay. In the seventeenth and eighteenth centuries, of course, most Africans forcibly brought to the Western hemisphere did remember their original homeland. But as time passed and slaves intermarried and/or were traded around, their knowledge of their homeland receded. Even more important, as black Americans adapted to the dominant society's values and political

economy—as they became an indigenous group—their sense of identification with Africa and its history diminished.[3] In a land whose
institutions and culture were permeated by an ideology of black inferiority and white superiority, the early struggles of slaves to defend
themselves, demand their freedom, and ultimately to seek inclusion
into the American polity further removed them from any conscious
identification with Africa.[4]

Nonetheless, black people did move in a collective fashion to name
themselves. In the early period of this country's settlement, free black
people referred to themselves as "Free African." In many instances,
the word *African* figured prominently in the names of churches or
social organizations, such as the African Methodist Episcopal Church
or the African Society of Brotherhood. During the eighteenth and
nineteenth centuries, whites often referred to blacks by their particular African ethnic group or country (Mandike, Angolan, Ibo, Sene-
gambian, and so forth) or, later in the nineteenth century, simply as
Africans. That whites used such appellations did not necessarily
mean, of course, that they were positively disposed toward blacks.
Slaveowners, for example, often held to complex racialist theories
about which "tribes" were best suited to what labor or stood the best
chance of surviving disease, harsh climates, and poor living conditions. Indeed, given the negative feelings that most whites harbored
about the African continent and their deep racism toward blacks, it
was no wonder that over time many black Americans shied away from
having the word *Afro* associated with themselves.[5] There was also a
good deal of racial mixing during and after the period of slavery, so
much so that the word *black* did not seem an appropriate name, on
top of which it was a term of derision often used by whites against
blacks. Hence, within AfroAmerica the term *colored* gained wide
currency.

By the turn of the century, the most commonly used terms in
AfroAmerica were *colored* and *Negro*. Black writers generally capitalized "Negro"; most whites did not. (Indeed, the struggle to have
the word capitalized, led by W. E. B. Du Bois, lasted until well into
the forties.) The twenties and thirties found the young blacks of the
Harlem Renaissance again searching for a name by which to know
themselves. The so-called New Negro showed a willingness to accept
Africanness, even though the mass of black people may have been

reticent about using "Afro" or "African" as a part of their identification. Thus Countee Cullen wrote of the "African," as did Langston
Hughes, while George Schuyler, in his leftist days, tried to get black
people to call themselves "Aframericans." Marcus Garvey's black nationalism was widely popular among the black masses and may have
encouraged a positive view of Africa for black people, although his
followers called themselves "Garveyites" not African Americans.

When the civil rights movement peaked in the mid-sixties, the long
accepted terms *colored* and *Negro* came under harsh criticism from
young blacks. Given that one of the catch phrases of the sixties was
"identity crisis," the renewed focus on nomenclature is hardly surprising. Under the influence of Malcolm X and a growing consciousness
of the newly won independence of the colonial African nations,
young blacks were discovering the richness of African history. These
young black radicals were trying to make connections between their
plight as an oppressed people in America and the plight of those who
were oppressed in South Africa (and in South Vietnam). Many of
them supported the use of the term *Afro-American*, inasmuch as it
underscored their African heritage as well as their identity as Americans. Others preferred to call themselves "Black" (later altered to
"black," which parallels "white") on the grounds that this was an
assertion of racial pride in the face of white power. It mattered little to
most Afro-Americans that they were not really black; what mattered
was that whites held the power to define who they were. The use of a
color designation, of course, served as well to call attention to the
problems of skin color and the racial polarization of the society. But it
did not openly address the systemic issues of class or gender.

By the mid-seventies, the term *Afro-American* had begun to be
widely used, while those adhering to a Pan-Africanist perspective
began using African American. The issue of naming reasserted itself
in the late eighties as the call for recognition of America as a multicultural society swept the nation.[6] By the late eighties, the tide was
turning in favor of *African American*, although there was some debate
over whether to hyphenate the term. This debate hinged on a subtle
distinction of ideological emphasis. By using the hyphenated form
African-American, as Jesse Jackson and Ramona Edlin began to do,
one is saying that black Americans are an ethnic group like so many
other ethnic groups, whereas the unhyphenated form places more

emphasis on the place of origin.[7] Ultimately, though, African American was deemed the name by which all blacks should call and know themselves. This in turn raised the question not only of whether the masses of blacks would accept the term but also of what it said about the state of AfroAmerica, black middle class ideology, and Afro-American culture.

This book attempts to examine the evolution and influence of a particular segment of AfroAmerica, the educated middle class. The black middle class, or the black bourgeoisie, has been an important force in AfroAmerica, both for good and for ill. Negatively, the black middle class has often served as a buffer between the black masses and white society in return for being allowed some entrance into mainstream American society. Positively, it has provided many fine examples of political leadership and guidance, and has worked to disseminate the cultural ideas of AfroAmerica. Of course, in any discussion of "class" there are bound to be sharp disagreements along ideological and/or disciplinary lines. In the twentieth century our notions of class have grown far more complicated than those of the traditional (though at times useful) Marxist paradigm. The definition of class used in this book is basically that of the social historian Edward Pessen, in his admirably concise and helpful essay "Status and Social Class in America." Class is seen not merely as economic and social but as political and ideological as well. The members of a given class have a particular way of viewing the world, given the material resources at hand and the historical conditions past and present. Moreover, from America's founding onward, race has been intertwined with class. It thus becomes crucial to seek fresh ways of understanding how the various Afro-American classes have emerged, behaved, and changed over time.[8]

In the eighties, within the expanded black middle class that was a legacy of the sixties and seventies, there has been a confusion of purpose and vision even as there has been a revitalization of African American cultural endeavors. The fruits of integration have been at once sweet and bitter. This book tries to examine why that is so. Throughout this book run two unifying threads. The first concerns the influence of the black middle class ideologically and culturally on the way that African Americans are perceived and presented to the larger American society. The second concerns the ongoing struggle of

African Americans to define themselves and their attendant vision of what America is and is becoming, a struggle that it has often fallen to the black middle class to mediate.[9]

The first chapter attempts a general characterization of the black middle class and how it has moved to prescribe solutions and ameliorate the condition of Afro-Americans. Given the greatly enlarged and diversified black middle class of today, it is often hard to realize that it still acts as a reflector and shaper of what is transpiring in Afro-America. That is to say that the modern black middle class continues to share the "twoness" or double consciousness that Du Bois so perceptively wrote about in connection with the early-twentieth-century black middle class. Indeed, where once the veil of segregation had rendered most of AfroAmerica invisible, integration has pulled that veil away, revealing a highly energetic culture, a separate "nation," as it were. This nation continues to struggle not only for the eradication of racism and the social acceptance of African-descended people as full American citizens but also for the preservation of their heritage, their "Africanness," which almost inevitably entails a redefining of what that heritage means in relation to being an American.

At the beginning of the twentieth century, Du Bois made the prescient statement in *The Souls of Black Folks* (1903) that the problem of the twentieth century would be one of "the color line." Now as AfroAmerica and America move rapidly toward the twenty-first century, there are intense, even rancorous, discussions within the community over whether integration has worked or failed, over the issue of Afrocentricity and questions of self-esteem, and over the merits of racial essentialism. In all of these arenas of debate the most fervent intellectual activity appears to originate in the expanded black middle class.

The black middle class has gone from being a small but committed group, which fought for racial justice and civil rights, to a much larger group currently grappling with the effects of integration and increased professionalization, and with new issues of racial identity. Both the nationalist undercurrent within that class and the white perception of Afro-Americans have been transformed since the successful passage of the Civil Rights Acts of 1964 and 1965. Among African Americans, that transformation has created a revived interest in racial identity and creative expressions of black culture that in many respects has had a positive impact on the professions, business, and the political world. White Americans have slowly become more aware of the vital part that African Americans have played and continue to play in the American experience. Chapter 2 looks at the struggle for civil rights and the key role of the black middle class in moving America to redress a century of legal discrimination and cultural racism.

But despite undeniable progress in race relations, the "color line" continues to haunt America and AfroAmerica. The increase in white supremacist activities and violence against blacks in the late eighties provided firsthand evidence that racism, far from having been rooted out of the society, is still very much alive. The resurgence of racially motivated attacks against blacks began during the Carter administration and heightened during the Reagan years. To make matters worse, the tone of the presidential leadership in the eighties seemed to encourage the idea that white resentment of black achievements through affirmative action and in politics was both reasonable and worthy of legal sanction. The confusion this neoracist stance produced in the black middle class was exacerbated by anxiety over the deteriorating prospects for young people, many of whose lives were being destroyed by drugs, lack of jobs, crime, and homelessness.

In addition, Islam was quickly gaining widespread currency among those newly arrived in the black middle class. But there was a danger here, as the embrace of the Moslem faith and values often went hand in hand with a potentially rabid fanaticism. The anti-Semitic exhortations of Louis Farrakhan (of the black nationalist and Shiite Nation of Islam) led to clashes with the nonracial Sunni groups headed by Warith D. Muhammad and Farid Muhammad.[10] The search for stability and strong moral values that the growing interest in Islam reflected was in keeping with the generally conservative temperament of the nation in the eighties. But at the same time, the embrace of fundamentalist religions or groups reflected the anger and fear of black Americans over the regressive treatment meted out to Afro-America during the Reagan years.

Furthermore, the black middle class leadership and black liberal intellectuals found themselves in a similar bind ideologically as their white counterparts: their ideas of the welfare state and of a government that would intervene to protect the less fortunate had not only grown stale but were deemed unworkable in an economy that was contracting. During the eighties, the United States, once the world's richest nation, became the world's largest debtor nation. Within that nation there were steadily widening disparities between the poor and the wealthy, and the middle class was increasingly being charged with the burden of paying off an enormous deficit.

The prescriptions put forth by black neoconservatives in response to this situation often amounted to an anachronistic call for self-help remedies. Indeed, the so-called neoconservatives often sounded more like the civil rights workers of the early sixties in their talk of a "color-blind" society and equity based on merit and character—and these particular intellectuals may have been misnamed, if only because their particular prescriptions owed more to liberal integrationism than to the hard-line, racially biased conservatism that has often permeated the far right. Black intellectuals more to the left also seemed trapped in the past, echoing the earlier New Deal liberals who downplayed racial matters and called for a restructuring of the economic system. (Very few blacks, however, called for the emergence of a socialist state, which may have been reflective of *perestroika* in the Soviet Union and, later, the collapse and dismantling of socialist societies in Eastern Europe.)[11] Chapter 3 explores the "conservative" cast of mind with an eye not only to raising questions about affirmative action and the viability of voices of dissent but also to demonstrating how the expanded black middle class has enriched the cultural diversity within AfroAmerica.

The remaining chapters of this book look at the continuing struggle of the black middle class to give shape and meaning to Afro-America's attempts to make America a humane and comfortable society in which to live. More than anywhere else, I would argue, this struggle is being carried out in the cultural realm. Through literature, music, motion pictures, and television, the black middle class has tried, in a variety of ways, to further the interests of African Americans. But it has not always been clear how best to do so, and the ensuing debates have raised critical question about racial and cultural identity. The black middle class (along with most white Americans) has traditionally been most comfortable with creative endeavors that seek to present positive images of AfroAmerica. But many creative artists have argued for a more honest and open approach, one that would not shrink from acknowledging the very real problems that exist both within AfroAmerica and the nation at large but would do so in a manner that preserves racial pride. There is, moreover, the issue of how to retain one's cultural identity in a world where artistic success is usually decided by the values of the mainstream, white society.

At their best, African American artists have presented a vision of integrated cultural diversity, a concept explored in chapters 4, 5, and 6. That is to say, they show us that America is a medley of distinct cultural voices that together define what this country is all about. This in turn allows these artists to demonstrate how the African presence has shaped American culture. Indeed, the ways in which writers, musicians, and filmmakers have presented Afro-American life and thought have had a profound impact on the way in which Americans identify themselves, especially in the postintegration period.

Yet even as I write, the struggle over the direction that the leadership within the African American middle class should take politically and economically is being contested. The NAACP's search for a new executive director, which culminated in their choice of veteran civil rights activist Benjamn Chavis, has revealed the factionalism within that organization; the new senator from Illinois, Carol Moseley-Braun, the first Afro-American woman senator ever and the first black senator since Edward Brooke, has not yet defined her position; Justice Clarence Thomas of the Supreme Court appears likely to downplay race in general and play up a strict constructionist reading of the Constitution. And intellectuals within the black middle class promise to continue to provide illuminating and vibrant, if not heated, discussions regarding the place of African Americans in the reenvisioning of America in the twenty-first century.

The overriding purpose of this book, then, is to raise questions about the ideology and culture of middle-class African Americans and place them in their historical context. Many of the issues discussed herein are very old—the question of integration versus nationalism, for example, or the literary question of which audience Afro-American writers should address. That these old issues are still being debated does not mean that Afro-Americans have not advanced; it means only that these issues have yet to be resolved. Hopefully, the conditions of black people and American society have changed sufficiently so as to enable Afro-Americans to find answers to those questions that have created war within their souls and begin a serious movement toward the realization of what it means to be an Afro-American, and what it means to be an American. For in the end this is what integrative cultural diversity is about: the recognition and understanding of the vital and intrinsic role that people of African descent have played in the creation of a culturally diverse America. Integrative cultural diversity, applied to the nation at large, seeks to understand the American identity as an essentially creolized one, in which the African presence is a vital component, although clearly African Americans are not so "assimilated" as to have disappeared. The notion of integrative cultural diversity, then, opens a way to get beyond the often muddled discussions of racial essentialism and confront the meaning of what it is to be African American. To do so, we must explore the important historical forces that Africans, Europeans, and Native Americans exerted to lay the foundation for our creolized American society. The larger project, that of a reconceptualized American history, would certainly include the important histories of Latinos and Asians and would not only help us better to understand what ethnic pluralism means but also expand and enrich the notion of integrative cultural diversity.

This book happens to focus on African Americans. Surely, we have all had our share (and more) of the Euro-American version of American history. Over the course of that history, the vital presence and the contributions of African-descended people have either been overlooked or, when recognized, belittled on the grounds of cultural and genetic inferiority. That racism has in some ways poisoned all of Americans, black and white. It is time that the African presence in America's soul be acknowledged, affirmed, and heard in all its variety.

Thus, in another way integrative cultural diversity is also about the many different voices that make up AfroAmerica, voices that in the postintegration period have been heard by the rest of America. For many Afro-Americans, this has been a source of consternation. Black folks, they argue, should not not air their dirty laundry before the nation, as it will only hurt the perception of the community and provide racists with further proof of black people's inferiority. Such controversial matters should stay within the family. But as African

Americans in the middle class increasingly call, whether implicitly or explicitly, for a more expansive and inclusive understanding of what it means to be an American, this can no longer be the case. And despite the heated discussions, it is indeed toward integrative cultural diversity that African Americans of the middle class, wherever they may fall on the political spectrum, are headed. This book hopes to suggest how and why.

The Fruits of Integration

CHAPTER 1

Leaders of Thought,
Missionaries of Culture

It was a spring evening in April 1984 at Cornell University when Clarence Pendleton, chair of the Commission on Civil Rights, delivered a talk on the need for putting "true equality" back into civil rights.[1] Pendleton's presence at the Cornell campus had stirred up the usual commotion, given his controversial stature as the conservative choice of Ronald Reagan to head the otherwise liberal commission. For several weeks, students had been demonstrating against the university's investments in South Africa, and yet now the speakers' board had invited a man who, even though himself a black, carried out policies under the direction of the Reagan administration that threatened to destroy the gains of the civil rights movement over the past twenty years, particularly in the area of affirmative action.

The audience was made up largely of academics—mostly white— along with a smattering of black and white students, plus a few members of Cornell's Board of Trustees who were visiting the campus for their spring meeting. Before Pendleton even began to speak, one sensed the air of tension and hostility. Apparently unfazed, Pendleton boldly put forth his position. Blacks no longer needed affirmative action, he asserted. In fact, affirmative action created more problems than it solved. Not only was it preferential treatment but in the hands of government it had become a catchall program for all minorities

including women, who, he correctly pointed out, made up the majority of the populace. Instead, black people needed to pull themselves
up by their bootstraps, take advantage of the opportunities around
them, and stop using race as an excuse for not making it. After his
talk, during the question-and-answer period, the perceived tension
and hostility manifested itself in harsh comments and questions from
the audience. Pendleton fielded the comments seriously if with a
certain theatricality. At one point, in response to a question about
black leadership, he stated fervently that he did not want to be seen as
a "black leader or a black anything." He just wanted to be seen as "a
man doing a job successfully."

Boos and catcalls greeted this statement. That Pendleton could
adhere to such a ruggedly individualist perspective (and be so openly
disdainful of women who entered the workplace as professionals,
thereby supposedly abdicating their duties as mothers and guardians
of the family) clearly demonstrated that by the eighties ideological
power had shifted to the conservatives after a long reaction to the
changes of the sixties. At the same time, despite the potentially harmful policies that he espoused on behalf of the Reagan administration
regarding civil rights and affirmative action, Clarence Pendleton held
true to one of the chief tenets of the early civil rights movement and
especially of its many black middle class participants: the need to see
past color and make real the abstract ideals of the American ideology,
such as equality and liberty. If, from the perspective of AfroAmerica,
Clarence Pendleton was out of step, it was only because he spoke not
of group achievement but of individual achievement. He chastised the
black community for relying on the federal government to redress
their every grievance when they should be voluntarily banding together as a group to improve the community and, as individuals,
taking advantage of the opportunities they had gained. Clarence
Pendleton thus appeared to hold two somewhat contradictory
positions—group solidarity and individual initiative—in tension. But
his emphasis was on individual achievement, which was perceived by
many established civil rights leaders as heralding more harm than
good for AfroAmerica.

Some two years later, another voice spoke on another campus to a
mostly black student audience. The Reverend Benjamin Hooks, executive director of the NAACP, was the last main speaker at the end of

an event-filled black history month at the University of Rochester.[2] For students of African American history, Hooks's oration was at once easily recognizable as fitting into the mold of the NAACP. It was a powerful justification of that organization's work through the legal system to achieve an end to racial discrimination and open the doors of opportunity for blacks, especially black youth in the nation's inner cities, who were enmeshed in a vicious circle of drugs, crime, and unemployment. Unlike Pendleton, however, Hooks spoke more of group solidarity and group accomplishment.

In this respect, Hooks seemed more in tune with the mood of black America than had Pendleton. Nonetheless, at what was perhaps the most interesting point in his speech, Hooks cautioned his audience against cynicism and anger at the American system. In a grandfatherly manner, using the cadences of black Baptist preaching, Hooks recalled how much black people had accomplished over the last twenty-five years. The civil rights movement had opened up new opportunities for young blacks—who could not, after all, be expected to remember what it was like to endure the humiliation of Jim Crow segregation. The fact was that careers in education, the professions, and business were much more accessible to black youth today.

Benjamin Hooks's oration stirred the audience. But there was also an unease at this recollection of the "bad old days." Hooks seemed to be overlooking the "bad new days." He spoke little of the increase in harassment of, and sometimes outright violence against, black students that was occurring on many college campuses. Nor did he address the resurgence of black pride as witnessed in the calls by some scholars and activists for an understanding of the world through an Afrocentric perspective.[3] At his best, Hooks inspired the students to push ahead and be all that they dreamed, although at times he lapsed into the standard platitudes about the virtues of living in an integrated ("culturally pluralistic") society. In some ways, then, the messages of Hooks and Pendleton were oddly similar. Both men operated on the premise that the American values—the work ethic, the seizing of opportunities at hand, and the principles of civil rights—were fundamentally good and worthy of respect.

The estimated 250,000 people who gathered at Madison Square Garden on October 7, 1985, did not seem to share this attitude. They had come to hear Minister Louis Farrakhan of the Nation of Islam (popularly known as the Black Muslims). Farrakhan was a former protégé of Malcolm X. When Malcolm X left the Nation of Islam in 1964, Farrakhan (then Louis X) became his antagonist. After the death of Elijah Muhammad in the mid-seventies, Farrakhan revived the Nation of Islam and, by the early eighties, had gained notoriety on college campuses. Although the Nation of Islam had traditionally never endorsed political candidates, Farrakhan backed Jesse Jackson for president in 1984, which won him the legitimation of media coverage and brought him into national prominence. He had also aroused deep emotions—and garnered plenty of media attention—with his apparently hostile references to Jews.[4] Whether these remarks were in fact taken out of context, they nonetheless carried a mean-spirited streak that appealed to the xenophobia of many newly arrived middle-class Afro-Americans. Farrakhan's rhetoric blended a message of racial solidarity based on racial essentialism with a steadfast exhortation to African Americans to adhere to bourgeois standards of cleanliness, respectability, and frugality. Any individual achievement or initiative was subordinated to the need of the African race.

At the Garden, Farrakhan arrayed himself on the podium with various black ministers, along with several progressives whose causes ranged from Palestinian liberation to Native American self-determination to Pan-Africanism—the last represented by Kwamè Toure, namely, Stokley Carmichael.[5] For anyone who had participated in the movements of the sixties and early seventies it was like an All-Star Revue of sixties' radicals. Most in the audience, however, had come to hear the pro-black message of Farrakhan. What was disheartening about the affair was that many of the short speeches preceding Farrakhan's address laid the emotional groundwork by making various incendiary references to the overwhelming power of the Jews, both nationally and internationally. The Palestinian, Said Arafat, called Zionism "cancerous." Russell Means of the American Indian Movement castigated Jews in Hollywood for their distorted cinematic representations of indigenous peoples. (The previous week, Farrakhan had created a similar stir, which had caused a great deal of tension between middle-class black leadership and the Jewish community.) Stokely Carmichael called for war against Israel. By the time Farrakhan finally made his appearance, the crowd was more than warmed up; they were in a frenzy.[6]

Farrakhan spoke for three hours, leading his audience on a rhetorical journey through his version of black history, which emphasized
that all the world's accomplishments were initiated by Africans and all
tragedies were introduced by whites, but nonetheless included a men-
acing criticism of black politicians. ("When a leader sells out the
people, he should pay a price for that. Should a leader sell out the
people and live?") Farrakhan also delivered a steady diatribe against
Jewish people, condemning them for attacking him and taunting
them that they will never get rid of Louis Farrakhan. This was a far
cry from the days at the beginning of the century, when middle-class
black leadership held Jewish people up as an example for Afro-
Americans to follow. Ostensibly, Farrakhan's address was to be about
the Nation of Islam's solution for the economic ills of AfroAmerica.
But that issue was covered in only ten or fifteen minutes of the three-
hour talk. Moreover, those prescriptions amounted merely to Farrakhan's ideas for marketing black-produced toiletries.[7]

One cannot say for certain how deeply those many thousands of
people felt about the content or meaning of Farrakhan's talk. Black
intellectual observers like Stanley Crouch talked to some African
Americans who were critical or suspicious of Farrakhan. Another
intellectual in attendance, Julius Lester, was frightened and ashamed
at the vociferous and enthusiastic response of the crowd. "What is
happening in Black America that it can revel in vicarious bloodlet-
ting?" he asked, noting accurately that the present generation of African Americans was not the first to have gone through the trials and
tribulations of racism, violence, and poverty.[8]

After more than two decades of growth, relative stability, and relative
prosperity, the black middle class was in crisis. Part of the crisis was as
old as the black middle class itself: political confusion, a dilemma of
identity, and alienation from the larger black community. But as the
twentieth century moved toward a close, the black middle class found
itself in an even more precarious situation. That situation arose not so
much from the gains incurred by the civil rights movement of the
sixties as by the failure to devise new ways to maintain a healthy
tension between individual and group needs and demands, and to
envision ways of moving beyond those liberal successes to address
fundamental flaws in American society.

The liberal achievement in easing discrimination in education, in public accommodation, and in the political process enabled the black bourgeoisie to flourish in the sixties and seventies. At the same time, however, the reigning liberal ideology's success in redressing long-standing visible discriminatory practices against blacks allowed all other excluded groups ("minorities") to press for alleviation of their injustices. A veritable Pandora's box was opened as the sordid underside of American history was revealed, which resulted in constant pressure for amends to justifiable grievances. The oppression and anger of women, Native Americans, and gay people were presented alongside the concerns of African Americans. Given the liberal vision of fairness and inclusion of outside groups into the fold of American society, it could not have happened any other way. But the staggering inequalities with which each group was grappling, inequalities that were in fact embedded in the political economy and culture, did not lead liberal politicians or intellectuals to ask fundamental questions about the social structure. Rather, each "minority" was treated according to the principles of the laws established by the successful struggles of African Americans for social justice. Thus a peculiar fiction was created, whereby the civil rights laws were rendered "color-blind" and extended to cover any and all minority grievances. As a result, attention was deflected from black people's remaining needs and concerns: institutional racism, vast unemployment among the youth, and debilitating poverty. Further, just as the various minorities were granted some political access, the economy (certainly a fundamental concern) began a precipitous decline. The late seventies and most of the eighties superficially began to resemble the end of Reconstruction, from 1877 onward, as the nation grappled with inflation, recession, mounting deficits, widening disparities between rich and poor, and a growing indifference on the part of the white majority to the those who had previously been discriminated against.[9]

This historical comparison may seem exaggerated, but there were deep consequences of both the failure of liberal ideology and the dilemma of the black middle class in the seventies and eighties. The major consequence was that after immense struggle and considerable success in eliminating blatant forms of discrimination and creating opportunities for inclusion and advancement in America, African Americans continued to experience racism (albeit in subtler forms), violence, and poverty, as well as dissension within their own community about how to remedy the situation. This dissension split the black middle class. Some—notably the established civil rights leadership—favored continued pressure on the federal government to enforce (and in some cases strengthen) the civil rights laws. Others, dubbed "black neoconservatives" by the predominately white media, aligned themselves with the Reagan administration's philosophy of cutting back government intervention into social issues, asserting that African Americans must instead rely on themselves and on existing opportunities to improve their condition. These neoconservatives were composed primarily of certain black intellectuals in the universities and in the urban communities and black political figures close to the Republican party. But, in their social prescriptions, they were part of a tradition that went as far back as the late nineteenth century. Still other African Americans—intellectuals, academicians, writers, and political activists—pushed for a more progressive reordering of the whole American society. They envisioned an American society and culture that was not only egalitarian but also multicultural and multiethnic. Composed of many who had been militants during the sixties, they retained a black nationalist vision of African Americans as having a unique culture and pressed for an "Afrocentric" understanding of the black perspective and situation in both America and the world. This particular view was neither as new nor as radical as it appeared. It followed in the tradition of W. E. B. Du Bois's Pan-Africanism. In short, it was often unclear, even patently confusing at times, just where the black middle class wanted to be. It was clear, however, that African Americans of the middle class sought a way not only to be included in American society but also to retain a distinct racial identity. That desire had informed black middle class ideology throughout the twentieth century.

The black middle class's promotion of AfroAmerica to the larger white society recapitulates a major theme of Afro-American history: the desire to uplift the race and be included in American society while still maintaining racial heritage and identity. That the Afro-American masses traditionally looked to the black middle class for leadership and inspiration only exacerbated tensions within that class over the best way to resolve the "Negro problem." Given white dominance in

American society, the goal of inclusion with racial identity intact, no matter how eloquently or forcefully articulated, was an impossibility. Thus different strategies for improving black people's lot, devised in the hopes that as blacks demonstrated their achievements white attitudes would eventually change from hostility to acceptance and significant reforms would be enacted, foundered on a major contradiction. The black bourgeoisie accepted that the political economy, as it stood, would work for African Americans. But capitalism, despite its encouragement of personal initiative and its promise of freedom through profit and accumulation, presupposed inherent inequalities between individuals that provided no assurance that Afro-Americans, as a group, would advance. Further, racist ideology and resistance to black advancement were deeply embedded in American society's history and culture. Nonetheless, the black middle class demonstrated what one black political scientist, Charles P. Henry, called the hallmark of black politics: an "ability to combine individualism and community as well as the sacred and the secular."[10] This ability allowed the black bourgeoisie to reject strong pulls toward extreme forms of black nationalism (separatism) yet at the same time retain essential nationalistic elements (racial solidarity) as a way of preserving race pride and consciousness.[11] Perhaps the best example of this is the fabled Du Bois-versus-Washington debate.

The simplistic, though popular, dichotomy of W. E. B. Du Bois and Booker T. Washington as symbolic of two opposed ideas on how to improve the condition of black people has been taught for years by teachers, black and white.[12] Despite serious scholarship that reveals that both men held complex views, initially very similar and only later totally opposed (even though Washington died in 1915 and Du Bois lived until 1963), the temptation to perpetuate this opposition remains a fixture of textbooks and classroom lectures. The expanded black middle class of the seventies and eighties seemed to have uncritically accepted the received wisdom of that opposition, despite old and new scholarship to the contrary. A lucid understanding of Du Bois and Washington's stances—along with an appreciation of their subsequent effects in the 1930s, which harbored the seeds for the civil rights movement and the future growth of the black middle class—might have prompted those in the new black middle class to pause before proffering solutions regarding the masses of blacks still left out of mainstream America.

In the 1890s, when the national atmosphere was thick with racist ideology and the economy, despite setbacks, was in most of the country steadily moving toward corporate capitalism, both Washington and Du Bois espoused industrial education, capital accumulation, and moral uplift for the masses of black people in the South. Despite Du Bois's later decisive critique of Washington, he, like Washington, placed much emphasis on education as a means for blacks to attain knowledge, skills, and moral strength in order to combat racism, enhance the standing of their race, and obtain economic justice. Du Bois was also concerned that black leadership come from those individuals who had achieved that knowledge and moral strength. Washington, however, was more intent on using education to create a peasant-proprietor class and therefore disdained the sole pursuit of the intellectual or political life. Du Bois agreed that all blacks should pursue industrial or vocational skills, but he never wavered from believing that a "Talented Tenth"—an articulate black bourgeois class— would lead the masses to greater consciousness in social, political, and economic matters.[13]

On the whole, it was ultimately Du Bois who contributed more to the intellectual foundations of the modern black bourgeoisie. In the first two decades of the twentieth century, Du Bois moved toward fusing race consciousness with class consciousness. He began to elaborate a cultural pluralism based not on Jeffersonian liberalism but rather on a cautious socialism that blended black nationalism and Marx. This cultural pluralism, when later fully developed in the thirties, envisioned an America composed of ethnic minorities and races that would prosper in an economic commonwealth and still be able to retain their identities and significant features of their respective cultural heritages.[14]

But given the historical context of the late nineteenth and early twentieth century, which saw the triumph of corporate capitalism, the massive growth of urban centers and the equally massive migrations of blacks to those cities, and a pervasive racist ideology in American society, it was not surprising that Du Bois was largely ignored. It was Booker T. Washington who was elevated to chief spokesperson for blacks in general and the black middle class in particular on the strength of his pragmatic assessment of the prevailing circumstances of the period. Inculcated through his education with nineteenth-century bourgeois values, this former slave projected those values onto the black masses. In elaborating a social theory of the black condition that borrowed heavily from the racist ideas of black and white intellectuals and social scientists, Washington urged blacks to lift themselves out of crime, poverty, and immorality by means of hard work, thrift, and rigid adherence to moral values. It was through education—through the use of the classroom to instill values—that Washington saw the middle class as being most useful to the black community.[15]

A cruel irony lay in the fact that the exhortations and prescriptions of Washington, Du Bois, and many other prominent Afro-American men and women of the black middle class tended not only to blame the victim but also to reinforce the racist beliefs held by so many whites. Of course, these prominent black middle class individuals never believed that black people were inferior; they had just been incapacitated by slavery. Although Washington secretly moved against the more vicious forms of white supremacy, his emphasis on education, self-help, and accommodation were geared toward shaping black people into workers imbued with the proper set of values, who would be able to compete with white workers on the basis of merit. Ultimately, color barriers in the marketplace would fall, and blacks would eventually earn those civil rights that whites had always had. The chief difference Du Bois had with this mode of thinking was that, in his opinion, there should already be civil rights for all blacks, regardless of whether they were demonstrating their abilities or not. This talented group of blacks would in turn serve as leaders for the masses and work to uplift them. Such a notion reflected Du Bois's upbringing in New England and his educational experiences there and in Europe, which had endowed him with a good dose of elitism.[16]

Thus, Washington's viewpoint was accommodationist with a streak of the meritocratic. It was also an accommodationist view that, by turning inward to AfroAmerica to provide uplift and self-help, tended to be evasive about many of the social and cultural realities of the late nineteenth and early twentieth centuries. Jim Crow legislation, lynching, and powerful pseudoscientific racist explanations for black behavior served to move Washington's intended goals beyond the realm of possibility. Moreover, it was an accommodationism that tied itself to the white philanthropy and corporate capitalism of the North while closely adhering to the mores of the South concerning the races.

Nonetheless, with the backing of white philanthropists, capitalist entrepreneurs, and politicians, Washington was able to create a strong base and to exert a strong hegemony over the direction in which black people, in or out of the middle class, moved.[17] Through all of this, Washington, however much manipulated by or a manipulator of the prevalent racist attitudes, clung firmly to an optimistic belief in the positive effects that the rapid industrial changes in the political economy and culture would have for black people. But black women activists, whom Washington seemed never to have paid much attention to, came forth with more trenchant analyses than Washington.[18]

Bourgeois black women, like all black women, had more than their share of burdens. Viciously stereotyped as promiscuous and immoral and generally believed incapable of rising to even the minimal standards of white bourgeois civilization, black women were easily the most exploited and abused members of the race, not to mention the larger society. Notwithstanding all this, Afro-American women demonstrated immense courage and endurance. Black middle class women, in particular, came forth loud and strong on issues of pressing concern to the black community. Josephine St. Pierre Ruffin of Boston, founder of the Women's Era Club, which produced the first black women's magazine, *The Women's Era*, was steadfast in her devotion not only to uplifting Afro-American women but also to seeking full citizenship rights for all women. Ida B. Wells's anti-lynching campaign, which galvanized black women in and out of the middle class, adhered poignantly to the ideas Du Bois was espousing about the need for black middle class leadership. More important, bourgeois black women, through the network of their local and national clubs, uncovered the intense exploitation of gender relations that went hand in hand with the debilitating racist atmosphere of the period. As Paula Giddings observed:

> If White women were frustrated, Black women were even more so. Although growing numbers of Black women had the opportunity to enter college and the professions, the masses of Black women were relegated to domestic and menial work. They were excluded from such job categories as clerk and secretary, newly opened to women (who were being hired to replace men at lower wages), because White women wanted them.[19]

Middle-class black women's valiant efforts, however, were often overshadowed by black males such as Washington, Du Bois, T. Thomas Fortune, Monroe Trotter, and others, who focused more on procuring black rights as evidence of manhood and establishing a stable social and economic climate in which black men and their families could prosper. In short, bringing black people into line with the bourgeois values of an industrialized democratic nation was the major priority of black middle class leadership. Gender relations were thus circumscribed by those premises, and many black women activists were hard-pressed in their efforts to initiate a dialogue on whether either black men or blacks in general would be best served by embracing such a system. Middle-class African American women activists nonetheless continued, through their regional clubs and national professional organizations, to provide inspiration and support for the main priority of inclusion. But the sting of gender inequality remained.

Despite the obvious tensions among black spokespersons in the late nineteenth century, though, they all agreed that the values of respectability, thrift, strict sexual morality, and adherence to the work ethic were necessary for the uplift and advancement of the race. Black intellectuals and activists of both sexes recognized that pervasive racism was the main obstacle preventing African Americans from progressing along with the rest of the nation. Thus it was "race consciousness" that received the greatest attention from the black middle class from the late nineteenth century through to the 1930s. This race consciousness was at once reactive to imposed laws and social Darwinistic studies that reinforced black inferiority and at the same time sought to instill race pride in black people through history, literature, and self-achievement.[20] The emphasis on race consciousness, however, was ultimately tied to the dominant ideology regarding work, morality, and advancement. This ideological stance in turn enabled black middle class leadership, engaged in protest, to mount effective arguments for the rights of blacks as citizens. Through organizations such as the National Association for the Advancement of Colored People (founded in 1909) and the National Urban League (1910), together with the help of sympathetic whites, the black middle class was able to tap into the Progressive movement's ongoing campaign of reform and adjustment to industrialization and urbanization.[21]

On the whole, though, very little was accomplished for the majority of African Americans who lived in the South. Strictly enforced Jim Crow laws, which erected a rigid caste system, allowed only for the inculcation of bourgeois values within segregated black communities. That meant little without an equal opportunity to fulfill the expectations such values inspired in the larger society. Furthermore, the South's economy was far behind that of the rest of the nation. At best, some among the black masses were able to own farms; but most were subjected to tenantry, domestic work, and other menial jobs that whites would not touch.

The small black middle class in the urban South held occupations in the helping professions—ministry, teaching, law, medicine—and participated in small business enterprises such as insurance, real estate, and undertaking. Their example permitted the values of uplift and achievement to be passed on to the masses. But in no way was this black middle class able to translate their achievements or positions into political power in order to increase opportunities for the masses. Hemmed in by the rigid Jim Crow caste system, only a few blacks were able to encounter whites of any stature. These more visible members of the black bourgeoisie acted as representatives of the community through their actions as responsible, well-mannered citizens. In turn, in the black community they obtained an exclusive market in goods and services within the segregated system. While this isolation dropped a veil of separation that reinforced racial stereotypes on the part of southern whites (and whites in general), it also acted to provide the black community with a cultural space through which the church, the press, social clubs, and small businesses that catered to the masses could instill the values of the dominant society.[22]

Nonetheless, the color scheme and the inequality pervasive throughout the system of segregation distorted the inculcation of true class values. As one sociologist of the black middle class, Bart Landry, aptly put it:

In the absence of class distinctions similar to those among whites, *status* distinctions predominated. Membership in the emerging black elite depended less on economic means or occupation than on such characteristics as family background, particularly white ancestry, skin color, and manners and morals patterned after middle-class and upper-class whites.[23]

Thus, without having the means truly to accumulate capital and become thoroughgoing capitalists, relatively privileged blacks retained features that resembled those of the old "black elites" but were not quite fully "middle class." Members of certain professions, such as undertakers, teachers, ministers, and insurance agents, were of service exclusively within the black community, while, for example, railroad porters, barbers, and caterers served the larger white community as well. Within AfroAmerica, these occupations carried high status, and it was to this group that the masses looked for inspiration and leadership. This was also the group that intellectuals such as Du Bois, Washington, Trotter, and Wells hoped to cultivate in order to put forth to the white community proof of the worthiness of black people to compete and be productive citizens.

For a time in the early part of the twentieth century it seemed that this middle class was making some headway in the urban areas of the South. In cities such as Atlanta and Durham, a visible black middle class did emerge in conjunction with the rise of the New South and its attempt to match the rapid industrialization of the North. But the South's agricultural economy and the reluctance of large planters to follow the lead of a corporate capitalist structure continued to lock the majority of black people into tenantry and domestic service. One scholar of the black working class in the South found that 86 percent of African Americans were either agricultural workers or domestic servants in 1890.[24] That situation had changed little by the twentieth century when W. E. B. Du Bois began his studies of the black worker in the South. Indeed, it was the major issue in a series of debates in late 1906 and early 1907 between Du Bois and Washington.[25]

Washington, thoroughly convinced that industrial education was the best route for African Americans, claimed that "I believe that enough facts can be given to show that economic and industrial development has wonderfully improved the moral and religious life of the Negro race in America." Du Bois, while not totally disparaging the necessity for industrial education for black people, countered by pointing out that hatred for black people was so intense that they were even denied the vote. "In modern industrial democracy," he argued—once blacks obtained political power and economic independence—such "disenfranchisement is impossible." But until then it made little sense to talk about any improvement in the South or among black people.[26]

Du Bois did, however, detect some improvement in the form of the "Group Economy" that had developed as a result of black migration from the fields into the cities and that reflected the deep aspirations of black people to participate in the American economy. The Group Economy, as Du Bois understood it, was a "cooperative arrangement of industry and service in a group which tends to make the group a closed economic circle, largely independent of surrounding whites."[27] But, although this situation provided certain opportunities, it had its drawbacks. On the one hand, it fostered a sense of group solidarity, encouraged economic growth among black professionals and workers, and allowed for the development of a black middle class that could not only uplift the community but also anchor it. On the other hand, a Group Economy that retreated from the view of a society dominated by whites harboring pernicious racial attitudes only served to reinforce those attitudes and at the same time unwittingly to provide justification for Jim Crow segregation. And should blacks try to move outside of that circle to compete in the general economy or otherwise challenge white dominance, the reaction could often be swift and deadly, as the Atlanta riot of 1906 revealed.

On September 22, after a recent racially heated gubernatorial primary and amid increasing interracial tensions stirred up by inflammatory newspaper reports of blacks allegedly raping white women, white men mingling with blacks in Atlanta's red-light district on Decatur Street turned on blacks. Throngs of whites subsequently rampaged through the inner city of Atlanta beating and shooting at black men. The police offered little protection. Walter White, who would be executive secretary of the NAACP in the thirties, was only thirteen as he witnessed a crippled Negro bootblack brutally murdered by a mob; W. E. B. Du Bois, who was in Lowndes County, Alabama, completing a study of a black community, rushed back to Atlanta to defend his family and home with a shotgun. Booker T. Washington, who had less than a month before he was to convene a meeting of his National Negro Business League in Atlanta, was in New York City. From there he called on the "best white people and the best colored people to come together in council and use their united efforts to stop the present disorder."[28]

What was remarkable about the riot was the determination of the black community, especially the middle-class section known as Brownsville, forthrightly to defend themselves against white attacks.

The black community had been discreetly arming itself as the racial tensions had steadily increased over the previous weeks. When roving bands of whites attempted to invade Darktown, the tough lower-class section of black Atlanta, they were repelled. When the action turned to the Brownsville area in south Atlanta, considered the most peaceful and "obedient" black community in the city, county sheriffs and vigilantes came in to arrest blacks for possession of firearms. They were met with heavy fire, in which the head of the posse was killed. That section of the city was sealed off, and more than three hundred blacks were arrested and two wagon loads of firearms confiscated. Later investigation by a white committee placed the blame for the riot on the press's overheated reportage of rapes by blacks in the city. Little was said about the social and economic conditions that made the riot in Du Bois' terms a "political-economic riot." Those conditions owed to the migration not only of Afro-Americans from the farm regions into the urban areas but also of white migrants to the city. The competition for jobs, coupled with the racist attitudes of the whites, made racial tensions inevitable despite the good intentions of the leading whites to make Atlanta the model city of the South.[29]

Perhaps the chief significance of the riot, however, was its impact on the thinking of black intellectuals in the middle class. The riot in some respects symbolized the futility of accommodation. For Washington, who endorsed the status quo in the South as a way of building a strong working class among blacks, the violently defensive reaction exhibited by the lower and middle class was counterproductive. At the time of the incident, he urged Afro-Americans "to exercise self-control and not make the fatal mistake of attempting to retaliate, but to rely on the upon the efforts of the proper authorities to bring order and security out of confusion."[30] But T. Thomas Fortune and other blacks from the North, who often sided with Washington, took the side of the Atlanta blacks. Fortune angrily stated to Washington's secretary Emmett Scott that "I would like to be there with a good force of armed men to help make Rome howl." Du Bois, whose scathing criticism of Washington's philosophy in *Souls of Black Folks* (1903) along with his participation in the oppositional Niagara Movement's civil rights–oriented manifesto in 1905 had pushed him far to the fringe of effective social discourse within the black community, said that the whole situation made him feel "pretty thoroughly disillusioned."[31]

Feeling unable to hold a middle ground between the dominant strength of Washington's accommodationist "Tuskegee Machine" and the strong assimilationism and race consciousness represented by William Monroe Trotter's Boston *Guardian*, Du Bois finally moved to an economic integrationist position that held to the most minimal nationalist position, that of group solidarity. That position was best expressed through the formation of the NAACP, which Du Bois felt would get at the real question (as he saw it) of "how far educated Negro opinion in the United States was going to have the right and opportunity to guide the Negro group."[32] In other words, how were black people in the middle class going to be most effective for AfroAmerica in realizing citizenship rights and acceptance in American society?

It was the impoverishment of the South, the closure of immigration, and the desire for labor in the northern and midwestern industrial urban centers prior to and during World War I that proved to allow hundreds of thousands of African Americans to escape the horrendous oppression in the South and to increase their opportunities to realize the American dream. But for the black middle class the migrations produced new hopes as well as new anxieties.[33] Without a doubt the North presented more varied opportunities in employment, politics, and social interaction. Nevertheless, the ingrained racism of the nation proved to be uncannily subtle north of the Mason-Dixon line. Black rural migrants often found themselves locked into urban ghettoes and working unskilled jobs that, after the war, were eliminated. Skilled black workers faced racism, as they were excluded not only from jobs but also from unions. To make matters worse, the North's black bourgeoisie was not always receptive to the vast influx of their rural brothers and sisters. And despite the introduction into the black middle class of entrepreneurs and professionals and some access to a measure of political power, the apparent success was, as W. E. B. Du Bois lamented, "disappointing since it has mainly served to further the political, social, and economic position of a few individuals. They seldom reach positions of real influence where they could take any decisive action to better the status of their people."[34]

At the end of World War I, as the nation tried to return to normalcy, AfroAmerica embarked on a major journey of redefinition. By the 1920s the race consciousness lauded by the men and women of the black middle class and encouraged in the masses found expression in Marcus Garvey's call for black purity and separation. Granted, as a class that contained a good share of mulattoes, the black bourgeoisie had always been careful about just how far to push the race conscious-ness idea. But now, out of desperation, frustration, and for some, serious belief, the idea of racial purity ("pure blackness") and separa-tion from white society became a fervent hope of many of the African American masses. Clearly, the black bourgeoisie's leading lights had not counted on the masses to rise to such appeals.

Within the black middle class, moreover, opinion was divided. Many young black writers and intellectuals were influenced by the Garvey movement culturally, writing proudly of the African past, black rural folk culture, and the "New Negro." Other Afro-Americans, though, the "aged race men," as the historian James O. Young has termed them, now began to downplay Garvey's race consciousness and instead to emphasize black people's "Americaness."[35] Pride in racial heritage was fine as long as it did not divert black people from becoming hard-working American citizens. Thus the black col-umnist George Schuyler, who flirted with leftist ideas and satirized race consciousness, proclaimed that Negroes were "black Anglo-Saxons"—white men in black skins. He wanted to forget color and viewed race consciousness as an absurdity. Schuyler was not alone; by the 1930s many young black intellectuals in the middle class would point to economics and class alliance, not race, as the best direction in which Afro-Americans could move in order to improve their status.[36]

The black bourgeoisie's shift away from race consciousness to mat-ters of class and economics was prompted less by a desire to rid black Americans of their racial identity than by the reality of the Great Depression. Never totally secure economically and politically disen-franchised in the South, black people were plunged by the Depression into extreme immiseration. They were not alone, of course; millions of whites also lost employment, savings, and homes. But for black people the opportunity to find a decent job, work hard, and build a life all but disappeared. The thirties thus brought the black middle class face to face with a difficult question. If, as so many intellectuals, both black and white, believed, capitalism was dead or dying, then what was to be done about the condition of black people?

The answer came from at least two groups in the black bourgeoisie. One segment, which can easily be called conservative, fell back on the old nineteenth-century bourgeois beliefs in individualism, hard work, entrepreneurship, and morality. Skeptical of capitalism's decline, these blacks exhorted the masses not to give up hope and, especially in the urban North, to cast their votes for those who could help them (more often than not the Republican party). Thus the black conservatives continued to instill race consciousness, larded with a sturdy belief in the American capitalist system. The second segment was composed mostly of liberals, left sympathizers, and leftists. The strategies settled upon by this group of the black middle class included efforts to obtain federal economic relief, renewed pressure for civil rights, and encouragement of the idea of "class solidarity" with white workers. A few among them espoused socialism or communism.

But, however promising or necessary such an alternative may have been, the black bourgeoisie as a whole never seriously considered left analyses and prescriptions. Likewise, the black masses did not rush to join the Communist party.[37] At most, intellectuals such as E. Franklin Frazier, Abram Harris, and Ralph Bunche endorsed an emphasis on economics and class. But this was more a tactic of downplaying a racial consciousness that might hinder resolution of the serious economic plight within AfroAmerica and the nation. As Robert Weaver, an advisor in the Roosevelt administration and himself a black liberal, recalled, America "was a middle-class society and those who fail to evidence most of its values and behavior are headed towards difficulties."[38] Weaver wanted America to acknowledge its discriminatory effect on blacks and initiate meaningful changes so that African Americans would be able to keep pace with the rest of America.

For Robert Weaver and other middle-class blacks such as Forrester Washington, Mary Mcleod Bethune, and Ralph Bunche, who served as advisors or program directors in Roosevelt's New Deal, the federal government was the force that would create such opportunities. However, as befitted the values of the black bourgeoisie, they were insistent that the African American masses be ready and able to seize whatever opportunities were available. They clearly recognized that the New Deal was at best only potentially beneficial to black people because among most politicians and policymakers there was a studious effort to ensure that the New Deal would not single out any particular group for special attention.[39] The New Deal's all-encompassing concern for the common man moved black intellectuals to soft-pedal race and emphasize economics and class alignment. But even here, as sympathetic as some were to left analyses, there was confusion if not outright division.

A good example of both confusion and division can be found in the debate between E. Franklin Frazier, the militant sociologist, and W. E. B. Du Bois, the leading intellectual of the black bourgeoisie. Although it took place within the context of the New Deal, the Frazier–Du Bois debate over the best economic direction for AfroAmerica also provides the best reference point for the continuing dilemma of the black middle class in the postintegration years of the eighties and nineties.

The principal differences between the two men were age and temperament. Du Bois, now in his sixties, remained a romantic and an elitist. Given the depth and breadth of his experiences, the thirties and the debate with Frazier can be seen as a period of creativity and maturation. Du Bois saw this time as one in which Afro-Americans could truly build an economic base on which they could proceed, politically, into the mainstream of America.[40] Frazier, who was in his early forties, was of the working class and newly arrived in the academic world, and was clearly sympathetic to a left analysis of the collapse of capitalism and the need for black-white workers' alliances. Not surprisingly, he was both highly critical and openly skeptical of the vision that a member of the "old guard" such as Du Bois presented.[41]

At the same time, despite his cautious approach to socialism, Du Bois was moving closer to a Marxist analysis. He supported the idea of collectivized consumer cooperatives that were culturally diverse. In the thirties he controversially advocated the creation of a "separate economy" whereby blacks could accrue sufficient economic power to compete in the marketplace, which would in turn encourage effective political participation. Blacks would thus go it alone and constitute a class of their own. Such a notion, which spurned any hope of a coalition between black workers and white workers (whom Du Bois saw as heavily imbued with racism) seemed to fit the communist directive that blacks should be seen as a nation and developed in ways that would aid the class struggle to remove capitalism. In this respect, Du Bois retained his influence among the young left-leaning black intellectuals who focused on economics while still maintaining a nationalist perspective.[42]

To his credit, Du Bois never lost sight of the racist tendencies in the white working class and deftly used his knowledge of the past when elaborating his scheme of consumer cooperatives. He knew full well that corporate capitalism transformed workers into consumers, incurred a massive growth of the middle class, and in a peculiar way refashioned the genteel bourgeois culture into a seemingly democratized mass culture. Shorn of any recognition of the rich racial and ethnic heritages that had made America, this mass culture (and society) existed only as a ready-made advertisement and environment for consumption. Du Bois's solution was to maintain racial heritage on the one hand, and, on the other, through the creative use of socialist principles to work toward economic justice, elimination of racism, and political equality for all.[43]

Frazier had at one time accepted the idea of black cooperatives in the South. In the thirties, however, he came to distrust Du Bois's concern with economic improvement and accordingly offered one of the sharpest critiques of Du Bois's economic ideas. Acidly observing that "the voice of Du Bois is genuine only when he speaks as a representative of the Talented Tenth," Frazier dismissed Du Bois's ideas of a black nation within a nation as so much wishful thinking.[44] Frazier also attacked Du Bois's socialism as hopelessly romantic, arguing that his vision of a consumer cooperative system was impractical. Frazier was further disturbed by what he saw as Du Bois's attempt to discourage the black masses from joining forces with white workers and economic radicals. The system that Du Bois proposed, Frazier noted, would "set up false hopes for the Negro and keep him from getting a realistic conception of capitalist economy and the hopelessness of his position within the system."[45] In his advocacy of a class analysis of AfroAmerica's economic dilemma and his polemical critique of Du Bois, Frazier adhered fairly closely to the Marxist program of class struggle favored by some leftists in the thirties. Nonetheless, Frazier parted company with the Communist party, which favored a progressive nationalist position regarding Afro-Americans—a position that recognized black Americans as a nation within a nation and supported the creation of a black state, which would then form a coalition with white workers.[46]

For Frazier, the final goal was instead to create a heightened class consciousness among Afro-Americans that would again lead to a co-alition with white workers, but one wherein the racial factor would be diminshed. Frazier's analysis of black status in the thirties was, how-ever, grounded in a complex but ultimately ahistorical and economi-cally mechanistic reading. Frazier drew on the sociological theories of acculturation and assimilation espoused by Robert Ezra Park, accord-ing to which outside groups would gradually adopt the mores of the mainstream society and, over the course of several generations, would become practically indistinguishable from the rest of the populace. But Frazier was overly optimistic about the creation of an urban black proletariat and the possibility of its coalition with the white working class.[47] E. Franklin Frazier believed that "the condition of the black worker is determined by the same forces in our economic system which affect the white worker." In the end, then, the race's salvation would come about "through its cultural disappearance, culturally and biologically."[48]

Frazier's desire to see racial antagonism swept away through the biological and cultural disappearance of African Americans was as provocative then as it is today. But despite his fierce independence in intellectual matters, Frazier was in fact deeply concerned with the condition of black Americans. Throughout the thirties and even in the twenties, Frazier held to a firm belief that African Americans, both as a people and a culture, could not be explained by referring to their African roots. "The manner in which Negro slaves were col-lected in Africa and disposed of after their arrival in this country would make it improbable that their African traditions were pre-served."[49] Frazier was well aware of the cultural relativist's argument, as presented by the anthropologist Melville Herskovits, that African Americans retained particular "Africanisms" that identified them as a unique culture. Although he maintained a long friendship with Her-skovits, he did not accept the idea of African survivals nor did he revel in the romantic sentiments of black nationalists (Du Bois included) who celebrated an African past. "In spite of those who would dig up his African past, the Negro is a stranger to African culture," wrote

Frazier in an early article on the black bourgeoisie.[50] Frazier instead saw political and economic integration as the best possible solution for African Americans. Even though he was skeptical of full assimilation or amalgamation ever taking place (and here he disagreed with Park), Frazier was intent on intellectually demonstrating "the processes by which the Negro has acquired American culture and has emerged as a racial minority or ethnic group."[51] Along with all this, however, Frazier remained a committed "race man" who politically and intellectually fought for the eradication of racism and the rights of African Americans. In his socialistic vision and his optimism about future race relations, he was clearly a product of the leftism of his times. At the same time, he was somewhat prophetic regarding the pitfalls that cultural relativism and exuberant Afrocentrism would hold for the black middle class.

The Frazier-Du Bois example provides a good portrait of the tensions within the black middle class over the attitudes and strategies that African Americans should adopt in order to improve their economic condition and social and political status. To be sure, both the conservatives and liberals of the thirties worried about unskilled and poor black people becoming overly dependent on the government and thus "wards of the state."[52] But the conservative wing of the black middle class clung tenaciously to a severely weakened Republican party, and to bourgeois notions of individualism, the Puritan work ethic, and respectability, while the masses of African Americans turned in droves to the Democratic party. Black liberals and radicals recognized that with the attention Roosevelt's New Deal gave to social problems, there was more hope for providing economic relief, political equality, and structural reform for blacks as a group. As historians such as Harvard Sitkoff and John B. Kirby have demonstrated, the seeds of the civil rights movement were planted in the thirties by the efforts of the liberal-left segment of the black bourgeoisie and their white sympathizers.

Those seeds would not flower until the sixties, and the fruition would follow in the seventies and eighties. But even then the disputes between black middle class leaders and intellectuals over whether African Americans should emphasize race or class would continue. Indeed, in the nineties, as AfroAmerica moves deeper into the post–civil rights era and the century draws to a close, the debate over priorities and approaches continues to rage.

One shift in the debate, whether for good or ill, has come about with the expansion of the black middle class. Within that class there has increasingly emerged a faction that had always represented a distinct minority voice: black conservatives who believe in individual achievement and community self-help as opposed to government intervention. The black conservatives (or "neoconservatives") of the eighties and nineties—of whom Clarence Pendleton provides a good example—have been among the beneficiaries of the struggles of the sixties. Their viewpoint has developed in reaction to the collapse of any coherent liberal program for structural reform, the ascendancy of the New Right during the Reagan and Bush administrations, and the devastating immiseration of the black masses amidst poverty, crime, and disease in the inner cities.

However earnest these conservatives are in their efforts to improve the condition of the black community, though, it would seem that the changes wrought by the civil rights–black power movements in the sixties and seventies still exert greater influence within the black middle class, as the remarks of (and reception accorded) the NAACP's Benjamin Hooks attest. Louis Farrakhan, for his part, spoke to an anxious and fearful side of newer members of the black middle class, who are wary of assimilation and are grappling with the need to find an identity that will at once be inclusive and distinctive. In short, the expanded black bourgeoisie is continuing, in a variety of ways, to work out the legacy of the civil rights–black power movements, movements that both contributed to the growth of the black middle class class and laid the foundation for new tensions in AfroAmerica and in America.

CHAPTER 2

From the Hollow to the High Ground and Back

The Civil Rights Movement and Its Aftermath

The 1960s saw America undergo social and cultural changes that still affect the nation and promise to do so well into the next century. For African Americans in general, and the black middle class in particular, the sixties were a time not only of change but also of expansion, of new opportunities. This was also a period of personal and cultural self-affirmation, in which black Americans as a whole began to reenvision America. That the massive movement of black people toward the attainment of civil rights and equal opportunities met with resistance goes without saying. It could not have been otherwise given the deeply entrenched Jim Crow system in the South, which African Americans resented but nonetheless had accommodated themselves to, and the subtle but widespread racialist belief on the part of white Americans that black people were somehow different, together with its racist corollary: that they were inferior.

With the ground-breaking Supreme Court decision in 1954 that undermined the doctrine of "separate but equal," not only was more than half a century of blatant racial discrimination declared unconstitutional but also the entire cultural and social landscape that all Americans were accustomed to living in was suddenly open to question and readjustment. If the key issues of the sixties were centered, as some scholars have claimed, on the question of identity, individual and collective, on a debate about authority and the role of dissent, and on the search for a new America, then African Americans of the middle class were once again to face serious challenges regarding their role and position in AfroAmerica.[1] Would they continue to strive earnestly to uplift the masses of their less fortunate brethren (mostly young urban blacks) and thereby actively work to dissolve the poisonous racial categorization that had oppressed black people for almost two hundred years? Or would the black bourgeoisie essentially turn its back on the masses and instead move to blend quickly into the mainstream of America's middle class, reassuring the nation as it did so about the beneficence of race consciousness and the glories of a truly egalitarian and multicultural America? Either path was fraught with traps that could cast the black community into confusion, frustration, and anger. What the black middle class needed to do was reenvision what it meant to be both black and American, viewing these not as alienated polar opposites but as positive dimensions of one's self that, when jointly embraced, could prove enhancing and empowering.

From the end of slavery onward most African Americans wanted to be treated "no different than the white man." But the racism of America was a hard-core reality that had to be faced. African Americans in the middle class wrestled mightily and in many cases courageously with questions of race and equality, and with the ultimate meaning of such concepts in an America that was undergoing rapid changes. The civil rights movement may have been their finest hour, but it was only the beginning of a new and in many ways more painful journey to real freedom. From the moment of the Supreme Court decision regarding segregated schooling to the emotionally intense and politically volatile questions of affirmative action and racial separatism in the eighties and nineties, the black middle class found itself in turbulent waters.

In his classic work, *Black Bourgeoisie* (1957), E. Franklin Frazier provided a stinging critique of the black middle class and a prescient view of the struggles within that class over the direction in which African Americans should move. From a historical vantage point, *Black Bour-*

geoisie was deeply flawed: it continued a long-standing debate over cultural survivals, found the black family severely disrupted because of slavery, and railed against the moral incapacities of the black masses. White scholars picked up on these themes and, through historical scholarship, sociological studies, and even public policy, promulgated a view of the black community as one devastated by a "mark of oppression" incurred through slavery.[2] The legacy of slavery thus became the explanation, for whites and for some blacks, as to why African Americans had been unable to assimilate into American society as easily as other immigrant groups. Slavery was the cause of personality distortions, broken families, and the inability of blacks intellectually and socially to measure up to the demands of modern day society.[3] The black community in the urban areas represented a "tangle of pathology," as Daniel P. Moynihan put it in a mid-1960s study that later found expression in the public policy recommendations on racial matters put forward as part of Lyndon B. Johnson's Great Society program.

Moynihan's study was based on Frazier's reading of the conditions of the Afro-American family and Afro-Americans in general.[4] But Frazier's real intention, at least in *Black Bourgeoisie*, was to send a loud warning, if not a rebuke, to black bourgeois leaders and intellectuals for their failure over the past two decades to provide concrete remedies for the plight of the black masses—remedies such as the creation of economic cooperatives and alliances with white workers, the inculcation of positive values that would enable black people to live in dignity, and the elimination of racial exclusion from American political, economic, and social life. Instead, as Frazier angrily noted, "the black bourgeoisie live largely in a world of make-believe, the masks which they wear to play their sorry roles conceal the feelings of inferiority and of insecurity and the frustrations that haunt their inner lives. In attempting to escape identification with the black masses, they have developed a self-hatred that reveals itself in their depreciation of the physical and social characteristics of Negroes."[5] The black middle class "cravenly" sought white recognition and acceptance even as it turned away from providing any real leadership or hope for the African American masses.

What was revealing, even poignant, about this passage, and indeed about the whole work, was its emotionalism, which in turn suggested the dilemma in which this brilliant black intellectual now found himself. This was the "economic radical," the serious student of acculturation and assimilation who, during the thirties, had argued that class solidarity must take precedence over race and yearned for the eventual disappearance of the African American race "biologically and culturally." Now, at the threshold of the sixties, Frazier not only excoriated the black middle class for racial self-hatred but stated that the "mark of oppression" had led many to internalize their feelings of inferiority to the point where they wished to be white.[6] Far from heralding African American salvation, the "disappearance" of race among the black middle class now seemed to threaten the entire community.

Feelings of inferiority implanted by years of racist ideology and behavior on the part of whites, as well as segregation in the South, affected the black bourgeoisie as it did all Afro-Americans. But Frazier's anger and frustration may have blinded him to the fact that the black middle class had assimilated enough of the positive traits of American individualism and the belief in equality and fairness to struggle against the onslaught of white supremacy and racist thought. The very institution that Frazier himself noted as being the bulwark of the black community—the black church—combined religious fervor with race pride and with a belief in the justice not only of God but also of the Constitution.[7] Moreover, AfroAmerica, as Frazier himself recognized, had long nurtured businesses, associations, and newspapers. These institutions, along with extended family networks, enabled many Afro-Americans to cope with the alleged feelings of inferiority and in many cases to transcend them.[8]

The foresight of Frazier's work lay in his description of a "new" black middle class. This group benefited from the job opportunities gained during and after World War II. The expansion of Afro-Americans into professional areas—teaching, medicine, law, and social work—along with an increase in clerical work and access to corporations laid a firm basis for the black middle class in the 1960s.[9] Despite the fact that the masses of blacks in the South remained disfranchised and locked into a vicious racial caste system, the black bourgeoisie was able to exert enough pressure through the courts, through boycotts, and later through Congressional legislation to break down some of the legal barriers to equal opportunity and political participation. But although the momentous occasion of the 1954 Supreme Court decision and the subsequent struggles for desegregation and voter registration provided great hope and proved exhilarating for all Afro-Americans, there were external forces that complicated the black struggle and the black bourgeoisie's efforts to eliminate the centuries-old problem of race relations.

Chief among these external forces were the changes in postwar American society. With the victory over Nazism and a recovery from the Depression, America entered into a period of relative prosperity and of world leadership. Although Roosevelt's New Deal, carried on by Truman's Fair Deal, provided some promise that the federal government was finally taking steps toward alleviating racial discrimination, most of the fifties found the liberal establishment on hold. The conservatism of the Truman years reached its peak in anticommunist hysteria, "police action" in Korea, and increasingly tense relations with the Soviet Union. For AfroAmerica, the one ray of hope lay in the Supreme Court's decision to declare school segregation unconstitutional. Yet even here the main issue, when closely examined, revolved around the notion that school segregation was morally wrong, that it hindered the psychological and intellectual advancement of black people. Encouraged by the legal briefs of the NAACP and by social psychological studies regarding black self-esteem, the Supreme Court declared it unhealthy for Afro-American children to be segregated. In the Court's apparently straightforward words:

> Segregation of white and colored children in public schools has a detrimental effect upon the colored children. The impact is greater when it has the sanction of laws; for the policy of separating the races is usually interpreted as denoting the inferiority of the negro group. A sense of inferiority affects the motivation of the child to learn. Segregation with the sanction of the law, therefore, has a tendency to [retard] the educational and mental development of negro children and to deprive them of the benefits they would receive in a racial[ly] integrated school system.[10]

But these words can be read in another way. Guided by personality studies of the Negro that stressed the psychological damage wrought by slavery and subsequent enforced segregation, the Court did not consider the ideological and historical dimensions of racism, which had reinforced an ethic of white supremacy. For all its radicalism in proclaiming segregation as a moral wrong, the Court also failed to address the detriment to the white population of its acquiescence to and continued perpetuation of segregation. Granted, to the joy of Afro-Americans, both in and out of the black middle class, the Supreme Court ruling pointed toward a vision of an integrated society free of racial problems. But the somewhat paternalistic tone in which the Court's decision was worded bespoke a refusal to deal with the reality of ideological and institutional racism.

Moreover, the black middle class, so restless and eager to enter into the growing American prosperity, did not consider the deep well of white resistance that could be summoned up by the Court's proclamation. The Supreme Court decision was lauded as revolutionary by the black middle class and, if anything, it had an even greater impact on the black masses, raising expectations for a truly fair and equal society. AfroAmerica was poised for results. Even when the decision was met with bitter white resistance, black enthusiasm did not dampen; expectations were only fueled. After all, had not the Supreme Court, the law of the land, spoken? Had their leaders not told them a new era had begun?

Thus the black middle class acquiesced in the Supreme Court's compromise, focusing on the immorality of race discrimination but at the expense of coupling this moral vision with a vigorous reexamination of a political economy that had enabled racism to exist for so long. Such an examination, of course, would have called into question the unwavering faith of liberals in the welfare state and almost everyone's faith in corporate capitalism (however much regulated), as well as revealing the institutionalization of racial ideology within those structures. This particular compromise, while perhaps the best that could have been made at that time, would return in the eighties to haunt the black middle class, especially the traditional civil rights organizations (the NAACP and the National Urban League) along with the newer Southern Christian Leadership Conference. The slipperiness with which discrimination operated in a volatile economic marketplace made the eradication of racism and the expansion of equal opportunity, whether through affirmative action or more stringent governmental regulations, even more difficult to sustain simply on the premise that African Americans had a strong moral right to economic justice.[11]

The presumed vindication of African American rights by the Supreme Court also had a psychological effect on the black community. Feeling certain that the government would protect them as long as they sought out long-desired opportunities, a new assertiveness began to emerge. The African American masses, young and old, participated in organized boycotts against segregated transportation in urban centers in the South and demanded desegregation of public facilities and accommodation. Inspired by the ethic of passive resistance advocated by Martin Luther King, Jr., the black masses fused the messianic vision of the black church with some of the richest and oldest traditions of American reformism. Not since the abolitionist movement was there such a moral fervor, a deep and strong conviction in the righteousness of a cause. Indeed, as long as the black community held the high ground of moral imperative, the civil rights movement could not be stopped. And it was through morality—the calls for black and white together and the vision of a beloved community, juxtaposed to the brutal racist violence that was the reaction of many whites—that white liberals in government were able to respond, however gradually, to the demands for justice and an end to racial discrimination. Such a stalwart belief could not go unnoticed.[12]

With liberalism reinstated to power under John F. Kennedy, liberals moved to enhance the country's image, improve the quality of life, and revive a sense of mission and will in the nation's citizenry. The continuing presence of racial discrimination was not only an obstacle for many liberals but also a potential threat for everything they were trying to achieve nationally and internationally. The credibility of the United States as a friend of underdeveloped nations, a proponent of liberal democracy, and a defender of freedom was in jeopardy as long as Afro-Americans were systematically denied their rights in America. Thus the ascendancy of Martin Luther King, Jr., as spokesman for Afro-Americans was greeted with approval among white liberals. As the appeal of King's moral suasion grew, white liberals responded in a variety of ways, from philanthropic donations to participation in many demonstrations. Liberal politicians moved more cautiously, but they too were eventually won over, whether through a fundamental, if previously hidden, belief in King's message or by fear of the unpredictable.[13]

The prophetic moral vision of Martin Luther King, Jr., mirrored the traditions of Afro-American history. The direct antecedent of that vision was Frederick Douglass, the nineteenth-century abolitionist, writer, and spokesman for black people. Just as Douglass was seen as an "exemplary colored man" for the black masses, so too was King cast as a role model for young blacks to emulate and follow. Douglass argued for the assimilation of blacks into American society on the strength of his belief in the viability of individualistic liberal democracy. King, many years later, echoed those beliefs eloquently and forcefully in his "I Have a Dream" speech in Washington, D.C., at what may well have been the moral height of the civil rights movement:

> When we let freedom ring, when we let it ring from every village and hamlet, from every state and every city, we will be able to speed up that day when all of God's children, black men and white men, Jews and Gentiles, Protestants and Catholics, will be able to join hands and sing the words of that old Negro spiritual. "Free at last! Free at last! Thank God Almighty, we are free at last!"[14]

The message of both men, however, was often threatened by the turbulence of the times. From the emergence of corporate capitalism and its crucial transformation in the later years of Douglass's life to corporate capital's dominance in King's time, the vision of a moral commitment to a just and humane society grew increasingly more remote. Added to this were all the received notions of racial inferiority, however contested and debunked, which lay deep in white America's soul. The real genius of Martin Luther King, Jr., lay in his ability not only to penetrate to the conscience and soul of white America but also to resurrect a meaningful vision of a nation that could purge itself of the poison of racial ideology and base itself, however pluralistically, on a shared belief in the message of the Declaration of Independence and the essential worth of the Constitution.[15] Most African Americans and many whites embraced that vision. But the strictures of racism, the ingrained characteristics of competitive individualism, and the excruciatingly slow movement of government in taking action created a frustration and anger that led ultimately to violent responses from some, mostly urban, black people.

The violence of the mid-to-late sixties was a long time in coming, but it was in many ways inevitable. No people can maintain a nonviolent posture indefinitely in the face of harsh resistance and overt violence, even death. That so much delay, so much political wrangling, and so much compromise were required in order for black Americans to be rewarded such elemental rights as free access to public accommodations, that America had to be so heavily pressured to provide laws that enabled black people to eat at a restaurant alongside whites or to vote for a candidate to represent their interests, stretched the patience of many African Americans to the breaking point. Moreover, as important as these measures were for breaking down a Jim Crow South, for those African Americans living in the northern, midwestern, and western urban centers, such limited reform was not enough.

By the sixties, a significant portion of black Americans were urban. As a 1989 updating of Gunnar Myrdal's expansive 1944 study of African Americans pointed out, since World War II black people had migrated to the North and West by the thousands, a migration that "eventually totaled 3.5 million blacks, more than one-quarter of the national 1940 black population of 13 million."[16] This massive migration, coupled with the long-standing settlement of African Americans in the North, had resulted in a black urban subculture far different from the southern rural landscape traditionally associated with black life. Northern black urbanites, unlike their southern rural brethren, had the right to vote, could, for the most part, use public facilities, and had been exposed to the diversity of other ethnic groups. If there was much promise and hope in those experiences, there was also disillusionment. What black urbanites could not attain revealed the true depth of the oppression of the northern black masses: access to a superior education, the chance to acquire higher skills in order to secure meaningful work, and the ability to afford decent housing. Northern urban black communities came to represent what the Kerner Commission of 1968 called the division of American society into two societies, one black, one white, one struggling, the other privileged.

The violent eruptions and "long hot summers" that plagued the nation's cities during most of the sixties were the result of the pent-up frustrations and anger of a black urban population that felt left out of the mainstream of America. But underneath those frustrations there was also emerging within this segment of AfroAmerica an angry nationalism that at least since the thirties had been submerged. This particular strand of black nationalism, which promoted bourgeois values as well as racial pride and purity, sought to lift up the black masses and encourage them to seize power for themselves. This was clearly a movement away from the moral vision of the early civil rights movement in the South, which, while attempting to remove visible barriers of racial discrimination, also tried to heal wounds and reconcile blacks and whites who had much in common historically and regionally. Most northern urban Afro-Americans, however, whatever their roots, had fully embraced the competitive individualistic ethos of an industrialized consumer society. And yet, as studies of AfroAmerica have repeatedly noted, these urban communities constantly faced frustration. Even though they had avenues such as the church, voluntary associations, and newspapers to provide them with a view of their world that white organizations and the media often excluded or distorted, black urbanites were unable to break down the racial barriers that prevented them from participating in political decisions affecting their communities. Despite the existence of a few small businesses owned by middle-class blacks that catered to specific needs within their communities, African American urbanites remained unable to amass sufficient capital or gain the necessary managerial experience to effect the creation of, or their advancement within, large-scale business enterprises. Granted, there were a few who had "made it," and those individuals who had managed to gain visibility in white America were held up as role models in the black community, whether it was a Jackie Robinson in sports, a Nat King Cole on television, or even, to the relief of many blacks and the consternation of many whites, an Adam Clayton Powell in Congress. These success stories, however, could not assuage a nagging feeling among African Americans, urban or rural, that America was not going to let them get inside. Indeed, there was a deep suspicion in AfroAmerica that white America really did not want black people around. But that feeling, which was vented by frustrated extremists on urban street corners, was sublimated by most blacks. Day after day, year after year, they struggled through their lives, trying, like all Americans, to do their jobs, to provide for their families, and to realize the American dream of prosperity, of hard work justly rewarded. But the American dream, however glorious a myth, proved very elusive for African Americans.

When the civil rights movement of the early sixties gained national recognition, it seemed for a moment in AfroAmerica that soon all would be well. But the psychological lift that hovered in the air from the time of the Supreme Court decision in 1954 to the march on Washington in 1963 rapidly began to sink as resistance against black people struggling to break down the barriers of racial discrimination mounted. As the daily papers and nightly news reports spoke of the murder of civil rights workers, the beatings of Freedom Riders, the cattle prodding and hosing of demonstrators, that nagging suspicion lurking in the back of most African Americans' minds about the value that white America truly placed on them kept coming forward.[17] Thus in the mid-sixties, when the movement turned to black power under the aegis of the young black middle class activists in the SNCC (Student Non-Violent Coordinating Committee), there began a psychological transformation that was at once angry, determined, and destined to be long-lasting. Various black writers saw that transformation as the birth of a new "black being." As one former SNCC member, Julius Lester, stated: "The Black Power phenomenon was not a political movement; it was a psychological cleansing and a baptism, a transformation and redefinition of black self and consequentially of white America." George Davis and Glegg Watson, in their analysis of blacks in corporate life, offered a similar assessment: "The [sixties] revolution can be called successful even though no one overthrew the dominion of white males over America and the world. We blacks, however, overthrew the rule of white men in our minds. We underwent a psychological revolution."[18]

That "psychological revolution" was in fact the flowering of an important but less dominant trend in African American history: black nationalism. Although middle-class black leaders such as Martin Luther King, Jr., and Adam Clayton Powell, Jr., drew on the traditions of the black church to instill race pride, they did so principally to build black self-esteem and solidarity in the face of the injustices of racial discrimination within American society. But younger African Americans, whether in the civil rights movement or in the urban enclaves of America, were influenced in the sixties by the quick-witted and angry voice of Malcolm X of the Nation of Islam. Popularly referred to as the Black Muslims, under the leadership of the Honorable Elijah Muhammad (Leroy Poole) the Nation of Islam was a religious sect that exalted black purity. According to its cosmological history, the black man was the originator of humanity but had been stripped of his birthright by the evil machinations of the white devil. The struggle of all black people, then, was a struggle to regain their birthright.[19] Shorn of its mystical and mythical trappings, however, the Nation was very much steeped in a strict adherence to bourgeois morality, holding to a stringent moral code and an emphasis on work and responsibility to family and community.

But many of the African Americans who immersed themselves in a new-found racial pride under the influence of the Nation and Malcolm X went further than the wearing of African dress, the adoption of African names, and the embrace of African traditions. They sought, as Lester aptly put it, a "psychological separatism." This retreat into the love of blackness was for the most part due to the inability of the civil rights–black power movement to deliver immediate relief from economic and racial injustices. But the rise of black power and its attendant cultural nationalism also served to further the black bourgeoisie. As Cornel West, the prominent African American philosopher and intellectual, pointed out, "The black nationalist movement, despite its powerful and progressive critique of American cultural imperialism, was principally the activity of black petit bourgeois self-congratulation and self-justification upon reaching an anxiety-ridden middle-class status in racist American society."[20]

West's strident critique, written from the vantage point of the eighties, may not be unwarranted. After all, as the sixties' civil rights movement spread out from the South, where racial discrimination had the most visible effects, the middle-class black leadership found itself up against an entirely different type of foe. The institutional structures in the North were not blatantly discriminatory. The subtle kind of racism that made blacks seem an "invisible people" operated on a more individual and psychological basis than did the rigidly defined and legally supported racism of the Jim Crow South. An educated African American, for example, could never really tell if she or he had been turned down for a job because of a lack of qualifications or because of race.

Moreover, by this time most whites in the America did not see Afro-Americans as a particularly oppressed group. From the mid-sixties onward, most white Americans took what might be called a middle-of-the-road position regarding segregation and race relations. They did not see themselves as hard-core segregationists, but they continued to balk at the idea of social contact with blacks as a group. As numerous studies of white attitudes undertaken by social scientists throughout the sixties and seventies have clearly demonstrated, while overt expressions of white prejudice against Afro-Americans decreased, a reservoir of dislike remained.[21]

Indeed, the popular refrain of the sixties among whites, liberal or otherwise—"What is it that they want?"—spoke volumes. It attested not only to an ignorance of the black experience and of African American history but also to a profound lack of understanding about how a supposedly fair and just society protected whites on the basis of skin color. As the black power advocates demanded economic improvement, increased educational opportunities, and better housing for all African Americans, many whites heard only angry rhetoric that suggested separatism and hatred for anything white. Liberals, black and white, did seem to notice the demands of black power militants had a decidedly conservative cast to them: calls for self-determination and control of community schools and economic enterprises were not particularly radical innovations. But by the end of the decade, what with eight straight summers of urban rebellion across the nation, a growing fear that there might be a race war, and the heightened rhetoric of black pride, tensions and fears had mounted. In the early 1970s, white liberals, stunned by the steady increase in racial antagonism, responded by providing programs, foundation money, and fervent promises to rectify the black problem. Thus, not surprisingly, by the mid-seventies (and perhaps even earlier) the black middle class had expanded. While by no means on a par with the white middle class in either income or range of occupations, it was steadily closing the gap.

The increase in the black middle class could be traced to the successful passage of the Civil Rights Act of 1964 and the Voting Rights

Act of 1965. As educational opportunities expanded, more and more working-class Afro-Americans began entering college, earning degrees, and subsequently moving into corporate, political, legal, and public sector jobs.[22] The growth of the black middle class was most visible in the areas of government and the lower managerial end of business. The private sector witnessed an increase in black salaried workers of 27 percent in 1970 and 37 percent in 1980—compared to a mere 2 percent in 1940. But the majority of black professionals held government jobs. As the Committee on the Status of Black Americans reported in 1986: "Overall, 27 percent of blacks were employed in government in 1980, compared with 17 percent of the total work force."[23] At the same time, the traditional professions of the black middle class, teaching and ministry in the church, to some extent declined.

The expansion of the black middle class in the sixties also brought with it a heightened concern among African Americans with race consciousness. Cornel West's remark about an "anxiety-ridden" middle class in racist America reflected the fear felt by many newly arrived members of the black bourgeoisie that they might lose their racial identity or their connection with AfroAmerica—that they might fall prey to what in recent years has been popularly referred to as "whitening up."

Perhaps in response to this anxiety, cries for black power resonated throughout the social and cultural institutions of America, in many cases providing the cutting edge for the questioning of the America's institutions and values. One prime example occurred on college campuses in the late sixties and seventies when African American students called for the creation of black studies departments or programs that would foster a sense of self-worth and community as well as demonstrate that the study of the Black Experience was a valid scholarly enterprise. Set alongside the rancorous student demonstrations against the war in Vietnam and the growing chorus of criticism of American imperialism, the struggle for black studies probably appeared to be more political than it actually was. The deepest desires of the students and faculty who demanded black studies programs were for the recognition of the contributions of African Americans to American society, the reevaluation of assumptions about who made civilization or world history, and the establishment of courses that would be revelant to African Americans in a rapidly changing society. Those intentions often dovetailed with or broke the ground for other changes that occurred throughout higher education: disciplines became more specialized, debates took place over objectivity—the need to maintain a critical distance from one's subject matter—and relativism, and the true purpose of the university in society was called into question.[24]

Whatever the intrinsic merit of such debate, however, the fact remained that its impact was confined largely to the academic realm. Once they moved into the business world, for example, African Americans again met with the elusiveness of institutional racism. As George Davis and Glegg Watson pointed out in an analysis of blacks in corporate America:

> All along we were concerned that within corporations there was not a great deal of talk about race. It is mentioned only when it becomes obvious that a racial problem must be dealt with. Subtle racial problems are ignored. Deep-seated ones are often treated as if they don't really exist.

On the surface, black and white workers seemed to get along well, but as Davis and Watson found "blacks are often oppressed by this silence on race. Their careers and morale are affected by this thing that they cannot mention."[25] The atmosphere became even more stifling as the criticism of affirmative action bgean to cast doubt on the adequacy of the training that participants in such programs received. In response, some African American intellectuals charged that this criticism—which came from all quarters—undermined the confidence of black professionals, who began themselves to grow suspicious of their merit and the quality of their work.[26]

The contraction of the economy owing to the oil crisis in the early seventies and the end of the Vietnam war, along with the reemergence of racial animosity aimed mostly at affirmative action, put a halt to what little progress had been made for African Americans. As the seventies closed, the picture for most black Americans was grim indeed. Unemployment reached staggering heights, almost rivaling conditions during the Depression. By 1984 the national unemployment rate for white males aged 25 to 54 was 5.2 percent; for black males in the same age group it was 16.4 percent. Among younger black males the figures were even more horrifying. In 1939, 32 percent of black males between the ages of 20 and 24 had no earnings, but neither did 27 percent of white males. During the sixties, the employment and earning status of young black males improved to some extent. By 1969 only 16 percent of black males aged 20 to 24 still had no earnings—half the 1939 figure. Among white males, however, the number had dropped to 8 percent. But by 1984 the situation had deteriorated: now 28 percent of black males in that age group had no earnings, whereas among white males the figure, now at 9 percent, had remained relatively stable. Moreover, job prospects for young black males seriously worsened throughout the eighties.[27]

The social consequences of this massive and ongoing joblessness were even more catastrophic. Black-on-black crime, infant mortality, and drug abuse increased in the black community to frightening levels, and with drug abuse came AIDS. Homicide became the number-one cause of death for black men between the ages of 15 and 34. In 1983, although African Americans made up only 11.5 percent of the population in the United States, 43 percent of homicide victims were black.[28]

If the number-one cause of death among young blacks was homicide, the birthrate among African Americans was two to three times higher than that of whites, which contributed to the burden of poverty. Moreover, the increase in the birthrate was most striking among teenage black women. In 1984, 20 percent of all teenage mothers were adolescent African American women as opposed to 11.1 percent for white adolescents. This was a marked change from the 1960s, when the birthrate for teenage black women had been falling. The Committee for the Status of Black Americans attributed the increase to several social factors: an early initiation into sexual activity (two years earlier, on the average, than among white females), very little use of contraception, and less recourse to abortion.[29] There was also an increase in the infant mortality rate. In 1985 the rate was 18.2 deaths per thousand for African Americans as opposed to 9.3 for white Americans. Perhaps for this reason, America had, overall, one of the higher rates of infant mortality among the developed nations of the world.[30]

These grim statistics pointed to the devastation that was ravaging AfroAmerica. They could also be used to mount an argument that the civil rights movement had not been as successful as everyone had hoped. But that was true only to a certain extent. Clearly, the black middle class had benefited from the movement, as had those working-class African Americans who had been able to take advantage of the legislative decrees that opened up educational and professional opportunities. And integration had succeeded in removing the most egregious forms of racial discrimination.

Indeed, at first glance it seemed at the time of Jimmy Carter's inauguration in 1976 that the struggles of the fifties and the sixties had paid off quite handsomely. Major cities such as Detroit, Atlanta, and Los Angeles had black mayors, and even southern counties and towns could boast of black sheriffs and elected officials. Southern schools were almost completely desegregated. In Congress, while there was no black senator (Edward Brooke of Massachusetts, the only black senator since Reconstruction, had lost his seat to Paul Tsongas in the early seventies), there was a Congressional Black Caucus, begun in 1971 with some twenty members and promises of future growth.[31] Moreover, the civil rights movement had had a salutary effect on the country as a whole, as all Americans were reminded of the ideal of a nation that purported to believe in freedom and equality. Even the black power movement, if at times divisive and polarizing, nonetheless was a necessary tonic for a country whose long history had often grotesquely stereotyped African American thought and behavior.

At the same time, African Americans as a group were still entrapped in a system that recognized individual rights as opposed to group or collective rights. A historian of the civil rights movement, William Chafe, has noted that "if the primary purpose of the civil rights movement is defined as individual freedom and the opportunity to secure personal gains previously denied on the basis of race, then the movement would have to be described as a success."[32] But of course the movement had a wider vision than just individual freedom and personal gain. Given the racism deeply embedded in the structures of the society and the discovery by young activists of the roles that class and power play, there was an earnest desire for the transformation of the society into one that would be more humane and just— one that would close the gap between the rich and poor as well as allow African Americans as a group to determine what was necessary for their communities. When these criteria are attached, the movement can safely be said to have failed, and perhaps not surprisingly. As J. Mills Thornton, another scholar of the civil rights movement, has argued, "Any effort to effect a collectivist egalitarian program . . . is doomed inevitably to failure by the entire weight of American History."[33]

Although liberals lamented the high unemployment rate among black youth and the rise of the "black underclass," they were at a loss for remedies. Given a contracting economy and an inflation rate that put many whites in financial trouble, any substantial remedy within the structure of corporate capitalism was bound to exacerbate tensions between competing groups. That, along with the rise of a ruthless individualism among many Americans (labeled by pundits the "Me Generation") in the late seventies and early eighties, only served to decrease the chances for successful mediation not only between African Americans and whites but between the poor and the rich in general.

Moreover, a subtle new ideology of racism was emerging that further promised to remove any hopes for reversing the increasing separation of the black community from the rest of America. Many white intellectuals, always uneasy at the demands of the black power advocates, began to mount what seemed a defense of American values such as fairness, individualism, and "equal opportunity." Their main goal, though, was to show that remedial actions based on race were themselves a form of discrimination, particularly against white males. Critics such as Nathan Glazer saw affirmative action as "disaffirmative action" that would tear apart the society from its traditions of fairness and its devotion to equal opportunity.[34] Given this climate of opinion, an Allan Bakke could successfully sue the University of California for discrimination against whites.

Under affirmative action, black youth had indeed entered college in increasing numbers, aided by federal and state funding for colleges and universities. In 1960 only 3.5 percent of blacks aged twenty-five or older had four or more years of college; by 1990 the figure had grown to 16.4 percent. (The comparable figures for whites are 11.8 percent and 23.5 percent.)[35] This increase in college attendance enabled many young African Americans, in and out of the middle class, to strive for an education of sufficient quality that it could lead to fulfilling careers. Yet as the seventies came to a close, the economy contracted sharply, with the result that job possibilities for liberal arts graduates rapidly became scarce. The attendance of African Americans at colleges also fell sharply. A major reason for this decline was the cutting back of scholarship funds and government loans during Ronald Reagan's eight years in office.

Those young African Americans who were in college in the eighties and nineties seemed to set aside the idealistic concerns and commitments of their predecessors and gravitated toward maximizing their material and economic well-being. Thus, many black college students and graduates, like their white counterparts, followed the prevailing market and pursued careers in business management, law, accounting and communications. When ten student leaders from historically black universities were asked what they expected to be doing in the year 2000, the majority pointed to those fields. But beneath their career goals these students revealed a deepening concern with the rest of the black community and once again with issues of racial identity. One student leader from Morehouse stated that "blacks need an identity so that they will know what they are about." Other student leaders seemed generally optimistic that there would be improvements in the condition of AfroAmerica over the next century. It was significant that these students, who represented a vital core of the black middle class, had chosen to attend historically black universities.[36]

African Americans attending predominantly white universities, both public and private, experienced a marked increase in campus aggression against blacks in the late eighties. Intense academic competition, a deepening resentment among white students over affirmative action, and a widespread sense of alienation encouraged many black students to separate themselves from the general student body and call for "culturally diverse" programs, which in turn created tensions that often exploded into racial confrontations. Despite all the advances during the sixties and seventies, the harsher realities of AfroAmerica remained.

These advances, moreover, were for the most part enjoyed by an established middle class that had for so long sought them. The overwhelming majority of black people, however, saw little, if any, improvement in their lot. True, during the late sixties and the seventies the black middle class had been strengthened and enlarged by the incorporation of some of the masses. But in the eighties reality became all too clear. Unemployment among black youth approached 50 percent, black male employment had stalled at 40 percent, and, perhaps most alarming of all, 40 percent of black households were headed by single women, a large portion of whom were still in their teens.[37]

The deterioration of black community structures and values sent shock waves through the black middle class, which, like the dominant middle class, was preoccupied with worries over the economy. While by no means unconscious of the new phenomenon of the emerging underclass, established middle-class black leaders persisted in clinging to New Deal ideas regarding the welfare state, equal opportunity, and racial justice. It must be noted that the black bourgeoisie of the seventies and eighties saw the fulfillment of the New Deal initiated by the Johnson administration's War on Poverty and Great Society programs. These programs, which built on Rooseveltian ideas, did provide some opportunities and monetary relief for African Americans. But they were markedly circumscribed by several crucial constraints: the reluctance of white liberals to engage substantive structural transformation, the threat of white conservative backlash, the fear of continued and ever more violent black uprisings, and finally the active compliance of black middle class organizations in discouraging any serious pursuit of societal transformation.

Granted, by the time of the Reagan years established black middle class organizations were very much on the defensive. Economic stagnation, the resentment over preferential treatment, and the rise of neoconservatism had placed civil rights organizations in the position of having to mount arguments for the continuation of policies that would build on measures such as the 1965 Voting Rights Act and parts of the 1964 Civil Rights Act.[38] As the American economic pie shrank during stagflation and worries over the rise of the underclass mounted, black middle class leadership and their white allies became concerned with finding cures for a potentially explosive social situation. As much as the sixties had held out a vision of what America could become, forces of retreat were already in motion.[39]

In an extended description and analysis of the origins of the black underclass for the *Atlantic Monthly*, Nicholas Lemann, a liberal white journalist from the South, asserted that "every aspect of the under-class culture in the ghetto is directly traceable to roots in the South. And not the South of slavery but the South of a generation ago."[40] According to Lemann, the roots of the black underclass had nothing to do with the debilitating effects of slavery, the standard liberal social science explanation of the Afro-American's status. Rather, the emer-gence of this class is better understood as a matter of "demo-graphics—specifically two mass migrations of black Americans." In Lemann's historical revision, the migration of blacks to urban areas during the forties, fifties, and sixties saw a rural black class system imported to the North "virtually intact."[41] A second migration in the late sixties saw the black bourgeoisie along with the more fortunate working-class Afro-Americans leaving the ghettoes, thanks to the civil rights movement. This flight left behind poor, ill-educated, and un-skilled blacks who, in a growing dependency on the welfare system, multiplied and fostered a pathological culture of poverty.

Lemann's detailed description of Chicago's black underclass could easily be generalized into a portrait of most urban centers in the North during the eighties and nineties. But Lemann also came dan-gerously close to blaming the civil rights movement for the rapid growth of the black underclass in the seventies and eighties. Lemann managed to avoid that conclusion, however, by pointing out that the "ethic of dependency" began as a result of racism and exploitation in the poor rural areas of the South, which, among other things, re-duced blacks to the status of second-class citizens. Transplanted to the North during the migrations of the forties and fifties, this ethic was further subsidized during the sixties by President Lyndon B. John-son's Great Society programs. Nonetheless, it was civil rights legisla-tion that enabled the black middle class to expand and ultimately to leave the inner city.[42] In Lemann's analysis, moreover, the black middle class subsequently abandoned its responsibility to provide a stable environment in which lower-class Afro-Americans, particularly youth, could aspire to uplift themselves.[43]

Many members of the black middle class were, of course, pro-foundly troubled by the worsening racial situation in America. After ten years of so-called Reaganomics, which produced spending cuts in the social programs of the sixties in order to finance tax breaks, AfroAmerica was clearly in deep crisis. While some African American intellectuals responded in a conservative fashion, as we will see, others

continued to defend the gains that were won in the sixties and pro-
pose ways that might lessen the harsh conditions under which the
majority of African Americans now lived. But no matter what ideas
were proposed by the liberal wing of the black bourgeoisie, they
ultimately failed to come to grips with the conservative revolution
that had swept the nation.

Lemann's own solution to the tragic situation of the black underclass illustrates the paucity of liberal ideas in the eighties. According
to Lemann, a resuscitation of the New Deal's Work Projects Administration was "the best solution for the ghettoes" a solution that "attacks their cultural as well as their economic problems."[44] This neo-
WPA would offer jobs at a lower minimum wage (in order to attract
private sector employers), in an effort to reach black teenagers who
were without skills. But the principal aim here was to "take people
out of the ghetto culture" and move them one step closer to the
national mainstream. Lemann even considered bringing black middle
class youth into the program, in the hopes that their bourgeois values
would rub off on their underclass sisters and brothers. It was unclear,
however, whether the black middle class would regard Lemann's solutions in the same positive light as did their author, especially given the
condescending manner in which he proposed them.

Lemann's attempt to engineer a social solution to the black underclass received a more detailed treatment in the *New Republic* from staff
writer Mickey Kaus. Kaus described the demise of the work ethic
within the inner city, which led him to offer a solution that was a
peculiar mixture of social democracy and the Puritan work ethic: the
Welfare State in the future must transform itself into the Work Ethic
State.[45] Unlike Lemann, who saw the underclass as emanating from
migrations, Kaus emphasized the legacy of cultural deprivations within urban AfroAmerica. As he put it, "Even if whites were a majority
of the long-term poor, it would be hard for them to create a poverty
'culture' because poor whites have never been confined to segregated
communities."[46] But Kaus's solutions were not that much different
from Lemann's.

Kaus would also remove black youth and single mothers from the
inner city, find them minimal employment, and somehow initiate
them into bourgeois society. Whereas Lemann was somewhat more
sensitive to the harms of long-term racism and exploitation, Kaus

eschewed any attempt to grapple with the nature of late-twentieth-century technological capitalism, notably its need for highly skilled workers and its consumption orientation, or the particular effects all this had on the social, political, and economic life of black people. Moreover, neither man seemed to have deeply considered what black intellectuals, such as William Julius Wilson, had to say about these matters.

William Julius Wilson, professor of sociology at the University of Chicago, shared more than just the institution of his intellectual fore-bear, E. Franklin Frazier. In his writings he demonstrated a complexity and independence of thought that was very much like that of his predecessor. In *The Declining Significance of Race*, written in the mid-seventies, Wilson astutely alerted America to the expansion of the black middle class and the growth of the black underclass, as well as to the problems that both posed for AfroAmerica and the rest of the United States.[47] The book caused a good deal of controversy. Wilson proclaimed that "class has become more important than race in deter-mining black life-chances in the modern industrial period." Moreover, now African Americans clearly belonged to one of two classes—the black bourgeoisie or the black underclass—instead of the traditional three classes that other sociologists, black and white, thought had previously existed (say, around the turn of the century). Wilson of course recognized that the civil rights movement had exerted a tre-mendous influence on the growth and stability of the black middle class. But, more important in his view, changes in the economy, along with the expansion of that middle class, had dramatically widened the gap between the middle class and the rising underclass. As Wilson himself concluded, "The ultimate basis for current racial tension is the deleterious effect of basic structural changes in the modern Amer-ican economy . . . changes that include uneven economic growth, increasing technology and automation, industry relocation, and labor-market segmentation."[48]

African American intellectuals were skeptical of, if not outright angered by, Wilson's highly controversial book. Particularly irked were those liberal and left scholars who read Wilson as eliminating race from the agenda of social ills that had to be remedied. The black scholar Manning Marable, who like many others held to a progressive nationalist viewpoint, argued that Wilson's "basic message was an updated version of the line developed by the NAACP and Urban League a half century before—that American racism could be understood as an aberration within American democracy; that with the end of legal segregation and Jim Crow, race consciousness remedies were no longer necessary." Marable saw the black working class as the saviors of AfroAmerica and called upon the black middle class to help forge "a new tradition of black nationalism" that would become "a class-conscious force for social transformation."[49]

But in the ideological climate of the 1980s, leftist proposals remained on the periphery of intellectual and political discourse. A more measured critique of William Julius Wilson, one that tried to understand him from the ordinary African American's viewpoint, was offered by Julius Lester, who commented that Wilson's "study seems divorced from the inner experience of blacks. It relies on economic data, omitting the experiences of the people the data represent." Lester noted that blacks' own perceptions varied greatly with Wilson's rather abstract conclusions on matters such as job discrimination and the experience of bias among black professionals. Furthermore, whereas Wilson's economic analysis seemed to emphasize class at the expense of race, Lester asserted that the continued need for affirmative action "underscores the fact that race is highly significant in America."[50]

William Julius Wilson's analyses and prescriptions came at a crucial moment, as the conservative wing of the black middle class gathered its forces within the general swing toward conservatism in the nation. As once staunchly liberal white intellectuals began to reassess their thinking on matters of race, black intellectuals also began seriously to reconsider the direction in which AfroAmerica should go. Wilson, who was often described by his critics as a neoconservative, was actually advocating a leftist social democratic approach to the issue of the underclass and to poverty in general. But the progressive nationalists eschewed integrationism in favor of racial autonomy, rejecting the need for coalitions with various constituencies such as labor and industry as well as women and various minority groups.[51] As for established civil rights groups, which had traditionally sought interracial cooperation and integration through the legal system, they had to some extent accomplished their goal: antidiscrimination and voting rights laws had been enacted. However, what stumped them through-

out the eighties and into the nineties was that, despite the expansion
of the black middle class, there was an increasing disparity between
the situation of those who had made it into the middle class and the
ominous emergence of a growing underclass. In other words, established black leaders were unable to move from thinking in terms of
civil rights to considering economic justice.[52]

In a study of middle-class black leadership written in the late
eighties, Harold Cruse accordingly argued that established organizations such as the NAACP had embraced a notion of "noneconomic
liberalism" as they attempted to redress discrimination through the
federal courts. By failing to address the economic problems that black
people faced, black leaders, with the exception of Du Bois, became
locked into fighting for social and educational opportunities. Economic equality and social justice quickly faded from the agenda.[53] As
far as he went, Cruse was on the right path. As John Dittmer, a
student of civil rights, accurately observed, when "viewed in a broader
perspective, the civil rights movement had been a referendum on the
principles of American liberalism, whether this country could at last
resolve Myrdal's 'dilemma' over the theory and practice of democracy."[54]

Cruse would have no doubt agreed. Because he based his argument
on a belief that America was a pluralistic society, though, Cruse himself had to admit that this nation was founded as a "white nation."
This raised a quandary of sorts as to whether a pluralistic democracy
such as Cruse envisioned was ever possible given the pervasive racism
so thoroughly embedded in the structure and institutions of the present society. However important a contribution Cruse's work was to
the critique of black middle class leadership, he nonetheless could not
come up with any alternative other than the creation of an independent black political party. To that end, Cruse criticized Jesse Jackson's
failed attempts to run for the presidency in 1984 for "neglecting the
more crucial and fundamental and *obligatory* task of political organization at the bottom, *the independent black political party.*"[55]

Cruse believed that this political party had to arise from the contemporary black middle class that the civil rights era had produced.
That class (and he by no means attached a particular ideology to it,
liberal or conservative) had to be willing to engage in the political,
educational, intellectual, and cultural leadership of AfroAmerica.
Contrasting the post–civil rights black middle class with the middle

class that E. Franklin Frazier had examined a generation previously, Cruse found the enlarged black bourgeoisie to be in even worse shape. The black middle class of Frazier's day had an awareness of their social responsibilities toward the more downtrodden of their race. Although the coming of integration and the enlargement of opportunities had created an expanded and more affluent black middle class, it was in Cruse's words "an *empty class* that has flowered into social prominence *without a clearly defined social mission* in the United States."[56]

Cruse's solution amounted to a more sophisticated version of encouraging the black middle class to take the reins of leadership and pull AfroAmerica out of its dismal situation. But given the economic environment of the period, the continued hostility to civil rights and affirmative action, and the resurgence of a markedly hostile racism among the white populace, it was hard to imagine how African Americans could possibly improve matters by resort to an independent political party. It seemed neither safe nor feasible.

In the end, perhaps William Julius Wilson's solution was the best that could be hoped for: fundamental economic reform and the creation of a "broad-based political coalition to achieve it." In Wilson's words, "the hidden agenda for liberal policymakers is to improve the life chances of truly disadvantaged groups such as the ghetto underclass by emphasizing programs to which the more advantaged groups of all races and class backgrounds can positively relate." That meant that there had to be a recognition on the part of the black leadership that "the poor minorities are profoundly affected by problems in America that go beyond racial considerations."[57]

That, in turn, meant that the time had come for African American intellectuals and leaders to move beyond their long-standing ties to the Democratic party's New Deal–Great Society liberalism. As the nation tilted more and more away from liberalism, the ideas of many black intellectuals who had fought for civil rights or who had benefited from them took on a conservative cast. Whether their prescriptions were distinctly conservative or simply called for the society to return to the fundamental principles of the early civil rights movement, their voices promised to restore a dialogue, as well as to renew tension, over the social responsibilities of the black middle class.

CHAPTER 3

To Preserve the Dignity of the Race

Black Conservatives and Affirmative Action

The conservative triumph of the 1980s signaled that there would be no further steps taken to resolve the extreme difficulties facing the black community. In the language of the New Right the solution to these problems was couched in phrases such as "law and order" and "enterprise zones," accompanied by calls for a return to "traditional family values." Taken at face value, of course, these phrases seemed to hold out some promise. The new emphasis on law and order perhaps meant that the federal government was planning to do something about the epidemic of drugs and crime that was ravaging the inner cities of America. "Enterprise zones," which were set up to provide tax breaks for private corporations in order to train and to provide jobs to unemployed and unskilled black youth, also seemed like an admirable idea. Even the New Right's stand on traditional family values—if largely a reaction against the permissiveness of the sixties, the effects of which were said to be tearing the social fabric apart—hardly seemed cause for alarm.

But if there was any doubt as to what the New Right actually intended, it was quickly dispelled by the vigorous, and at times heavy-handed, attempts by the white conservative government to severely curtail, if not eliminate, government assistance to poor black families, including legal services and employment programs, as well as what had become a most volatile issue, affirmative action. By the late eighties, President Ronald Reagan was calling for a study of how to completely revamp the welfare system and seemed determined not only to roll back the civil rights measures of the sixties but also to eliminate the basic programs of the New Deal.[1] In reacting to this new spirit of conservatism, the black middle class revealed its ideological division—but it also demonstrated a striking diversity of thought for which most of white America was probably unprepared.

Throughout the eighties the most controversial sociopolitical issue was that of affirmative action. As the nineties began and the George Bush administration attempted to deal with the mounting social and economic problems that had emerged from the Reagan years, the issue of "quotas" and "preferential treatment"—affirmative action—increased polarization between African Americans and white Americans. At the same time, however, the controversy provided an excellent, if ironic, illustration of how "cultural diversity"—so highly lauded by the liberal left—worked.

Affirmative action was intended to be a corrective to many generations of entrenched racial discrimination in educational institutions and in the workplace. In what was undoubtedly the most daring and innovative use of the federal government to secure a measure of social justice, the erection of affirmative action procedures under the Johnson administration in the sixties also moved, unwittingly, toward a transformation of gender relations and class alignments within the United States. Had they been carried to their fullest extent and strictly enforced, it would have been only a matter of time before affirmative action programs caused institutionalized racism and gender discrimination to wither away. New class alliances or, as traditional Marxists would maintain, objective class interests would arise, further calling into serious question the economic configuration of the society.

But social forces working to undermine affirmative action were set into motion at almost same time those policies were being developed. To begin with, most affirmative action policies were peculiarly skewed toward the needs of the black middle class, while the black lower class received but minimal attention.[2] Entrenched racism, an expensive war in Vietnam coupled with the onset of dramatic shifts in the economy, anxiety over the new demands of women for equal rights, and the inability of liberals and policymakers to choose between two goods—fairness and social justice—caused serious efforts to implement full affirmative action to falter. Moreover, from the late sixties to the mid-seventies, when some affirmative action measures were just beginning to make progress toward providing opportunities for the black masses, strenuous and mean-spirited opposition to such remedies began taking its toll.

This opposition came from several quarters: hard-line conservative politicians who had never wanted any civil rights legislation enacted in the first place, a growing number of disaffected liberals (neoconservatives) who were fearful of the economic and political consequences that full implementation of affirmative action would entail, and white male workers who, faced with a contracting economy, perceived affirmative action as "reverse racism" on the government's part.

For the neoconservatives, both black and white, affirmative action represented all that was wrong with the liberal domestic policies of the sixties in particular and the welfare state in general. In their view, affirmative action did more harm than good. Instead of redressing past discrimination, they claimed, the government policies reinstituted race in the forms of quotas and preferential treatment. Some even argued that the inclusion of women in affirmative action programs took jobs away from able-bodied black men, thus further contributing to the breakdown of the black family and hastening the rapid deterioration of gender roles in society. Black conservatives echoed these charges, but, as we will see, found other flaws with affirmative action that betrayed its supposed benefits.[3]

Black and white liberals who favored affirmative action became increasingly defensive about the subject. They argued that there was a need for such policies in view of the past discrimination against minorities and women. Some liberals, leaning slightly to the left, spoke of the need for economic redistribution. But, in the end, given their inability to move beyond an ideological commitment to capitalism, with its inherent structure of inequality, and individualism, liberals could only continue to argue for equal opportunity while clinging to their faith that the existing mechanisms were sufficient to achieve that goal.[4] Moreover, issues of gender and class, which are notoriously difficult to separate from those of race, served only to entrap the liberal architects of the Great Society in dense thickets of contradiction and obfuscation. An understanding of the historical circumstances that led to the liberals' inability to make affirmative action work again reveals how perceptions (and misperceptions) of race among whites have continued to blind them to any vision of a truly free and democratic society.

By using affirmative action as a means for redressing past discrimination, liberals in the federal government hoped to enable black individuals and other members of minority groups to enter the mainstream of American life. Although never explicitly directed at African Americans, all the measures of affirmative action rested on the idea of including those previously excluded from the dominant ideology of individualism, democracy, and equal opportunity on the grounds of race. The very first announcement of equal employment opportunity, Franklin D. Roosevelt's Executive Order 8802, came in 1941 after intense pressure from black organizations for civil rights and equality. Directed at wartime defense contractors, Roosevelt's order called for fair employment practices "regardless of race, color, creed, or national origin." But this goal—like the goals of so many New Deal reforms—was compromised by a concerted unwillingness to confront grim realities, in this case of racism, head on.[5] Fear of upsetting lily-white southern Democrats was the reason most often given for this reluctance by participants in the New Deal and, later, by historians. But a deeper reason was the belief of the New Deal liberals that social relations could be reformed (so as to allow the "common man" a secure future in America) within the context of a refurbished liberal capitalism.

Moreover, adhering firmly to the doctrine of individualism, New Deal liberals were extremely cautious about appearing to favor one group over another, with the result that black people were lumped in with the common man. Without a doubt, Afro-Americans did receive some benefits from this approach. Many Black Americans were able to receive federal relief and in some cases were employed through the Works Project Administration, the Civilian Conservation Corps, and the Federal Theater Project. Importantly, however, the historical conditions that gave rise to racism, whether institutional or attitudinal, were never really addressed.[6]

Throughout the thirties, even as the New Deal politicians wrestled with the issue of discrimination in government contracts and relief programs, counties and states (particularly in the South) continued to practice racism, either through wage differentials or outright segregation. Southern politicians seemed firmly set against providing black people with equal pay for equal work, preferring to maintain a racist status quo. And even in Washington, despite various executive orders amending Executive Order 8802 in an effort to halt discrimination in the unions, the mood remained cautious. Indeed, the fear of provoking a retaliatory blockage of New Deal bills by powerful southern Congressmen caused liberal politicians to move very slowly, if at all, in this area. Thus, Southern influence in Congress served to dampen any meaningful attempts to sharply reduce discrimination, on top of which the national union leadership was reluctant to educate its rank and file.[7]

World War II, with its ideological struggle against the twin evils of fascism and Nazism, provided a crucial opportunity for those liberals to push through antidiscrimination measures. There could be no unified action against the enemies of freedom, they argued, so long as the charge of overt racial discrimination could be brought against the United States itself. Many Afro-Americans, however, were skeptical about whether these measures really signaled an end to discrimination. The racism that America displayed against the Japanese kept their perspective in order. Moreover, at least some African Americans felt a certain solidarity with the Japanese. As one black sharecropper was purported to have said the day after Pearl Harbor, "Boss, I understand them Japanese done declared war on y'all white folks."[8] Similar sentiments regarding the Japanese attack on "white" America may have lurked deep in the minds of many African Americans. In fact, several nationalist groups, like the Black Muslims, took an open stand against the war in the Pacific. Black newspapers, Afro-American intellectuals, and the black middle class leadership, however, urged the black masses to rally around America's fight for freedom. To be sure, the majority of African Americans did rally but, in all likelihood, largely out of a hope that the struggle to preserve democracy and freedom would this time ultimately result in real freedom and improvement for themselves.[9]

In some ways that hope looked as if it would be fulfilled. World War II did provide thousands of black people with jobs in defense-related industries, thus enabling many hitherto unskilled black workers to acquire skills. And given the necessity for manpower in the military, black women, like white women, entered the industrial workplace in massive numbers. As black labor historian William H. Harris noted, "Indeed, 'Rosie the Riveter' was as likely to be black as white."[10]

But the economic relief for African Americans would not continue unabated. The war's end demanded readjustments in the economy. If the war had opened up opportunities for black workers, during the postwar period opportunities were shifted back to returning white soldiers. African American workers, the majority of whom were the lowest on the seniority rolls, were quickly laid off. Throughout the fifties and into the early sixties, the unemployment rate among blacks was twice that among whites.[11]

Significantly, however, the war years were responsible for instilling a renewed sense of spirit and energy among Afro-Americans yearning for an end to overt discrimination. The seeds of the civil rights movement, sown in the thirties, began to sprout during the war years. And although there were setbacks in the fifties, there seemed to be a growing conviction that change was about to occur. How that change would ultimately affect all black people obviously could not be understood at the time. Nor could African Americans foresee how their subsequent struggles during the civil rights movement—with its attendant calls for justice, racial harmony, and affirmative action— would shake the moral, political, and economic foundations of America and provoke a more sinister and disturbing form of racism in reaction.

In 1954, when the Supreme Court banned segregated schooling, African Americans rejoiced. But they would continue to struggle for the next ten years to put an end to nearly a century of overt racial discrimination. The Civil Rights Act, strenuously debated, lobbied, and filibustered, was finally passed in 1964. Interestingly, however, it was essentially a replacement of the 1875 Civil Rights Act put into law during the Grant administration, only to be struck down by the Supreme Court in 1886.[12] Nonetheless, liberals congratulated themselves and worked earnestly on behalf of the Voting Rights Act, passed in 1965, which would later be called the triumphant victory of the civil rights movement.[13]

But seen from another angle, the Voting Rights Act of 1965 was in some ways a trade-off. On the one hand, the act ensured that the black masses in the South would be able to vote, which strengthened the hope that Afro-Americans would finally enter the political mainstream and participate in the democratic process. There was also the hope that, through the legal dismantling of the Jim Crow system, the South, long trapped in economic doldrums, would be forced into some sort of enlightened civility and economic rationality that would eventually contribute to economic revival. On the other hand, the successful passage of the Voting Rights Act tended to dampen the grass-roots radicalism that had existed as far back as the thirties and was now emerging through the activities of the Student Non-Violent Coordinating Committee.

In working with the black masses in the South, young middle-class black and white students hoped to foster a participatory democracy and instill a sense of community that was quite different from the suburban alienation of an affluent, technologically advanced society. The "beloved community" envisioned by SNCC members was certainly American enough—its roots went back to the more constructive aspects of the abolitionist and populist traditions. There was belief in the perfectibility of the individual and in the sustaining power of individual examples of moral suasion and nonviolence. But there was also a belief in the creation of a community—a community that respected the rights of others and, most important, took pride in the collective memory of who they were as a people and where they came from. Clayborne Carson, who studied the growth of the SNCC, provided an apt description when he stated that "black communities mobilized not merely to prod the federal government on behalf of blacks but to create new social identities for participants and all Afro-Americans."[14] But perhaps Julius Lester, who was one of those who helped in forming new social identities, summarized it best:

Perhaps, if I had not been one of those who had believed in the "beloved community," I would be content with changes wrought by the passage the 1964 Civil Rights Act and the 1965 Voting Rights Act. I would be content with the number of black lawmakers in Congress, state legislatures, city halls, and city councils. I would have found Jesse Jackson's campaign a sign of hope as did so many other blacks. But I didn't. . . . Did I acquire an ulcer in Mississippi just so somebody black could be president? Do I still mourn Chaney, Goodman, and Schwerner, Liuzzo and Daniels and Moore for a dubious integration wherein Mayor Wilson Goode of Phila-delphia can keep the Eagles from leaving town?[15]

The term *affirmative action* was first introduced, rather casually, in John F. Kennedy's Executive Order 10925 of 1961, which also stated that it was federal policy to use "positive measures" with regards to federal funding of grants to building contractors and subcontractors. The order, however, did not specify exactly what "affirmative action" meant.[16] Judging from previous presidential executive orders, Ken-nedy's intention was to remove discrimination from federally funded work projects. But what this would mean in terms of the training, hiring, and advancement of workers was problematic. Speaking in 1967, amidst increasing rebellion in the urban streets, Edward C. Sylvester, Jr., an African American and director of the Office of Feder-al Contract Compliance Programs under the Johnson administration, stated that "there is no fixed and firm definition of affirmative action. I would say that in a general way, affirmative action is anything you have to do to get results."[17]

The inability of liberal politicians and intellectuals to clearly define what affirmative action was and how it was to be rigorously applied was an important, and stark, reminder of the limitations of a system built on racial, gender, and economic inequality. Furthermore, the growing antipathy to an increasingly wasteful war in Southeast Asia only served to exacerbate an already polarized situation. In the span of six years—from Kennedy's introduction of affirmative action in 1961 to Sylvester's uncertain definition in 1967—American policymakers and intellectuals had failed to come to grips with one of the most critical problems in the nation.

Even as Lyndon Baines Johnson appropriated the hallowed slogan of the civil rights movement, "We shall overcome," in a speech at

Howard University and inaugurated his Great Society and affirmative action programs, there were clear signs that the masses of African Americans were losing patience with gradual reforms. Black Americans vented their frustrations at the continuance of racism and their inability to find employment throughout four years of long hot summers. Behind the scenes, white liberals, fueled by guilt and fear of social disruption, continued to base the rationale for affirmative action on the need to redress past grievances. For black intellectuals, this notion of the reparation of past discriminations was only fair and just. The problem (or rather the eventual flaw) lay with the ways to arrive at that result within the given capitalist economy.

The rise of black power, with its pride in racial heritage, demands for black autonomy, and rejection of liberalism, was unsettling for most liberal white politicians and intellectuals—so unsettling that they could not listen seriously to the demands of black radicalism or abandon their ideal of the elimination of poverty within the structure of capitalist society. Encouraged by an economic expansion (that was at best shallow) and clinging to a heartfelt belief in the essentially piecemeal approach of the civil rights movement, liberals pushed ahead with their antipoverty and affirmative action programs.[18]

At the core of the white liberal intellectual sensibility (which often found expression in anguished guilt) was the long-held belief that the collective personality of black people had been ravaged by slavery and racism. Slavery—that blot on American history—had wreaked havoc on America's soul. Its legacy—racism and Jim Crow restrictions—cast African Americans out of American society, and, as outsiders, black people were stereotyped and abused. Worse, they were deprived of the rights that were at the very foundation of the nation. The result was a tragic caste system in the rural South and a "tangle of pathology" in the urban areas of the country.[19]

White historical scholarship dealing with the African American experience came to fruition during a crucial transition period, when black intellectuals traversed the terrain from the racial harmony of civil rights to the nationalist autonomy of black power. Whereas black historians had traditionally written histories in order to uplift the race and countermand overtly racist interpretations of their presence in America, white historians in the late fifties and sixties provided histor-

ical analyses which refuted those earlier racist studies and detailed the
debilitating effects of slavery on blacks (and, indirectly, on whites).[20]
The intellectual climate of the Kennedy-Johnson years nourished a
flow of liberal ideas about the race problem. Drawing first on the
foundations laid by Gunnar Myrdal in *The American Dilemma* (1944),
explanations and analyses from all areas were refined and put forth
either to explain the black condition in America or to provide guidance for policymakers. In terms both of historical perspective and
social policy, these descriptions and prescriptions dovetailed with
white liberal programs, although they caused consternation within
some segments of the black community.

It was no accident, of course, that historical studies of slavery were
used to bolster intellectual rationales for implementing civil rights
reform and affirmative action policies. That African Americans had
been harshly treated and cruelly exploited during slavery called for
some form of reparation. Furthermore, the legacy of slavery—racism,
the distortion of the black personality, the deterioration of the black
family—was a burden the nation had either to relieve or else pay the
price in social disruption and loss of credibility internationally. Finally, were not blacks, to paraphrase historian Kenneth Stampp's sincere
but controversial statement, nothing more or less than white men in
black skins?[21]

Academic studies of African Americans were quickly appropriated
by presidents and other government officials. Kennedy, in a bold and
precedent-setting address to the nation after the 1963 murder of four
little black girls in a Birmingham church, drew on the moral dimension outlined in Gunnar Myrdal's massive study. "We are confronted
primarily with a moral issue. It is as old as the Scriptures and is as
clear as the American Constitution," Kennedy stated. He then went
on to deliver a moral lecture to the nation, upbraiding it for its
discrimination against blacks in public accommodation, in schools,
and at the ballot box. "Who among us," Kennedy asked rhetorically,
"would be content to have the color of his skin changed and be in his
[a black person's] place?" Ending his televised address, Kennedy
again emphasized the ethical dimension of the situation, characteriz-
ing it as a "moral crisis," and calling for action by the "Congress
. . . your state and legislative body, and, above all, in all our daily
lives."[22]

Kennedy's moral approach was in line with historical and social science scholarship that emphasized the attitudinal nature of racism and the moral bankruptcy of discrimination. But more, important, these remarks demonstrated liberalism's belief that governmental reforms were possible and that amends could thereby be made.

Thus, when President Johnson spoke on May 22, 1964, he clearly indicated that the civil rights movement's agenda was the government's agenda. "The Great Society rests on abundance and liberty for all," Johnson proclaimed. "It demands an end to poverty and racial injustice, to which we are totally committed in our time."[23] Speaking shortly later at Howard University's commencement on June 4, 1965, Johnson revealed the intellectual position that liberalism was prepared to take regarding the racial dilemma in America. Armed with a report on the black family by Harvard-trained sociologist Daniel P. Moynihan, Johnson made it clear that the goal for racial reform was "equality in fact." It seemed that the preceding years of struggle had not been enough to close the widening gap in education, employment, and poverty between blacks and whites, particularly in the urban North. The cause of this affliction in the black community, the Johnson administration concluded, rested within AfroAmerica itself, specifically in the plight of the black family. Basing most of his talk on Moynihan's report, *The Negro Family: A Case for National Action*, Johnson declared that more must be done and proposed a summer conference on the matter to be called "To Fulfill These Rights."[24]

That conference was never held, and we can only speculate as to what might have or should have developed out of that gathering. But in spite of the fact that Lyndon Johnson's words and actions marked a dramatic and welcome change in presidential pronouncements on race, the intellectual premises were flawed. The convictions that liberals, black or white, held about the black community, whether culled from historical scholarship or policy studies such as the Moynihan report, did not come to grips with critical issues: institutionalized racism, the possible need to redistribute resources in the economy so as really to achieve equality in fact, and the need for the moral and political reeducation of a white majority steeped in a centuries-old belief in white supremacy.

Moreover, during the Kennedy-Johnson years, the black middle class leadership faced its greatest ideological challenge since the 1930s.

Locked into what Harold Cruse described as a "non-economic liberalism," civil rights advocates relied heavily on court actions to push through reforms that Congress had often been unable or unwilling to enact. Black bourgeois success in desegregating education was indeed a major achievement for a class that believed strongly in integrated education as a means to improving the conditions of the masses. But when the fervor of the civil rights movement demonstrated that southern black communities were ready and willing to challenge overt discrimination and to choose their own leaders, tensions arose among the movement's various organizers. Established middle-class organizations such as the NAACP, the National Urban League, and the Congress of Racial Equality (CORE), as well as newer organizations such as the Southern Christian Leadership Conference (SCLC) and the SNCC, quickly scrambled to figure out how to best coordinate the movement for civil rights.[25] But there were even greater tensions. Superficially, these appeared simply generational, but in actuality they bespoke fundamental ideological and cultural differences between civil rights leaders and young people.

The young black activists of the SNCC initially pursued a vision that was squarely within the goals of SCLC and CORE. They were never very comfortable, however, with what they perceived as a condescending attitude on the part of the established organizations toward the masses. Indeed, it had always been a tendency of black bourgeois leadership not only to speak for the masses but also to use them to advance integrationist goals.[26] For the young blacks (and whites) of the SNCC, integration was also important, at least initially. But it was also important for those young blacks that the civil rights movement was not just about creating a racially harmonious society. It was a freedom struggle. That freedom struggle was at first grounded in obtaining access to public facilities—the right to buy a hamburger at Kresge's. But true freedom, the activists soon learned, could only come about when the black community was able to determine its own direction and to have an equal voice in the policy-making decisions that directly affected its well-being.[27] Thus their support for participatory democracy, which would allow each individual a political and social equality unheard of for many generations, along with the right to organize politically, placed SNCC workers on the radical side of matters long before black power made its inevitable appearance.

The SNCC's visionary conception of a new society, imbued with values that could actualize the ideals of equality and freedom that all Americans supposedly believed in, was naive with respect to its faith that America could be morally persuaded to change for the better. It was only through experiencing harsh political betrayal at the Democratic National Convention in Atlantic City in 1964, the accumulated deaths of co-workers and friends at the hands of racist violence, and the bitter realization that white liberals in power were only going to go so far on behalf of African Americans that the SNCC moved to revise its tactics. In doing so, it also moved further left with its biting analyses of racism, class, and militarism.[28]

But even as the SNCC revised its stance to embrace black nationalism, it did not entirely forget or reject its fervent belief in participatory democracy and its vision of a new society. The tragedy of the SNCC was not in its espousal of black nationalism but rather in the way it angrily excluded white allies. The new leaders of the SNCC, "the nationalist faction," proclaiming that whites must rid their own communities of racism before any meaningful coalitions for change could begin, ejected whites from the organization.[29] That was a serious mistake, for there was no way that a serious reeducation of white America away from its belief in white supremacy could be accomplished by white radicals alone. Most white activists, though certainly antiracist, were profoundly alienated from their own communities. Radical African Americans, their justified anger notwithstanding, thus left liberals with little alternative but to attempt to forge an integrated society along the lines envisioned during the early days of the civil rights movement. Indeed, many of the white activists went on to construct the anti-Vietnam war movement, the women's movement, and the counterculture generally. But, sadly, the deep racism of the system remained largely unaddressed, in part because no one had a clear idea of what a multiracial, nonracist society would look like.[30]

The black middle class leadership essentially accepted the premises of the dominant capitalist ethos and liberalism's New Deal coalition politics. Now, however, they were forced into the somewhat uncomfortable position of seeking to curb the youthful desire for what they perceived as overly radical action, on the one hand, and, on the other hand, using the ideas and angry critiques of youth as a means of pressuring the liberal government for more moderate gains. Thus, for example, Executive Secretary Roy Wilkins of the NAACP and Executive Director Whitney Young of the National Urban League could, behind closed doors, effectively win concessions from corporations or politicians for programs by threats that "black militants" might generate social disruption. In public, though, the two men disavowed such radical tactics. Martin Luther King, Jr., who later in his career moved more toward the left, often used this tactic, although probably for more responsible ends than Wilkins or Young. King held firmly to the vision of a new society, but he never resorted to the harsh rhetoric of the nationalists or the advocacy of violence. However much he moved to the left, he tried to hold a center that was rapidly disappearing.[31]

It was not surprising, then, that the established civil rights leaders approved of President Johnson's Howard University commencement address. The goals outlined in that speech were what they had been struggling to attain for many years: this was the center that King wanted in place. The intellectual analyses as put forth by Moynihan concerning the tragedy of the urban lower-class black family were well within their traditional view of the downtrodden masses in need of government support for their uplift.[32] With white liberals apparently eager to erase past injustices and provide aid to the distressed black family, the black middle class leadership obtained programs for greater access to higher education, along with promises of steady employment and adequate measures to ensure equal opportunity. As long as black radical rhetoric, no matter how angrily anti-white, remained merely rhetoric, the black bourgeois leadership was able to finesse federal programs and corporate grants that would provide some visible examples of progress.[33]

That the chief beneficiaries of Johnson's Great Society were mainly members of the existing black middle class has long been noted, but it must be stressed that the middle class did expand.[34] In particular, the use of affirmative action in higher education saw a marked increase in black student enrollments and a slight but visible increase in black faculty. But affirmative action was a concept that, even in the apparent safety of its vagueness, liberals handled gingerly. Clearly, if rigorously applied, affirmative action programs would inevitably undermine the fundamental premises of a capitalist society—a society founded on inherent inequality coupled with the promise of reward for individual effort. Liberals chose instead to base affirmative action on the idea of redressing grievances for past discrimination and the prevention of future discrimination. But even this failed to solve the problem. Moreover, were not women grievously discriminated against? And Native Americans? And Hispanics?[35]

By the seventies, affirmative action had been extended to all minorities, and, by the late seventies, to women, who, although not a minority, were now recognized as a particularly disadvantaged group, especially in view of their increased presence in the workplace and a marked rise in single-headed households and female poverty.[36] In short, everyone was eligible for affirmative action except white males.

For African Americans who continued to carry the hope of a racially and socially just society, affirmative action was at least a minimal reparation—"a means of keeping white folks honest" and allowing a few worthies (mostly from the black middle class) into the system.[37] But affirmative action was designed to fail less because it allowed only so many blacks to benefit from equal opportunity than because it systematically refused to confront the full implications and consequences of affirmative action on a mature capitalist system. By not facing the multitude of contradictions that affirmative action posed for all aspects of the society's institutions, economy, political thought, and social relations, liberals provided more than enough ammunition to the most vicious critics of affirmative action (and the rights of Afro-Americans in general) for its demise. Notwithstanding the historical reality of a shrinking economy, the increasing growth of a large population of unemployable people, and the slippage of America's international economic power—all of which signaled the end of the American dream—it was questionable whether affirmative action, as constructed, could ever produce meaningful results.[38] Several factors mitigated against even the most bland versions of it.

Perhaps the most critical factor involved the premise upon which affirmative action was based. As Elizabeth Fox-Genovese cogently argues, "Historically our society has privileged the ideal of individual freedom of self-determination as the highest good." In a society convinced so deeply of the "myth of individualism," any ideas regarding the redress of past discrimination that took into account the collective histories of a group were immediately questioned. Such a consideration of group rights went against the grain of individual liberty and the idea of meritocracy. At worst, such an approach meant the introduction of categories that would, in effect, create new discrimination.[39]

The conservative opponents of affirmative action correctly saw the implications of the concept: a frontal challenge, if not a brutal assault, on cherished social structures that have served to maintain particular gender relations, race relations, and economic practices. The conservative (and neoconservative) attacks on what they termed "preferential treatment," "quotas," and "reverse discrimination" displayed a familiar desire to accommodate racism and white male supremacy but in new and more sophisticated ways. But liberals, faced in the eighties with the loss of political power, a splintering of the New Deal coalition, and an extremely shaky economy, continued to try to justify affirmative action in terms of individual fairness. Silently refusing to question the principles of individualism on which the concept was founded, much of the left even retreated to the position of arguing for the preservation of what little gains had already been won under affirmative action.[40]

In fairness, it was extremely difficult to press the transformative nature of affirmative action given the hostile political climate of the late seventies and early eighties. Nonetheless, the inability (or unwillingness) of liberals to think through affirmative action—not merely as a course of retributive justice but as a means of restructuring a faltering welfare state—allowed hard-line conservatives and the New Right to use the very same principles of individualism and "fairness" to dismantle affirmative action. Throughout the eighties, the Reagan administration used the Justice Department and the U.S. Civil Rights Commission to do just that.[41] Nowhere was this more successfully undertaken than in the areas of black access to higher education and the comparable worth of women's work.

In his insightful cautionary tale "The DeVine Gift," Derrick Bell, an African American Harvard law professor, uses fiction as a means of addressing complex issues surrounding affirmative action. In his story, Bell relates how Geneva Crenshaw, a brilliant civil rights lawyer-activist and consummate bearer of common sense, struggles with her university's disinclination to hire black faculty.[42] The university had been able to obtain a number of highly qualified black law faculty through Crenshaw's extensive connection to the Afro-American community. But a seventh candidate of superior qualifications is rejected, whereupon Crenshaw realizes that

> if and when the number of blacks qualified for upper level jobs exceeds the token representation envisioned by most affirmative action programs, opposition of the character exhibited by my law school could provide the impetus for a judicial ruling that employers have done their "fair share" of minority hiring. This rule, while imposing limits on constitutionally required racial fairness for a black elite, would devastate civil rights enforcement for all minorities.[43]

Bell's fable illustrates a familiar truth: affirmative action could be and often was used as a form of tokenism and to put a ceiling on the "black elite." But the fable is also ironic. Behind it lies a hard reality: as of 1988 only 4 percent of the faculty in higher education was black, in part because the number of blacks earning Ph.D.s, which had seen a significant increase in the seventies, began to drop precipitously in the eighties. With such a small pool to draw from, colleges and universities were in fact extremely hard-pressed to find qualified black candidates for their faculty positions.[44]

The main point here, however, is that the pursuit of true affirmative action would have exposed how deeply embedded racist ideology was in American society and how entwined with ideas concerning capitalism, individualism, merit, and standards of quality and excellence. But as long as white society refused to confront and destroy its white supremacist beliefs (however subtle or deeply rooted), affirmative action would be continually thwarted, weighted down by the contradictions of a capitalist society firmly grounded in inequality. While positive affirmative action procedures did begin to shed light on the depths of racism and the belief in white supremacy, its illumination of the inequality in gender relations proved even more revealing. This was especially so interracially for black women as the black middle class expanded.

The reemergence of the women's movement in the sixties and seventies emanated from the civil rights–black power movements and the birth of the New Left.[45] That movement was largely white and middle class, although professedly antiracist. But tensions between black women (a minority in the movement and largely middle-class also) and white women were present from the start.[46] Nonetheless, the claims of white women that they, too, were discriminated against and therefore deserved equal treatment under affirmative action procedures were justified enough to convince the courts and the government to include them under the guidelines.

But the mainstream women's movement fell into the same trap as that in which the black bourgeois leadership was ensnared by not thinking through the contradictions that affirmative action presented when grounded in individualistic terms. Moreover, when women proposed in the eighties that the value of their work should be commensurate to that of their male counterparts (the doctrine of comparable worth), they simultaneously added a new dimension to the notion of equality and to the vision of what a new American society could be. At the same time, they again avoided critically analyzing the individualistic and class premises in which affirmative action was enmeshed.[47]

Indeed, many of the arguments about affirmative action tended to neglect the dimension of class. The content of the arguments was too far removed from the day-to-day realities of working-class and poor people: they were at once too abstract and too concerned with the impact of these policies on specific individuals, as opposed to larger groups. But affirmative action for blacks mainly benefited the black bourgeoisie, and it was no different for women. That is to say that the prime beneficiaries of affirmative action and comparable worth were middle-class women, black or white, rather than lower-class women. Thus the masses of poor women were relegated even further to the margins of a society that in the eighties increasingly saw more women in the workplace and more female single-parent households (disproportionately so in the African American community), which added to the polarization between the haves and the have-nots.[48]

The hue and cry over comparable worth, however, nevertheless exposed the entrenched male antagonism toward women's rightful claims to an equal and participatory status in the society. Further, the challenges that women brought against the values and the social structure of America unveiled some of the more sophisticated, and insidious, forms of racism yet to be seen. George Gilder, a notable conservative intellectual in the early Reagan years, called for a halt to the women's movement *and* affirmative action on the grounds that both were destroying the black family. The women's movement and affirmative action forced men out of jobs, the argument went, thus accelerating the disintegration of the family and ruining the moral and social fabric. More specifically, affirmative action procedures favored black women over black men, thereby robbing those men not only of stable employment but also of a male sense of self-esteem that would enable them to head a stable family.[49]

At the same time, there was a group of newly arrived middle-class African Americans who were labeled neoconservative and were courted by the Republican New Right in the eighties. These black neoconservatives joined together black traditions of self-help, racial uplift, and a nationalist belief in racial solidarity with conservative beliefs in an absence of governmental interference, in entrepreneurship, and in individual achievement. There was also an emphasis on moral rectitude and the preservation of the black family. But what was more interesting about the black neoconservatives was their faith in economic integration and individualism. This faith rested, however uneasily, on a studied belief that African Americans as a group could improve themselves given a sound education, bourgeois moral values, and opportunities to achieve. Thus Clarence Pendleton, chair of the Civil Rights Commission during the Reagan years, frequently remarked that the notion of comparable worth was a "looney tune" and that affirmative action was unnecessary for, if not outright detrimental to, black people.[50] From Pendleton's viewpoint, comparable worth had the potential to wreak havoc with traditional work roles of men and women. But, even worse, the rewards of comparable worth did not really extend to those poor women, black or white, who might really have benefited from it.[51]

The ideas and prescriptions of the black neoconservatives set a new tone for discussion about how to solve the increasing problems that the majority of black Americans faced in the eighties and nineties. In many ways, these ideas harked back to the early years of affirmative action. But a closer look at those black neoconservatives revealed an interesting blend of integration and nationalism, as well as a determination to think independently of the received wisdom, whether of the Democrats, the Republicans, or the civil rights leadership.

There had always been African Americans who embraced the economic and ideological ideas of conservatism. Even as these people took pride in racial accomplishments, it was almost always within the context of an adherence to the doctrine of individual achievement and racial improvement within the prevailing social and economic norms. Thus, in the thirties, for example, many black middle class conservatives opposed Roosevelt's economic relief program, arguing that blacks would become dependent on the dole.[52] Yet those same conservatives, unlike their later counterparts, seemed uninterested in providing relief for the masses or in effecting any real improvement of their lot. Indeed, they distrusted them or, at worst, held them in contempt. Their main concern was to maintain order—to raise those who were impoverished to a level of social and economic "civility" where they would not attract unwarranted attention.

The neoconservative blacks of the eighties were far different from their predecessors in that they felt a real desire to seek some remedies for the black underclass.[53] In part, this was because many of those now in the middle class had come from the inner cities or from working-class families and had benefited from affirmative action policies that had opened the doors of education and professional opportunity to them. There was also some nationalistic belief in black solidarity. After all, most of those who belonged to this generation (sometimes referred to as affirmative action babies) had been influenced by, or could at least remember, Martin Luther King, Jr., Malcolm X, and the Black Panthers. But these neoconservatives also betrayed a decidedly integrationist streak. For black neoconservatives the question of race was not the main concern. Indeed, the whole notion of racial pride as a tie with which to bind the community together was considered good only so long as the community itself replicated or mirrored dominant ideological imperatives.

During the eighties, the rise of conservatism generally had the effect of highlighting those African Americans who espoused the ideas of the New Right. But black conservatives who criticized affirmative action or complained of the dependency of blacks on the

welfare system had been around as far back as the early days of
the civil rights movement. In particular—and a likely precursor to the
new generation of black conservatives in the eighties and nineties—
was George Schuyler.

Schuyler had a long career as a journalist and gadfly of the civil
rights leadership and the black left, a career that dated back to the
twenties. At that time, he had aligned himself with A. Phillip Randolph, whom he considered "one of the finest, most engaging men I
have ever met." Schuyler worked at Randolph's socialist-oriented
journal, *The Messenger*, as well as at the *Pittsburgh Courier*, into the
thirties. By the early thirties, however, he found himself increasingly
disagreeing with the "Reds" and the "Black mouthpieces that they
were corralling."[54] By the middle of the thirties, Schuyler had
dropped any pretense of being on the left and for the rest of his life
moved further and further to the right. By the fifties he was convinced
that the civil rights movement was part of a communist conspiracy.

But despite Schuyler's drift into a virulent anticommunism, there
were several features of his thought that remained consistent
throughout his life and to some degree have informed the new black
conservatives of the late twentieth century. Those features were a
strong belief in integration, both politically and socially, a total disdain for separatism, and a strong belief in individualism. Schuyler was
not anti-black, but he certainly was not in favor of Afro-Americans
using race as a crutch to solve their problems. As far back as the
thirties he wrote that Afro-Americans hurt their chances for improvement by "an overstressing of race, by fostering chauvinistic isolation,
by developing exaggerated race patriotism and seeing the whole
world and its problems through black spectacles."[55]

Schuyler maintained that Afro-Americans were, first and foremost,
Americans: "Our language, our culture, our training, are not African
or Negro, but American." In fact, Afro-Americans were nothing
more than "lamp-black Anglo-Saxons."[56] These particular ideas could
not be said to be held by all black conservatives, new or old. But
Schuyler also attempted to maintain the delicate balance between the
two identities that Du Bois wrote about even if it meant going back
and forth between Africanness and Americanness in a somewhat
schizophrenic and satirical fashion, as can be seen in his pulp fiction
and his novel *Black No More* (1931) as well as in his work for the

Pittsburgh Courier later in the thirties. Indeed, this was another hallmark of Schuyler's thought that was passed on to the new conservatives: the effort to find a balance between one's identity with the group and one's individuality and/or Americanness.

In many respects, then, the black neoconservatives of the early 1980s were descendants of a tradition of black conservatism that reached back beyond even the 1930s to the closing decades of the nineteenth century. Wedded to the nineteenth-century ideas of laissez-faire economics, bourgeois morality and respectability, and possessive individualism, most of these neoconservatives implicitly or explicitly rediscovered Booker T. Washington as a hero. Washington's strong hegemony over AfroAmerica has deeply influenced even black liberals and radicals. But for the black neoconservatives of the late twentieth century, Washington came to symbolize a form of "pragmatism" that would enable the black community to come to grips with being politically forgotten, on the one hand, and would serve to inspire community self-help and improvement, on the other. Robert Woodson, president of the National Center for Neighborhood Enterprise, a grass-roots organization dedicated to black community self-sufficiency, demonstrated that pragmatism when he stated, "I think of myself as a pragmatist because I'm more concerned with concrete prescriptions than with labels. My views contain certain elements of liberalism, conservatism, black nationalism, and American patriotism."[57] But drawing on the legacy of Washington provided little, economically, that was of any help toward resolving the increasing immiseration of the black majority. Washington's ideas were more fervently put to use to encourage African Americans to see that depending on the government to solve all of their problems was quickly becoming a waste of time. And it was here that affirmative action came under the most fire.

In the mid-seventies, a bright young black economist from Harvard, Thomas Sowell, emerged as the leading figure among the new black conservatives. Sowell consistently portrayed African Americans as an ethnic group that had unfortunately not been able to match the degre of assimilation achieved by other ethnic groups.[58] Sowell, in several books, compared the social and economic history of various ethnic groups with that of black Americans, and, in part 1 of his *Preferential*

Policies: An International Perspective, did what no one before had thought of doing: examining and comparing the preferential hiring practices in other societies with those of the United States. In comparing these ethnic economic and social histories with the history of blacks, Sowell discovered that slavery had severely handicapped black people, adversely affecting their motivation, self-esteem, and ability to achieve success. Of course, some individuals had succeeded. From Sowell's viewpoint, these successes were the result of the absorption of middle-class values and the existence of a strong traditional family that encouraged educational achievement, self-reliance, and morality. The masses of blacks have yet to achieve such success, Sowell maintained (along with other black neoconservatives), because of misguided civil rights legislation, welfare dependency, and affirmative action.[59]

Thomas Sowell's analyses and prescriptions were based on the common belief that talent, individual effort, and strong encouragement from one's family were the keys to achievement, a belief that, in the past, many African American middle-class parents had tried to instill in their children. One could also make the case that, at least to some extent, the values of the black middle class had been inculcated among working-class and poor blacks. In the South of the Jim Crow era, for example, forced enclosure segregation enabled working-class and poor blacks to encounter middle-class African Americans. In their roles as teachers, small shop-owners, and ministers, these petit bourgeois blacks were in a position to show that education and hard work could count for something. At the same time, those same middle-class blacks were engaged in trying to break out of the stifling environment that was suppressing their potential. Whether African Americans adhered to Washingtonian accommodationism or responded to the appeals of Du Bois and Ida B. Wells to stand up and demand their rights, they did so as a group that was viewed, by whites, as outsiders and declared by the prevailing racial ideology to be inferior. But that was then, and now the recent civil rights movement had produced a new situation in which the black middle class was freed from the suffocating circumstances of the past. The question, then, that Sowell and other middle-class black neoconservatives struggled with was how to stem the increasing deterioration of the poorer black community and give individual blacks an opportunity to lift themselves up.

For a long time, Sowell was seemingly a lone voice in calling for a reexamination of affirmative action policies. The accepted thinking in AfroAmerica during the civil rights movement had been that only the federal government was able to ensure the rights of blacks and that the federal courts would pave the way not only for equal opportunities but also equal results.[60] But twenty years later, with the society moving further to the right under the Reagan administration, younger voices in the enlarged black middle class raised doubts about the received wisdom of the established civil rights agenda. These bourgeois African American intellectuals, who came of age during the civil rights–black power era and subsequently embarked on careers in the academy and government, sought to redefine AfroAmerica's problems and the direction it should take. That many of them were aided and even praised by the conservatives in power should not obscure the fact that, in most cases, these individuals were neoconservative only to the extent that they questioned whether government agencies and programs like affirmative action were really helping the entire black community as opposed to the relative few that were already in the middle class.

As Stephen L. Carter had pointed out, accurately, there was something of an odd alliance with the black left among conservatives such as Sowell, inasmuch as the black left in the sixties was also opposed to government agencies making blacks dependent on them. Their vision was of a society in which African Americans, who culturally and socially constituted a nation within a nation, would have empowerment and self-determination.[61] But, whereas for the black left this vision presupposed a socialist state, for black neoconservatives the way to attain that empowerment lay within the system as it was presently structured and rested on individual initiative. The most notable presentation of this view, at least in the eyes of the white press, was made by Harvard political economist Glenn Loury in the mid-eighties.

Loury, who came from the streets of southside Chicago, had been another beneficiary of affirmative action education policies, advancing through prestigious schools and into a professorship. Loury reformulated the plight of African Americans in analyses that not only drew upon the insights of Thomas Sowell but also reflected the deep concern of many black intellectuals about the widening gap between middle-class blacks and the burgeoning black underclass. In a much talked-about article, "Beyond Civil Rights," which appeared in the *New Republic*, Loury offered an explication of his and other black neoconservatives' analyses and prescriptions.[62] In both his premises and conclusions Loury revealed how a growing segment of the black bourgeoisie was not only taking a dissenting and often rightward turn away from the position of established civil rights leaders regarding the black community but was also attempting the rehabilitation of the black middle class in accordance with a more conservative and individualistic view of society and morality. Thus Loury downplayed civil rights activism, arguing that "many, if not most, people now concede that not all problems of blacks are due to discrimination and that they cannot be remedied through civil rights strategies or racial politics. I would go even further: using civil rights strategies to address problems to which they are ill-suited thwarts more direct and effective action."[63]

Loury maintained that previous approaches to resolving socioeconomic inequality (namely, civil rights legislation and government agencies designed to enforce those laws) had not been able to eliminate racial discrimination because, in the end, the government was unable to legislate attitudes and morality among individuals or even within communities. In Loury's view, "As a result the nondiscrimination mandate has not been allowed to interfere much with personal, private, and intimately social intercourse." For Loury, the crucial key lay in the importance of "family and community background in determining the child's later success in life. Lacking the right 'networks,' blacks with the same innate abilities as whites wind up less successful."[64]

Having declared that civil rights had failed to influence the private lives of Americans, Loury then turned to the public policy implications of the civil rights approach. "Even in this area, the efficacy of this strategy can be questioned," Loury asserted. "The lagging economic conditions of blacks is due in significant part to the nature of social life *within* poor black communities." Despite two decades of civil rights efforts, the situation of the black masses had considerably worsened, but, Loury maintained, "white America's lack of respect for blacks' civil rights cannot be blamed for all these sorry facts. This is not to say that, in some basic sense, most of the difficulties are related to our history of racial oppression but only to say that these problems have taken on a life of their own, and cannot be reversed by civil rights policies."[65]

Like other black middle class neoconservative intellectuals, Loury attempted to explain white America's continuing acceptance of racism, economic inequality, and sexism by declaring that the tactics employed by the civil rights movement had been only partially successful and had outlived their usefulness. At the same time, thanks in no small measure to that movement, African Americans now have opportunities that were never before available, opportunities that it is up to them to pursue. Black thinkers like Loury thus appeared to have reverted, in perhaps a more positive fashion, to the older black middle class's mission of exhorting the masses to lift themselves up and their embrace of concepts such as individualism and liberty—a refashioning of the old black middle class's dictums to fit the post–civil rights era. Thus, for example, Loury stated that while "blacks continue to seek the respect of fellow Americans . . . it becomes increasingly clear that, to do so, black Americans cannot substitute judicial and legislative decree for what is to be won through the outstanding achievements of *individual* black persons" (my emphasis).[66]

The question immediately arose, of course, of what was to be done to resuscitate the black community. Like so many in the black bourgeoisie, Loury and his compatriots betrayed an age-old ambivalence about providing any concrete solutions. Part of that was not their fault, for, by the eighties, the black middle class was moving further away from having significant contact with the masses. As a 1991 study released by the Population Reference Bureau, *African Americans in the Nineties*, stated: "Among African Americans, opportunities continue to open up for the educated middle class while the urban poor appear stuck in a quagmire of unstable families, intermittent employment, welfare dependence, and the temptations of crime." The report went on to say that "the middle class blacks of the future may feel little in common with poor blacks because their experiences will have been dramatically different in so many ways."[67] Given the increasing gap between the black middle class and the black masses, it is not surprising that intellectuals like Loury were at something of a loss for answers.

Thus, for Loury and other black intellectuals who leaned to the right, it was only through the "outstanding achievements of individual black persons" that black people could gain, in Loury's words, "what ultimately is being sought . . . the freely conveyed respect of one's peers."[68] The black bourgeoisie had once again to become role models for the black masses. This meant that it was the duty of successful black middle class professionals to show that they had gotten where they were by the process of hard work and personal responsibility. According to Shelby Steele, an impassioned defender of this view, members of the black middle class could not be good examples "until they are released from a black identity that regards that example as suspect, that sees them as 'marginally black.'"[69] In other words, while overt racial discrimination was not to be tolerated, neither was racial separation or self-segregation.

Here the task of the black middle class was to exhort young blacks to seize the opportunities that were available instead of capitulating to what Steele called "the tendency to minimalize or avoid real opportunities, to withhold effort in areas where few blacks have achieved."[70] On the subject of the avoidance of responsibility, Jeff Howard, a black social psychologist, and Ray Hammond, a black minister and physician, argued that the avoidance or minimalization of real opportunities stemmed not from the devastating intellectual inferiority "rumored" to be found in blacks but in the internalization by Afro-Americans of this racist belief. They stated that "because of the gains in education, economic status, and political leverage that we have won as a result of the civil rights movement," the black middle class is "in a position to substantially improve the conditions of our communities using the resources at our disposal."[71] Thus, argued the black neoconservatives, the black middle class must attempt to inspire their less advantaged brethren to adopt the values of hard work, a good education, and bourgeois morality, rather than looking to the government to solve their problems.

Thus, even as the black left called for the empowerment of the black community based on the historical oppression that African Americans had received, black neoconservatives and other dissenting intellectuals called for commonality that would be enriched by differences in ethnic groups and races, arguing for many of the same goals as had the early civil rights movement: racial harmony and a color-blind society characterized by equal opportunity and fairness. Moreover, regardless of how rigidly confined or mired down affirmative action had become, there could be no doubt that some form of it would continue. At the same time, the successes of the civil rights movement and the passionate energies of the black power movement had brought forth a generation of young African American intellectuals who were willing to raise challenging questions not only about affirmative action but also about the value that American society held for African Americans. No matter how they were characterized by the white media or by black liberals, the neoconservative middle-class blacks, together with those other African Americans who took them seriously and who also dissented from the established civil rights agenda, were not traitors to the race. They evinced a serious concern for the plight of those in the underclass and were deeply worried about the widening gap between the black middle class and the urban black poor. Nor could they be said to be seeking a disappearance of the race along the lines envisaged by E. Franklin Frazier. Although the black neoconservatives were certainly integrationist in their desire for a color-blind society, they revealed a very real concern for the black community that carried with it a streak of nationalism and pride in being African American.

If anything, the black neoconservatives of the eighties were a significant part of the fruits of integration. They demonstrated to white America that there was more diversity within the black community than their one-dimensional view of "black." They also made it amply evident that black intellectuals were more than capable of addressing the problems besetting not only their community but also America in general and of suggesting new directions for both. In the following chapters we will see how this diversity of thought and spirit of creativity has found expression in literature and in music, television, and motion pictures. It is in these cultural areas that the black middle class has moved toward the greatest fruit of integration, which I call integrative cultural diversity.

CHAPTER 4

Integrating the Many Voices

The Continuing Growth of
African American Literature

As a nation within a nation, a people imbued with a double consciousness, AfroAmerica underwent a series of rebirths during the twentieth century. African American historians generally tend to focus on the years between 1919 and 1935 as the period in which the "New Negro" emerged. For our purposes, this era provided the foundation on which the black middle class would build its cultural representation of AfroAmerica as a race and as a nation within America. The period was called the Harlem Renaissance because of the vast migration of black people into Manhattan's northwest sector and the subsequent outpouring of poems, plays, and art. Many northern cities saw an influx of black people from the South, but Harlem was considered the capital of AfroAmerica.[1]

Harlem was a magnet that drew black people not only from the deep South but also from the West Coast and the Caribbean. It was to Harlem that Langston Hughes, Zora Neale Hurston, Jesse Fauset, Wallace Thurman, Countee Cullen, and many others came. Arriving in Harlem, these black writers immersed themselves in the street life, the clubs, and the salons and as writers bore witness to, and thus exposed some of America to, the cultural diversity of AfroAmerica.

AfroAmerica was a "nation" whose core was deeply American yet whose people were excluded from the power conferred by capital and political participation—a nation whose cultural values, forged through suffering and survival, provided a valuable alternative to America's growing love affair with material consumption and leisure. Those cultural values consisted of a desire on the part of Afro-Americans to attain full humanity through folk wisdom, the exuberance of the black church's rituals, and the creation of music, secular as well as spiritual, and literature. They provided a much needed spiritual mooring for the nation at large, which, weary from the effects of World War I, was torn between a desire for "normalcy"—a return to the traditional values exemplified in the rural town setting—and an eager embrace of carefree, fast-paced urban life.

Perhaps this particular period should not be burdened with so much historical significance. But it was in this period that the essential groundwork was laid for the subsequent movement of the black middle class toward what I call integrative cultural diversity. The cultural productions of the Harlem Renaissance, along with the rise of the New Negro, provided the initial means by which AfroAmerica would come not only to influence the American cultural landscape but also to reveal the various voices that together made up the black experience in America.

African American literary scholars of the late twentieth century have traced the evolution of AfroAmerica's literary culture to this period. One scholar, James De Jongh, saw the period's writers and artists engaged in what he termed "vicious modernism"—an intense and highly creative ferment that brought forth the New Negro and gave expression to the cultural force exerted by AfroAmerica within American society. Other scholars, notably Houston Baker, Jr., go as far back as Booker T. Washington to find the roots of literature in Washington's inspired manipulation of white America's peculiar conception of African American culture as nothing more than a minstrel show. Still others went even further back, citing the slave narratives as ways in which an oppressed people recreated themselves as a nation with a distinct culture.[2] These various scholarly perspectives on black literature, whatever their intrinsic worth, speak to the deep and enduring imprint that Afro-American culture has made on the larger American society. For even though African Americans were relegated to the status of outsiders by white Americans in the most blatant political and economic ways, their culture afforded spiritual nourishment. It also evoked troubling questions, which in turn led to suggestive ideas for the re-creation of the entire society.

AfroAmerica's cultural landscape was always inseparable from its political context in both America and the world. From whatever perspective one views the African American experience, this consideration of politics remains inescapable. It is crucial to the idea of integrative cultural diversity as well as to the way in which African American culture has shaped political and cultural perception and discourse. For example, Booker T. Washington's manipulation of white America's conception of Afro-American culture as minstrelsy was, in Houston Baker's argument, a brilliant form of "speaking back and black." Baker finds examples of this tactic throughout Washington's autobiography, *Up from Slavery*. As Baker acknowledges, Washington rose to prominence as the spokesperson for African Americans, but he was also the chief proponent of the dominant society's ideology to AfroAmerica. Given his accommodationist stance, Washington could provide AfroAmerica with a measure of visibility to the American nation, visibility that was at once relatively unthreatening to white racists and congenial to northern philanthropists and liberals. But, in Baker's view, the chief hallmark of Washington was less his alleged Uncle Tomism than the deftness with which he was able to juggle the bizarre perceptions that whites had of blacks. It was this ability that allowed Washington to advance the cause of AfroAmerica while seeming not to disturb the overall social fabric.[3]

Though whites saw Washington as the leader of his people, and despite the fact of his strong hegemony over AfroAmerica, African American culture was by no means summed up in Booker T. Washington. Washington's strength came in part from his identity as a black southerner at a time when the majority of African Americans resided in the South. However, considerable numbers of African Americans lived in the North, and their lives, while certainly influenced by Washington's presence, were markedly different from those of their rural brothers and sisters whom Washington wished to uplift. Then as now, African American culture was not so monolithic, and far from easy to define.

The class construction within AfroAmerica, which was similar to the dominant society's, was also shaped by the variegated regional experiences of black Americans and their degree of education and material wealth. By the turn of the century, there was a small but recognizable black middle class in most of the major cities of the nation. In areas outside the cities in northern states such as New York, Massachusetts, and New Jersey, enclaves of African Americans coexisted, however uneasily, with the predominately rural white society. And, of course, there were also the all-black towns of the South and the West.[4] The various adaptations to white culture that these black people made in no way negated the essence of African American culture but rather added a richness and texture that in many ways challenged, from within, the "mastery of form" that Baker ascribes to Booker T. Washington's handling of white cultural symbols about African Americans. That mastery of form, however, which worked well enough in the Jim Crow South, had to be revised in order to accommodate the experiences of, say, black northerners or African Americans who grew up in relative racial isolation. The most prominent examples here are W. E. B. Du Bois, who grew up in Massachusetts, Zora Neale Hurston, from Eatonville, Florida, and Langston Hughes, who came from Cleveland, Ohio.

W. E. B. Du Bois spent his early life in Great Barrington, Massachusetts, and is almost a textbook example of how Afro-Americans growing up in integrated settings come to discover their racial heritage. In his autobiography, *Dusk of Dawn*, Du Bois describes his family history, which he learned from his mother and grandparents:

> The number of colored people in the town and county was small. They were all, save directly after the war, old families, well known to the old settlers among the whites. My family was among the oldest inhabitants of the valley. The family had spread slowly through the county, intermarrying among cousins and other black folk with some but limited infiltration of white blood.[5]

Du Bois goes on to lay out the cultural context of his upbringing and, by extension, that of other black people in similar situations. Du Bois first realized the depth and vitality of African American culture when he attended an all-black gathering at Rocky Point on Narragansett Bay:

I had attended an annual picnic beside the sea and had seen in open-mouthed astonishment the whole gorgeous gamut of the American Negro world: the swaggering men, the beautiful girls, the laughter and gaiety, the unhampered self-expression. I was astonished and inspired. I became aware, once a chance to go to a group of such young people was opened up to me, of the spiritual isolation in which I was living.[6]

This amounted to a profound experience of how integrative cultural diversity worked on a localized level. Upon completing his education, Du Bois went to the South to live, teach, and work among his people, inspired by the cultural and political realities of that "American Negro world" within white America.

Significant as well about Du Bois were his perceptions regarding black culture and Booker T. Washington's representation of it, perceptions he shared with many Afro-Americans from the North. Du Bois recognized that "there was no question of Booker T. Washington's undisputed leadership of the ten million Negroes in America," but he quickly sided with the young black middle class intelligentsia. He pointed out that his dissatisfaction with Washington did not so much mean that he was "entirely against Mr. Washington's ideas"; rather, it stemmed from an "insistence upon the right of other Negroes to have and express their ideas." In other words, Afro-American culture, and its diverse range of political opinions should not be hemmed in by the dictates of one man who ingeniously manipulated the mask. AfroAmerica was too expansive, too multidimensional, to be strait-jacketed into an accommodationist mode that subordinated black political necessities to the good graces of well-meaning white philanthropists and black cultural imperatives to the often distorted and grotesque sterotypes of an unknowing white America. Du Bois's thought on this matter continues to resonate deeply in an integrated America that must still wrestle with the professional and political successes of the black middle class in the face of a deepening crisis among those many African Americans locked into unemployment and poverty.[7]

If W. E. B. Du Bois valiantly fought for the right of AfroAmerica to be heard in all its voices, political and cultural, then two important and enduring examples of the variety of those voices can be found in the works and lives of Langston Hughes and Zora Neale Hurston.

Both Hughes and Hurston could be said to be representatives of an integrative cultural diversity that encompasses racial identity and of how that racial identity expands or redefines the notion of what constitutes being an American. Furthermore, the examples of Hughes and Hurston dramatically show how the tensions over group loyalty as opposed to individual belief, over assimilation versus race consciousness, and over the role of middle-class black intellectuals and artists continue to form the core of issues that the expanded black middle class of the present day is attempting to address.

Langston Hughes's background was similar to that of Du Bois. A distant relative of the black Reconstruction politician John Mercer Langston, Hughes nonetheless grew up in a predominantly white world. His grandmother and mother provided him with the cultural foundations for his identification with his race, but these were severely tested by a father who not only abandoned the family but also proved to be bitterly anti-black.[8]

The supreme love and devotion that Langston Hughes had for his people could simply be explained as an active rebellion of a son against a father, a son who felt an urgent need to be accepted. But such psychological explanations, whatever their merits, ultimately fail to explain the ever-deepening journey that Hughes made through the African American world and the colorful multifaceted portraits that he produced through his prose and poetry.[9] Starting out as a marginal man caught between two worlds, Langston Hughes traversed AfroAmerica, returned to America laden with the riches of African American culture, and proceeded to articulate a vision of a new America. When Hughes wrote the poem "Let America Be America Again," he not only presented the situation of AfroAmerica in bold clarity but pointedly suggested what America as a whole had to become:

> O, let my land be a land where liberty
> Is crowned with no false patriotic wreath,
> But opportunity is real and life is free,
> Equality is in the air we breathe.
> (There's never been equality for me,
> Nor freedom in this "homeland of the free.")[10]

Zora Neale Hurston represented an even more striking perspective on AfroAmerica than that either of Hughes or of Du Bois. Hurston was born in the all-black town of Eatonville, Florida. Unlike Hughes and Du Bois, then, Hurston grew up surrounded by rural black folk culture, so much so that the excruciating pain with which that world had been made and forced to survive would not be known to her until later in her life. In many respects, it was the Harlem Renaissance that not only opened Hurston's eyes to the cruel reality of racism's effect on AfroAmerica but also led her to return to that world in order both to recreate herself and to preserve and present its treasured cultural forms to America.[11]

Hurston's autobiography, *Dust Tracks on the Road*, opened a terrain that only in the eighties was given the serious literary and historical attention it deserved: the role of women in AfroAmerica's culture.[12] More so than most of the Afro-American female writers of her time, Zora Neale Hurston came from deep inside of AfroAmerica. Her insights, pains, and visions were more immediate, and thus less likely to be misinterpreted, than those of her contemporaries Nella Larsen and Jesse Fauset, who were more concerned in their writing with combatting vicious racial stereotypes of blacks while presenting portraits of genteel black middle class culture and gender/race conflicts that stressed commonality with white middle class culture.[13] But Hurston made plain the tensions and anguish that gender inflicted on the black world. Especially in her novels *Jonah's Gourd Vine* (1934) and *Their Eyes Were Watching God* (1937), Hurston eloquently told of the trials and tribulations of black men and women. In an Afro-American culture that was continuously striving to prove its manhood in the face of white racist emasculations, Hurston stood as a stark, and crucial, reminder of the damage such striving unleashed within AfroAmerica.[14] Her novels, as well as her life, captured the ways in which black men and women related to each other. Eerily, those depictions were still valid at the time of her rediscovery in the eighties.

The writings and lives of key figures in the Harlem Renaissance not only laid the foundations for later twentieth-century African American writing but also pointed to the integrative cultural diversity that was quickly evolving in American culture. Texts by writers such as Hurston and Hughes challenged the ways in which white America perceived AfroAmerica, on top of which Hurston also challenged the hegemony of male patterns within black culture. These writers set the pace and the standards for future Afro-American literature. As a result of the work of Hurston and others, Afro-American women writers would eventually attain recognition and equal status within the canons of that literature. Another, perhaps more important result would be the presentation of the multifaceted nature of AfroAmerica and the implicit prescription for an integrative diversity that would continue to emanate from within AfroAmerica and to provide the means by which, to borrow Hughes's apt title, a way might be found to "Let America Be America Again."

The Harlem Renaissance flowered amid fervent African American quests for pride, rediscovery, and conflicting visions of what the "New Negro" meant. The great migratory trek that brought so many black people to the urban centers of the North created a cauldron of intense activity, cultural and political.[15] Despite the fact that the majority of people of AfroAmerica continued to reside in the South, the urban subculture that emerged in the North would set the stage for a new flourishing of African American culture and intellectual life within the larger American society.

For African Americans, the end of World War I, the return of black troops from Europe, and the sense that a new day might be dawning overshadowed the fact that from 1915 to 1954 AfroAmerica was perceived as "leaderless" by the dominant society. The death of Booker T. Washington in 1915 removed the genial manipulator of the mask. Washington's political accommodationism and relatively circumscribed vision of economic equality gradually receded as two other visions appeared that would course through the black middle class down to the present. The first was the black nationalism of Marcus Garvey, who carried out Washington's message of uplift but in a more forceful and explicitly racial manner. "Up you Mighty Race!" he proclaimed, encouraging Afro-Americans to recognize and embrace their Africanness.[16] The second was the Du Boisian vision of the service-oriented segment of the black middle class—the educated, civil rights–minded "Talented Tenth." Although strong supporters of integration, they certainly did not denigrate the past heritage of black people, but they did choose to emphasize the Americanness of AfroAmerica.

The cultural displays that ensued, whether in the form of the ornate parades arranged by Garvey's United Negro Improvement Association or the awards given by the NAACP and the National Urban League to gifted artists, announced to America that there was indeed a "New Negro" in motion. But while the political rallies and exhortations of the Garvey movement had a stimulating effect on the urban black masses, in the long run it was the writings that came out of this period that had a greater impact on African American culture. In diverse ways the novels, poems, and essays of black writers attempted to fuse the two seemingly disparate visions placed before Afro-America. Some of these writers, Langston Hughes and Claude McKay for example, were certainly more political than others. Other writers, like Jean Toomer and Jesse Fauset, sought to explore the complex and rich tapestry of AfroAmerica within the broader context of American society, while an examination of black folklore led Zora Neale Hurston to a rediscovery of African patterns in the Caribbean.[17] But if anything, it was Jean Toomer's monumental (and only really successful) work *Cane* (1923) that proved a landmark in this attempt to reconcile the two visions—the nationalist and the integrationist—ever at war within Afro-Americans.

Cane was a complex interweaving of verse, prose, and drama that spoke lyrically and poignantly of a transplanted Africa on a strange new soil. It was concerned with the fading of the South that had so long been the home of the American Negro. Even though he himself came from the upper echelons of the Washington, D.C., black middle class, Toomer felt intensely the passing of the simple rural life that southern blacks had managed to eke out. He knew well that the forces of industrialization, which had forced black people into migration, portended a new future, in which African Americans would be absorbed into the general populace, just like any other ethnic group. The Afro-American, Toomer wrote, "is in solution. . . . A few generations from now, the Negro will still be dark, a portion of his psychology will spring from this fact, but in all else he will be a conformist to the general outline of American civilization, or American chaos."[18]

Toomer's ominous forecast might have proved true had middle-class Afro-Americans ultimately chosen to relinquish their historical heritage in America and its connections with Africa in order to integrate themselves into white America. But this did not happen.[19] At the time, however, the writers of the Harlem Renaissance—most of

whom were of the middle class—were disdainful of what they perceived as the overly assimilationist stance of the black bourgeoisie.
They refused to be "conformist." Consistently in their works they
juxtaposed the world of AfroAmerica to that of American society
more generally and almost unanimously pointed subtly toward an
alternative to complete assimilation.[20] Nowhere was this more evident than in the work of Langston Hughes and Zora Neale Hurston.

More than any other writer of the Harlem Renaissance, Langston
Hughes, sketched the contours of AfroAmerica and pointed to the
alternative of integrative cultural diversity that would strike a balance
between the two warring visions. Hughes was of mixed heritage.
Early in his life, he recognized the importance of history in understanding the unique situation of black people in America. From his
maternal grandmother (a strong believer in racial justice whose roots,
by best accounts, were Native American and French, with a little
African) he learned of the bravery of blacks during slavery and their
achievements during Reconstruction.[21] His mother, Carrie, was a
black woman who impressed the young Langston Hughes with her
strength under hard times and her earnest desire that he become
somebody of importance.[22]

Although he went to an all-white school (at the insistence of his
mother) and spent one year at Columbia University (with some help
from his father), Hughes understood that his racially mixed background consigned him to marginality in white America. He thus
soon discovered that he would prefer to be a chronicler of Afro-
America. Immersing himself in the black nation within a nation,
Langston Hughes emerged not only as a genuine poet of the people
but also as an astute and gifted intellectual who probed from many
angles the absurdities of racism in America. His travels to Africa and
Europe, the Caribbean, and later the Soviet Union and Asia increased
his awareness of the various experiences and life-styles of the world's
colored population. But more important, his contacts with the black
peoples of Africa and the Caribbean instilled in him an essential
internationalism whereby Hughes could situate Afro-Americans in
the larger context of diasporic African peoples. Hughes's eagerness to
absorb the many different facets of African cultures in diaspora, including Afro-American culture, provided him with a crucial perspective that would allow him to demonstrate AfroAmerica's integral im-

portance not only to American society but also to all oppressed people who struggled to be free. This perspective had the potential to bring a balance to the warring visions within AfroAmerica and, more important, to sketch the contours of an integrative cultural diversity within which Afro-Americans could proudly take their place in American society.

Unlike Hughes, Zora Neale Hurston grew up squarely within AfroAmerica. Through her research into black rural life and folklore, carried out under the anthropologist Franz Boas at Columbia University, Hurston uncovered the African roots of the deep South and the Caribbean. But her most immediate connection to Africa came about when she spent three months with an old ex-slave, Cudjoe Lewis, an African illegally smuggled into America prior to the Civil War. It was from Lewis that Hurston discovered that African Americans were not the victims uniquely of white people. "White people had held my people in slavery here in America. They had bought us, it is true, and exploited us. But the inescapable fact that stuck in my craw was: my people had *sold* me and the white man had bought me."[23] This realization dispelled the romanticism of folkloric tales Hurston had heard in her youth about Africans being lured or snatched away by whites. Africans had been as responsible for enslaving their own people as had whites.

> I know that civilized money stirred up African greed. That wars between tribes were often stirred up by white traders to provide more slaves in the barracoons and all that. But, if the African princes had been as pure and as innocent as I would like to think, it could not have happened. No, my own people had butchered and killed, exterminated whole nations and torn families apart for profit before strangers got their chance at a cut.[24]

In a way that most black intellectuals at the time probably could not have fully understood, Zora Neale Hurston broke through the bonds of a debilitating victimization syndrome.

In a variety of ways the writers of the Harlem Renaissance were engaged, throughout their lives, in a process of re-creation, a re-creation that hinged on the reconciliation of AfroAmerica with America. These writers understood that black literature needed to find a voice. Langston Hughes, for example, found that voice in the every-day experiences of urban black men and women, often employing in his poetry the cadences of black language and jazz (which originated in the South and bore within it African rhythms) in order to evoke the emerging subculture of black urban life. But even as Hughes described and celebrated this voice found in the urban black masses, there was still an uneasy tension between AfroAmerica and American society. This tension was most clearly visible in the evolving debate over who the audience for black literature should be.

Hughes, of course, was not the only writer who wrestled with the important dilemma of audience and representation. Black writers mapping out the terrain for their literature were continuously in the process of, as Michael Cooke eloquently suggests, finding a voice and seeking intimacy.[25] The question of the audience to whom this litera-ture should be addressed—whether it should be principally black or white, or both—has been an ongoing concern of black literature throughout the twentieth century. It was, and remains, a concern suffused not only with critical literary matters but also with political and social ones, all three of which are interconnected, as the writers of the Harlem Renaissance revealed.[26]

In the June 23, 1926, issue of the *Nation*, there appeared an essay by Langston Hughes entitled "The Negro Artist and the Racial Moun-tain." Often thought of as a manifesto for the times, Hughes's essay was intended as a sharp rebuttal to George Schuyler's article "The Negro Art Hokum," which had appeared in the *Nation* a week earlier. Schuyler rejected any claims to a distinct black writing and felt that African American art should fit within the mainstream of Western literature. After all, according to Schuyler African Americans were nothing more than "lamp-black Anglo-Saxons." In adopting this as-similationist stance, Schuyler was not necessarily rejecting race con-sciousnesss altogether. He merely wished to eliminate race as a cate-gory by which writers (and politicians) should be judged, a stance that was not out of line with the prevailing orientation of the black middle class.[27]

In his eloquent and passionate article, Hughes argued that black writers must write out of their own experiences. In so doing, Hughes elevated race consciousness to a level that involved racial re-creation. Referring in his essay to Countee Cullen's assertion that he wanted to be a "poet—not a Negro poet," Hughes countered that this statement meant "I want to write like a white poet." For Hughes the rejection of one's race in artistic endeavors was the "mountain standing in the way of any true Negro art in America." It was "this urge within the race towards whiteness, the desire to pour racial individuality into the mold of American standardization, and be as little Negro and as much American as possible," that incurred Hughes's ire.[28]

By embracing race as an integral component of art and yet demanding individual creativity Hughes to some extent found himself straddling two worlds. As Hughes put it, "We younger Negro artists who create now intend to express our individual dark-skinned selves without fear or shame."[29] Here Hughes was implicitly attacking the "smug" black middle class, which felt that literature should depict only "clean," morally virtuous, and inspiring representations of black people. Indeed, Hughes reserved his sharpest barbs for them. As for white readers, if they liked the work of black writers, fine. If they did not, well, that was fine, too—and the same could be said for the stodgier elements of the black bourgeoisie. The point was that black artists had to be free "within themselves" to express their vision.

But if some of these visions were perhaps more equal than others, it was clear that Hughes opposed any monolithic view of the black world. He certainly recognized that the experiences of African Americans were varied and multifaceted. At the same time, Hughes's impassioned call for black writers to create out of their own experiences did not necessarily alleviate the tensions that Afro-American writers and artists faced in producing their work. The problem remained of how Hughes's strongly individualist vision of black art would be disseminated in an American culture in which often grotesque stereotypical images of African Americans continued to hold sway. The patrons, publishers, and (later) agents that black writers depended on were white. No matter how liberal (and in many cases eccentric) these patrons were, the specter of standardization remained: works that departed too far from prevailing norms were excluded from publication. Even in the late eighties and nineties, when African Americans of an enlarged black middle class attempted to found their own publishing houses for the express purpose of reaching a black audience, the economics of the publishing industry generally, along with distribution processes, still posed a formidable obstacle.[30]

George Schuyler's assimilationist approach would have made it easier for black authors to get published. But its long-term effect would have been to close off a vital force in American culture. AfroAmerica would have been rendered forever invisible, subsumed under a "universal" notion of "America." The reality of American society—its history and the development of its culture, and of the role that people of African descent played in both—would have been lost. Far from alleviating the deeply entrenched white supremacy of the nation, such an eventuality would have served rather to validate the notion that blacks were indeed inferior, inasmuch as their own culture had no intrinsic worth.

Despite the difficulties inherent in the position that Langston Hughes took in "The Negro Artist and the Racial Mountain," his assertions created the space for an integrative cultural diversity, that is, a space wherein all black writers, artists, and intellectuals could combine their many voices to portray the contours of American culture and AfroAmerica's important place within it. Such a space enabled Afro-American writers to present a newly complex image of AfroAmerica that not only challenged American society's view of its people but also suggested a vision of what American culture might become. Simply put, Afro-American writers strove to fashion a literature that gave voice to their perceptions of a society that must break the chains of racial oppression and rise to a level where differences are treasured and shared.

The search for audience and voice in African American literature, with its concomitant concern over how best to present AfroAmerica to the larger nation, produced a peculiar ideological struggle within AfroAmerica, as the civil rights–oriented sector of the black bourgeoisie confronted the rebellious young black writers. The legal fights of the NAACP for equality, the efforts of the National Urban League for the improvement of black urban life, and the embrace of race pride and nationalism by thousands of African Americans framed the confrontations between the New Negro writers and the traditional spokespersons of the black middle class. Critics such as Benjamin Brawley were representative of many middle-class African Americans who felt that literature should present the best of the race and provide portraits of uplift and moral dignity. Brawley, a southern black who edited the *Southern Workman*, found the notion that a renaissance in African American literature could take place in Harlem somewhat overblown. He felt that only after experiencing life in the South could black writers create meaningful literature. Of course, Brawley was a southerner, but William Stanley Braithwaite, a black critic from the North, echoed Brawley's concerns. Braithwaite lavishly praised Jean Toomer's moving tribute to southern black culture, *Cane*, but found Claude Mckay's work that of an "angry propagandist" whose choice of material—the black working class of Harlem—left much to be desired. As a proponent of the middle-class view of literature, Braithwaite also praised Jesse Redmon Fauset's work, which was hardly surprising given that Fauset's novels dealt with (if not the South) the everyday life of the northern black bourgeoisie.[31]

Jesse Fauset wrote her novels with a single-mindedness of purpose: to show that black middle class people were really no different from whites of the same class. As she commented, blacks were "dark Americans who wear their joy and rue very much as does the white American." Fauset's women and men, depicted in rich detail, strove to uphold the ideals embodied in the American dream. In their identity as Americans first, Fauset's characters tried not to "think anything about being colored."[32] Fauset's work accordingly contained two principal messages, each addressed to a distinct audience. On the one hand, she wanted white readers to understand that blacks were not some sort of foreign species, that "there are times when Blacks work, love, and attend to the demands of living without thinking of the [race] problem." On the other hand, Fauset's message to her black audience was that one's social and economic well-being was to be found not in "passing" utterly over into the white world but in pursuing a stable and productive life while remaining a member of the black race.[33]

Fauset's novel *Plum Bun* (1929), for example, centers on two sisters from a well-to-do Philadelphia family, Angela and Virginia Murray. Angela possesses sufficiently Caucasian features to be able to pass as white, whereas Virginia is distinctly Negroid. At once ambitious and yet ashamed of her racial background, Angela goes to New York, "passes," and attempts to become a painter. She meets a wealthy white man who ends up exploiting her as his mistress, even though she tries everything to get him to marry her. Meanwhile, Virginia has

come to Harlem, has taken up teaching black children, and has married a black man. Angela eventually goes to Harlem, makes an uneasy
peace with her racial self, and marries her new boyfriend, a mulatto.
Virginia is Jesse Fauset's prime example of what black people in the
middle class should do. She accepts her racial identity—it is not an
"issue"—and simply gets on with building her life, as would a white
American.

Jesse Fauset continued this message in her subsequent novels *Chi-
naberry Tree* (1931) and *Comedy, American Style* (1933). She denied the
prevalent notion of authors who wrote about the "tragic mulatto"
caught between two worlds, namely, that mulattoes were superior to
blacks because of the presence of white blood. Rather, Fauset played
down race in favor of issues of class. Her novels described a life-style
and a morality to which she was accustomed and which she hoped
whites would recognize as a reality among blacks and blacks as something to emulate. In her view, the virtues of "marriage, security, family, and respectability," led the list, along with pride in one's self and
one's race. Jesse Fauset believed that Afro-Americans could only gain
power by building up their racial pride around a distinct recognition
and acceptance of those middle-class values. As Addison Gayle cogently put it, "the symbol of power is no longer whiteness but class,
and one is more capable of exercising power in the race into which he
is born than in the other where entry can only be gained through
passing"—and, one could add, where there would be a rejection of all
the history and experience that came from being black.[34]

Jesse Fauset's works could be described as an entreaty to the black
middle class to look inward to the community and cease pursuing the
privileges that a white skin might bring. Looking inward to the community meant that the black middle class should act as a "role model
class," demonstrating to the lower-class black masses not only racial
pride but also the ability to overcome the disadvantages of race (as
negatively defined by white society) through education, material ac-
quisition, and respectability. In that regard, it was no surprise that
Fauset found a comfortable ideological niche for a while with Du
Bois, the leading exponent of the "Talented Tenth," or that she would
be at ease with the bourgeois orientation of the NAACP. The goals
she promoted in her works were firmly within the service orientation
that proper middle-class blacks upheld. Furthermore, her novels con-

tained a strong streak of cultural pluralism, in addition to integration-ism, that would re-create itself in the integrative cultural diversity of the closing decades of the twentieth century.

At the same time, the work of Renaissance writers such as Langston Hughes, Claude McKay, or Wallace Thurman raised eyebrows. The general distress with these writers was not so much personal—although Zora Neale Hurston joked that the young black writers were the "niggerati"—as it was with the themes those writers selected and how they were presented. For example, Claude McKay's intention in *Home To Harlem* (1928), a novel that celebrated the urban subculture of black Harlem, was to present the feelings and thoughts of working-class Harlem. McKay felt that the book was a "true proletarian novel." Du Bois, however, was outraged at the novel's vulgarity and its description of what he termed the "debauched Tenth."

McKay's book appeared not long after Carl Van Vechten's sensational and provocative novel, *Nigger Heaven* (1926). Van Vechten, a white, was not only a close friend of many in the black middle class but also an earnest supporter of younger Renaissance writers. His novel revealed his own perceptions of urban AfroAmerica of the period. Although his descriptions certainly were not designed to appeal to black bourgeois sensibilities, and were even offensive to many, Van Vechten's work was nonetheless praised by members of that class, notably James Weldon Johnson and Charles Chestnutt. Johnson wrote to his friend Van Vechten that "you managed to get what many Negroes will regard as 'family secrets'" and was happy about the novel's success. That happiness, however, was more reflective of the fact that, at the time, little about AfroAmerica was being written for a mass white audience. Despite the novel's unflattering title and to some extent troublesome contents, those in the black bourgeoisie knew that Van Vechten was basically a friend of blacks and hoped that some of the more complimentary aspects of *Nigger Heaven* would arouse sympathy among white readers. These black middle class literary critics, however, were not so willing to extend the same leeway to black writers, on whom they frequently passed harsh judgment for presenting similar themes and material.[35]

The central issue here, which continues to this day to inform debate about almost all African American cultural representations, was one of presentation as well as taste. In the minds of Du Bois, Brawley,

Braithwaite, and Fauset, the purpose of black literature was to uplift the race through positive images and thereby to combat racist stereotypes. These critics and writers certainly did not eschew race consciousness, but they often downplayed the force of race (whether as racial pride or as discrimination) in favor of providing African Americans with an alternative vision. That vision, of course, was the world of the black middle class, a world that somehow sought to retain a racial solidarity through uplifting service to the masses even as it disassembled a racial identity rooted in the nationalist connotations of an "AfroAmerica."

The younger writers of the Renaissance, however, far from attempting to "get beyond" the effects of race, celebrated their racial identity within AfroAmerica.[36] As such they not only accepted but in many cases actively explored the nationalist connotations of AfroAmerica and the origins of their racial heritage. Langston Hughes' evocative poem "The Negro Speaks of Rivers," for example, poignantly draws the connection between Africa and America:

> I bathed in the Euphrates when dawns were young
> I built my hut near the Congo and it lulled me to sleep
> I looked upon the Nile and raised the pyramids above it
> I heard the singing of the Mississippi when Abe Lincoln went
>   down to New Orleans,
> I've seen its muddy bosom turn golden in the sunset.[37]

Zora Neale Hurston examined AfroAmerica by tracing the folklore of southern black people to the Caribbean and to Africa, while Claude McKay, who was born in Jamaica, wrote out of a background that was still firmly rooted in an African identity despite a heavy overlay of British colonialism.[38]

During the 1920s the exploration of race through the immersion in racial experience thus became (and has remained) the paramount concern of black writers. Black literature that focused on a wholesome and inspirational presentation of black society and contained messages aimed at the elevation of the race was often preempted by the desire of younger generations to write out of their own particular experiences as African Americans in an often hostile society. This mode of writing was, however, itself entangled in a bourgeois concept of individualism. Although a few post-Renaissance African Americans were able to transcribe the thoughts and feelings of AfroAmerica in a collective fashion, the emphasis was generally on a particular individual who bore the weight of the vision of what AfroAmerica should be seeking. Two black writers who shaped the terrain for the period between the Renaissance and the resurgence of black literature in the sixties and eighties were Richard Wright and Ralph Ellison.

Richard Wright's work was a fascinating lesson in how Afro-American culture was able to fuse such disparate themes as individualism versus collectivism and art versus politics. A Mississippian who migrated to Chicago, Wright came from a southern black working-class upbringing that clashed with the rapidly evolving black urban culture of the twenties and thirties. Recounting his life in Chicago in his autobiography, *American Hunger*, Wright bore witness to the complexities and confusions of what it meant to migrate out of the segregated AfroAmerica of the South and into the black urban ghettoes of the North, which were often surrounded by an equally hostile white society.[39] "Culturally the Negro represents a paradox," Wright reflected. "Though he is an organic part of the nation, he is excluded by the entire tide and direction of American culture." Wright realized that any confrontation of racism in America would be heavily traumatic. "If the nation ever finds itself examining its real relation to the Negro, it will find itself doing infinitely more than that; for the anti-Negro attitude of whites represents but a tiny part—though a symbolically significant one—of the moral attitude of the nation."[40]

The appearance of *Native Son* (1940), a somber tale of a young black youth's existential liberation through an act of murder, was prescient in its description of the turmoil among young inner-city black males. In the introduction to a 1966 reprint of the novel, Wright wrote that its protagonist, Bigger Thomas, was "attracted and repelled by the American scene": "He was an American, because he was a native son; but he was a Negro nationalist in a vague sense because he was not allowed to live as an American."[41] Although the book had garnered prestigious awards and was even made into a (quickly forgotten) motion picture starring Wright himself, it appeared that the immediate message had been missed by most white readers. The continued ghettoization of African American males, combined with years and years of anti-black prejudice, had produced Bigger Thomases throughout the nation, the result as well of the values that characterized an industrialized consumption-oriented urban mass culture. In retrospect, Bigger Thomas prefigured the vast wasteland of the black urban underclass of the eighties and nineties. In choosing to focus so intensely on the alienation and oppressed life of a young urban black, however, Wright also merged individualistic notions of American culture with the collectivist impulse in AfroAmerica. In the eighties and nineties, that merger may have again been evident to some degree in the notion of hip-hop culture (itself a black middle class formulation), but the violence appeared more pandemic.[42]

Like Langston Hughes, Wright stood at the crossroads of two worlds, but Wright was more deeply influenced than Hughes by the radical analyses of society that percolated throughout the thirties. The radicalism of the thirties, especially pronounced in the antiracist activities of the Socialist and Communist parties, enabled Wright to navigate the murkier waters of a race-conscious nationalism cut through with the currents of bourgeois aspiration. Wright was, like Hughes, concerned with the devastation that industrial America had wrought on the soul of AfroAmerica. Racism was, in this capitalistic setting, a psychological construct through which black people were abstracted into nonentities (or, at best, inferior beings) who were in turn exploited as cheap labor or objects of amusement. Richard Wright strove to show the effects of this exploitation. The results were some of the sharpest and most painful examinations of AfroAmerica yet to be published.

In *Uncle Tom's Children*, his first collection of short stories, Wright probed the black world, showing how African Americans tried to live out their lives amid stifling segregation and, often, racist violence.[43] The human element—the yearning to be free of oppressive definitions and arbitrary exploitation—was present throughout these stories. But the cost of freedom for many of these southern black characters, when it was not death, was often a retreat from the carefully and defensively structured way of life erected in AfroAmerica that had somehow protected black people from the worst that southern white society meted out to them.

In the final story in the collection, "Bright and Morning Star," Wright suggested that the possibility for true survival in AfroAmerica would come when Afro-Americans rejected white definitions of race, affirmed their own humanity, and reached out for dignity. Wright presented the possibility of this transformation through the eyes of a working-class black woman whose sons were organizers for the Communist party in the South. Undoubtedly influenced by his own membership in the Party, with its strong belief in interracial class struggle, Wright nonetheless told the story from the perspective of a woman steeped in the rural black culture of the South.

Sue, the mother of Sug and Johnny-Boy, is a deeply religious woman who firmly places her faith in the Resurrection of Christ, "an imagery which had swept her life into a wondrous vision." But there is "a cold white mountain, white folks and their laws" that constantly threatens to shatter that vision. Sue, however, clings to her belief and tries to pass it on to her sons. But when they grow up, they reject the religious vision that has sustained her and present her with a more secular humanist vision, one in which "the wrongs and sufferings of black men and women had taken the place of Him nailed to the Cross."[44]

When Sug is killed by the local authorities after refusing to name members of the Party, Sue becomes fearful for her remaining son, Johnny-Boy. Yet she is also adamant. "Lawd, Johnny-Boy . . . Ah ju wan them white folks t try t make tell *who* is *in* the party n who *ain*! Ah jus wan em t try. Ahll show em somethin they thot a black woman could have" (185). When the sheriff learns that a Party meeting is to take place, Sue's words are soon put to a severe test. Warned by Reva, the young daughter of the white man at whose house the meeting is to be held, and seasoned by years of knowledge regarding the violent nature of white racism in the South, Sue tries in turn to warn Johnny-Boy, but to no avail. "Johnny-Boy's too trustin, she thought. Hes tryin t make the party big n hes takin in folks fastern he kin git t know em. You cant trust ever white man yuh meet" (185).

Johnny-Boy is subsequently apprehended by the white sheriff and a white mob, who brutally beat him to make him talk. Sue then learns that one of the new white members of the party, Booker, is on his way to tell the sheriff what he wants—the names of other Party members—and thereby save Johnny-Boy. Anxious to put her son out of his misery and fearful that he might give in and betray the Party, Sue hides a gun in a sheet and sets out to kill both Booker and Johnny-Boy. When she arrives at the scene, the sheriff attempts to make her persuade Johnny-Boy to reveal the names. When she refuses, the sheriff forces her to watch as Johnny-Boy's knees and eardrums are shattered. When Booker belatedly appears, Sue shoots him but fails to kill Johnny-Boy. Instead, Sue herself is shot. As she dies, she taunts her tormentors: "Yuh didn't git whut yuh wanted! N yuh ain goona nevah git it! Yuh didn't kill me; Ah come here by mahsef" (185).

Sue dies in peace, knowing that she has saved the spirit and integrity of the black community. But her death also heralds a "bright and morning star," for it holds out the hope that change will come about and that, given their history of heroic resistance, Afro-Americans can be a central force in that change. Wright demonstrated, in this story, how an individual managed to merge the collectivist ideals of a political ideology with the communal ideals of AfroAmerica. Sue's final words, spoken in proud defiance, suggest that, through retaining their dignity and fighting spirit, Afro-Americans may someday get beyond the racial and class exploitation of American society.

Wright's artistic wrestling with the individual versus the collective ultimately collided, however, with his belief in materialism and communism. The struggle to adhere to the Party's belief in the subordination of race to class clashed with Wright's literary vision of the ways in which the African American experience could be described, with the result that he eventually left the Party. Wright later told Ralph Ellison, a protégé of his, that "after I broke with the Communist Party, I had nowhere else to go." In his remembrance of Richard Wright, Ellison commented that "I think he was telling me that his dedication to communism had been so complete and his struggle so endless that he had to change his scene, that he had to find a new ground upon which to struggle." Wright went on to discover that ground and continued to mature as both an artist and an intellectual.[45]

Those who followed Wright, such as Ralph Ellison, Chester Himes, and James Baldwin, emphasized the individual experience of being black in America. While not necessarily shunning a leftist critique (Ellison and Himes were sympathetic to the ideals of the Communist party), these writers focused more on the interconnections between Afro-American and the larger American culture. Ellison drew on the blues, jazz, and black rural folk culture, along with the literary techniques of Herman Melville and Nathaniel Hawthorne, to give texture and tension to his widely acclaimed novel, *Invisible Man*.[46] Although Ellison was treated with scorn by militant black nationalists in the sixties, his work marked an important step in the evolution of integrated cultural diversity and has, more recently, been the focus of renewed appreciation.

Chester Himes, who was brought up in a midwestern black middle class family, used his novels to examine the psychological ravages wrought upon African Americans who not only attempted to exist in America but who also joined with sympathetic whites in an effort to bring true equality and humane values to American society.[47] His detective novels, set in Harlem, painted a portrait of the diversity with AfroAmerica. Although he dwelled at times on the psychological wounds inflicted by racism, Himes displayed a humor in his stories that was somewhat comparable to that of Langston Hughes. But it was James Baldwin, the youngest of the four writers, who was the most pivotal in creating a bridge between the themes espoused by Wright, Ellison, and Himes and those of the New Renaissance of black writing from the sixties onward.

James Baldwin's distinguished literary career, his powerful essays and books on race relations in particular and American society in general, embodied insights that were not only prophetic but also commonsensical in their prescriptions. In Baldwin's view, white America had shielded itself from itself through the creation of an Other. But the image of the black image that white America had fashioned through enslavement, Jim Crow invisibility, and popularized stereotypes diminished not only African Americans but also whites. "Our dehumanization of the Negro then is indivisible from our dehumanization of ourselves: the loss of our own identity is the price we pay for the annulment of his."[48] So wrote Baldwin as he critically examined Richard Wright's *Native Son* in 1949. This was a young Baldwin who challenged Wright's representation of Bigger Thomas as a symbol for an angry AfroAmerica: "Bigger . . . serve[s] only to whet the notorious national taste for the sensational and to reinforce all that we now find necessary to believe" (73).

The themes in that essay, "Many Thousands Gone," would resurface again and again in Baldwin's work: the necessity that whites confront themselves regarding racism; the crucial importance of blacks for whites and for American society; the white need of love from blacks. Baldwin masterfully turned the dilemma of race relations on its head; it was no longer the "Negro Problem" but intrinsically it was the White Problem. The most powerful statement of this theme was registered in "The Fire Next Time," published in 1963 amid the turbulent struggle for black civil rights, and, like so many of Baldwin's essays, directed toward white liberals. But Baldwin spoke with confidence in the knowledge that AfroAmerica assented in his voice. That many black militants later in the sixties would scorn the tone Baldwin took did not matter. The essence of what Baldwin had to say stood head and shoulders above what any black writer had written about the wrenching dilemma confronting blacks and whites.

"America, of all the Western nations, has been best placed to prove the uselessness and the obsolescence of the concept of color. But it has not dared to accept this opportunity, or even conceive of it as an opportunity" (373–74). America, according to Baldwin and contrary to historical belief, was not a white nation. The only way that America could truly become unified and "bring new life to Western achievements" (374) was to unconditionally free black people. That could be done only when whites confronted their fears and their guilt and learned to love. Baldwin's notion of love was in no way sentimental. It was a "state of being, or a state of grace—not in the infantile American sense of being made happy but in the tough and universal sense of quest and caring and growth." White people had projected their fears and desires onto blacks, but it was now necessary for them to release their "tyrannical power" over black people. And the only way for that to be done was, "in effect, to become black themselves, to become part of that suffering and dancing country" (375).

This was a tall order indeed, and bound to be misinterpreted, as it was, by both blacks and whites as a call for integration. Yet Baldwin was not stumping for integration, any more than he was trying simply to scare whites with his delicate and generous description of the Honorable Elijah Muhammad's Nation of Islam. At its most plain and simple, "The Fire Next Time" was a call to America for moral regeneration and social transformation. The political categories of liberal, conservative, and radical were not important, given that they connoted struggles for power rather than necessary changes in the way human beings treated each other. Thus, for example, anticommunist hysteria, which at once clouded much of white liberal thinking regarding racial demands for social progress and agitated white conservatives into a frenzy, was finally an obfuscation that allowed whites either not to confront racism or to cast the blame elsewhere. As Baldwin put it:

> It has not occurred to us that we have simply been mesmerized by Russia, and that the only real advantage Russia has in what we think of as a struggle between East and West is the moral history of the Western world. Behind what we think of as the Russian menace lies what we do not wish to face, and what white Americans do not face when they regard the Negro: reality—the fact life is tragic. (372–73)

In coming to grips with the most noted nationalist force within AfroAmerica (at least according to the national media), the Nation of Islam under the Honorable Elijah Muhammad, Baldwin sketched the outlines of a firm but balanced black response to the cultural and political crisis engulfing both Afro-American society and the American nation as a whole. While he was excited by what the Black Muslims had put forth and accomplished, Baldwin clearly saw that their agenda could not ease the racial strain that lay deep in the American soul, the impatience of black youth notwithstanding. As he summed it up near the end of "The Fire Next Time":

> In short, we, the black and the white, deeply need each other here if we are really to become a nation—if we are really, that is, to achieve our identity, our maturity, as men and women. To create one nation has proved to be a hideously difficult task; there is certainly no need now to create one black and one white. But white men with far more political power than that possessed by the Nation of Islam movement have been advocating exactly this, in effect, for generations. If this sentiment is honored when it falls from the lips of Senator [Robert] Byrd, then there is no reason it should not fall from the lips of Malcolm X. . . . They are expressing exactly the same sentiments and represent exactly the same danger. There is absolutely no reason to suppose that white people are better equipped to frame the laws by which I am to be governed than I am. It is entirely unacceptable that I should have no voice in political affairs of my own country, for I am not a ward of America; I am one of the first Americans to arrive on these shores. (375–76)

Baldwin continued this theme throughout the sixties and seventies, and into the eighties. Although he eventually slipped into an angry nationalist stance of the sort that often erupted within the expanded black middle class of the eighties, it was a forgivable slippage. The swift tide of events and the stiffening white resistance to black demands for economic justice and a change in the nation's priorities was enough to pull anyone off course. The true value of James Baldwin's presence, however, was best seen in how his message influenced a wide range of black writers from the turbulent sixties onward. Baldwin died in 1987, but his impact continues unabated.[49]

The themes touched on by Baldwin in his writings were certainly not original to him. It was his ability to articulate them to all Americans that was paramount to his importance as a writer. Emulating Baldwin's deportment, young African American writers were able to break through barriers, reach white audiences, and enlarge the scope of black readers. The pains and joys of being black, the struggles and paranoia of being a human being in a society that consistently defined one as an inferior "Other," were given full play in many novels, short stories, and poetry. Baldwin, of course, was not solely responsible for this upsurge; significant political events provided much of the momentum. But from the artistic and intellectual standpoint, Baldwin's courageous statements provided one importance cornerstone for what became known as the black aesthetic.

The black aesthetic—an outgrowth of the black arts movement of the sixties—was also closely connected to the civil rights–black power movement. It represented the nationalist perception of an angry AfroAmerica unwilling to stifle its voice any longer. It was also a distinctly black middle class perception. The young black students in the civil rights–black power movement came, in the main, from middle-class backgrounds. The Student Non-Violent Coordinating Committee was perhaps the best exemplar of that orientation.

Without a doubt, the SNCC made its share of mistakes. However, two significant points about that organization stood out. First, within the prevailing vision of an integrated society, they were the only organization that truly encouraged the black masses in the deep South to organize and empower themselves.[50] Second, the SNCC, because of the youth and intellectual training of its members, was on the cutting edge of social change. The insights and ideas of the SNCC sowed the seeds that led to the growth of new progressive groups that criticized the existing society and attempted to articulate a vision of a new, more inclusive one.[51] It was one of the tragic ironies of the eighties and early nineties that, as the analyses of the SNCC had to some extent predicted, the nation stood witness to government policies and social actions that sought to eliminate the achievements of socially enlightened civil rights groups under the guise of fostering a "color-blind" society.[52]

Given the SNCC's trajectory and extensive influence on events throughout the sixties, it was no surprise that some of the most creative talent came from its ranks. Indeed, black writers such as June Jordan, Alice Walker, Julius Lester, and Michael Thelwell not only wrote during that period as active participants in the SNCC but continued long afterward to produce some of the most engaging fiction and critical writing since the Harlem Renaissance. The later, more mature works of these authors reflect both their experiences while involved in the civil rights movement and their experiences as members of the middle class. These works, as well as those of younger writers during the eighties and nineties, pointed to a integrative cultural diversity that, although grounded in the particular experiences of AfroAmerica, also attempted to transcend stifling categories and envision a more human and inclusive society.[53] The writings of these young African Americans succeeded in large measure to accomplish the central goal that had motivated writers of the Harlem Renaissance: to provide a clear mirror of AfroAmerica from which white America, if it chose to look, would not be able to flinch.

While the movement itself produced these writers, whose legacy stretched back to the twenties and thirties, it also heavily influenced black writers outside of its immediate circle. Writers like Leroi Jones (Amiri Baraka) plunged deep into the nationalist purview of the movement. Initially a bohemian Beat writer, Baraka was tranformed into a fiery, charismatic theoretician of cultural nationalism and the black aesthetic. More explicitly than most writers, Baraka attempted to fuse the notion of Negritude (as articulated by the French-speaking African writer Leopold Senghor) with the African American concept of "Soul." The point was to show that AfroAmerica in its role as "outsider" in America was really a convenient illusion fostered by a racist and imperialist nation. In reality, AfroAmerica was part of the black diaspora, whose roots lay ultimately in Africa, the home of human civilization.[54]

Other writers who surfaced during the sixties and seventies continued the themes of those directly involved in the movement. What seemed to be common to all these literary works was a filtering of cultural nationalist concerns through a black middle class lens. John A. Williams's *The Man Who Cried I Am* (1965), a novel of stunning intensity, chronicled the life of a black novelist, Max Reddick. Famous black writers (most notably Richard Wright, who appeared in the book as Harry Ames) provided the backdrop for Reddick's journey through the white world of journalism, literature, and politics. Williams's book thus constructed a fascinating fictional bridge between two generations of black male writers. But Williams's primary concern lay elsewhere. In having Reddick exposed to the ravages that racism wreaks upon human beings, black and white, Williams not only revealed the paranoia that black Americans felt toward a conspiratorial white America but also demonstrated how that paranoia affected a middle-class African American.[55]

A similar theme appeared in Sam Greenlee's *The Spook Who Sat by the Door* (1969). On the surface, this book appeared to be little more than a commercially forgettable spy novel concerning the first black CIA agent. What made the book worthy of consideration was the transformation of the protagonist, Freeman, from a working-class black man into a middle-class black nationalist who trains young "bloods" to defend themselves and subvert the system. Early on in the book, Greenlee comments that Freeman "was not middle class"; being a "Negro-Firster" did not interest him in the least. He merely wanted to get the CIA job, do it well, and learn from "the MAN"— the white man—so as to be of service to the oppressed black masses.

Freeman's attitude accurately reflected not only the romanticization of the notion of black revolution but also the basic irony that lay behind this apparently radical idea. In the late sixties, frustrated and angry, the young militants of the black middle class summoned up a race consciousness, seeking to arouse AfroAmerica against an enormously racist white America. Yet the goals toward which the "Revolution" strove were clearly bourgeois: money (a good job and a nice home), status (the respect of the larger community), and a healthy environment in which to raise children (good schools, safe streets, and control of the community). What overwhelmed these goals and subsequently derailed the movement was the unleashing of deeply held, pent-up rage against white racism. All too often that rage not only caused the cultural nationalists to spurn white allies but also turned inward on itself, as these cultural nationalists excoriated the very same black masses they were trying to arouse for attempting to "integrate into a burning house."[56]

In retrospect, this furious activity resembled the heated debates among Garveyites and the black bourgeois liberals and radicals of the twenties and thirties. Then, the black bourgeoisie held fast and emerged triumphant. The political realities of the Great Depression and the New Deal, the emergence of radical alternatives such as the Communist party and the example of the Soviet Union, and finally the war to end fascism gave an impetus to those in AfroAmerica who aimed to have black people fully included in the American nation. Nationalist sentiments were certainly not washed away, but the separatist tendency was overshadowed by a spirit of integration, which sought to preserve black uniqueness (the concept of Negritude and the Pan-Africanism of Du Bois) within a pluralistic America.[57]

From the late sixties onward, however, the cultural nationalists ruled the day in literature, even though, politically, the nationalist voice, as absorbed by the middle class, seemed to wane as more and more black people began to derive some benefits from the early successes of the civil rights movement. But it remained a fact that the vast majority of African Americans were still mired in significant, often abject, poverty. Black novels of the period revealed three distinct trends that mirrored some of the realities of AfroAmerica and some of the confusion within the black middle class, and suggested some tentative proposals for the black community.

One trend, which, although in some ways disruptive, can only be seen as positive, was the growing emergence of black women writers. Of course, there had always been black female novelists, poets, and intellectuals, but in the struggle for civil rights the attention was almost always placed on male self-esteem, on the need for black males to achieve true manhood. The appearance of black women's literature, aided by the women's movement, exposed long festering resentments between black men and women. The intrusion of gender thus proved divisive, and the issue was one that many black writers refused to confront. Many African American male writers either placed black women on pedestals as African queens who stood behind their men (the nationalist version) or encouraged women to be ardent supporters middle-class virtues (a long-standing and respected tradition). Only Zora Neale Hurston had challenged this pattern, although, given that she was ahead of her time, she was not taken seriously in the twenties. Even in the late seventies and throughout the eighties, when Hurston enjoyed a much deserved reconsideration, she remained a problematic figure in black literary circles.[58]

Zora Neale Hurston's sensitive exploration of gender relations within AfroAmerica provided, in Charles Johnson's words, "the platform and the framework for black feminist writing in the 1980's."[59] Her politics presented a problem for African American women writers, however, most of whom were feminists (or, in Alice Walker's term, "womanists"): although Hurston prefigured many feminist ideas, she ended up a Republican conservative. Despite this political problem, black women writers expanded on much of what Hurston wrote about. During the seventies and early eighties, writers such as Toni Morrison (*The Bluest Eye* and *Sula*), Gayl Jones (*Corrigedora* and *Eva's Man*), Alice Walker (*Meridian* and *The Color Purple*), and Toni Cade Bambara (*Gorilla, My Love* and *The Salt-Eaters*) presented the continuing struggle of what it meant to be black, female, and brutally subordinated in a society that distorted the image of women generally.[60] For black women, there was the added burden of wrestling with the attempts of black men to triumph over the degradation imposed on them by white male society, who, in so doing, often fell back on that same society's view of gender relations. The difficulties this posed for black women provided a running theme throughout much of their literature.

With varying degrees of subtlety and historical nuance, African American women novelists (especially Toni Morrison and Alice Walker) reconstructed the black world through the particular lens of race, gender, and class. The furor raised by their writings was not so much over the depiction of the brutal consequences of racism for the black community; this had been a constant theme in black literature. The anger was over the way in which these novelists deconstructed the middle-class verities that earlier black writers had cherished. They presented a portrait of the psychological damage suffered by black women at the hands of black men, who were themselves under the sway of white male society.[61]

Thus Celie, the central character in Alice Walker's widely acclaimed novel *The Color Purple*, suffered one humiliation after another throughout the story at the hands of black men, particularly sexual exploitation by "Mister." Celie managed to survive these trials by bonding with black women. Her sister and Shug Avery led Celie into a world of self-esteem and assertiveness, intimacy, and eventually love for all of humanity. Even if the novel was not entirely convincing (especially in its historical specifics), Walker did succeed in exposing much of the damage done to African American gender relations as a result of that community's absorption of the bourgeois dictates of gender.

Unfortunately, the making of *The Color Purple* into a Hollywood motion picture undid much of the good Walker had set out to do. Steven Spielberg, the wunderkind Hollywood director, chose to bring Walker's novel to the screen. It was hardly surprising that Walker acquiesced in the venture. After all, the making of such a film not only affirmed the value of black literature but also provided a long-awaited opportunity for African Americans to be presented artfully and truthfully before a mass audience of white Americans. But this proved a serious miscalculation, given the formulaic nature of the American movie industry. The only gain made by *The Color Purple* was that it was hyped so positively; what emerged on the screen was far less positive. Perhaps not surprisingly, in view of Hollywood's commercial ethos, the brutal exploitation of black men had been considerably softened from the book. But what was most alarming was how the film trotted out nearly every stereotypical representation of African Americans familiar from Hollywood movies of the past. (The most egregious example was probably the grand scene where Shug Avery sings her way from the juke joint to the church, with half the county's blacks trailing behind her, to confront, and eventually reconcile with, her father.) The furor of middle-class AfroAmerica over the negative portrayal of black sexual relationships may have been predictable. Far more disturbing was that little, if any, comment was made about the resurrection of racial stereotypes. And the film was filled with them.[62]

The brouhaha over Spielberg's *The Color Purple* and the intense attention given to African American women's writing nearly overshadowed the other two trends in black literature that emerged out of the black aesthetic movement of the sixties. Although women writers participated in both trends, the themes these writers worked on were more academically inspired and oriented than those of Walker or Morrison, for example. Owing in part to the at least minimal success of affirmative action in higher education, there appeared a school of black literary criticism, which systematically studied black art forms and challenged the received canons of Western literature. Black literary theorists such as Houston Baker, Henry Louis Gates, Hazel Carby, and Hortense Spillers were able to ground the African American world of literature firmly in American literature yet demonstrate its distinct voice.[63]

Novelists such as Gloria Naylor, David Bradley (*The Chaneysville Incident*, 1982), and Richard Perry (*Montgomery's Children*, 1984) wrote works that in many ways reflected their academic sensibilities. Gloria Naylor's prize-winning novel *The Women of Brewster Place* (1984) was as much inspired by feminist theory as by the desire to produce sociologically descriptive novels along the lines of Richard Wright. Her examinations of the lives of black women walled in an inner-city neighborhood nicely captured the commonly held notion of two Americas—one white, one black. Yet while Naylor's central characters—all black women—were forcefully and poignantly rendered, they did not ultimately engage the world around them. By contrast, James Alan McPherson's two short-story collections, *Hue and Cry* (1972) and *Elbow Room* (1974), had covered similar ground— urban black society—but using a more varied cast of characters. Although McPherson, a protégé of Ralph Ellison, is himself ensconced in academia (in 1981 he was awarded a MacArthur fellowship), his work manages to avoid the self-conscious theoretical sophistication of many "academic" novels, which lends a sharper edge to his insights.[64]

There has been, then, a certain "academicism" to much recent black writing. Whether it drew on the deconstructionist spirit of black literary theory or the brave but demanding experimental fiction of a Clarence Major or Ishmael Reed, the fictional world of Afro-Americans quickly became abstract and confused—emotionally out of touch, it seemed, with the reality of AfroAmerica. Michael Cooke was indeed correct when he wrote that Afro-American literature had not yet reached "intimacy."[65]

The other trend that came out of the sixties and early eventies seriously tried to engage the duality of AfroAmerica. It could be said that many of the writers working along this path were engaged in a meditation on history. Their works sought to make sense of Afro-America, not just for white audiences but also for themselves and their enlarged black middle class readership. These writers produced works, often complex in structure, that pointed to a new vision of how African Americans saw themselves in an America of Reagan popularity, resurgent racism, and calls for a revival of the civil rights movement. In some respects, this trend was a fruitful blend of the experimental, the feminist, and the academic. Above all, though, it was deeply grounded in the African American revisionist view of American history, which was gradually achieving recognition within that discipline and encouraging a thorough reconceptualization and rewriting of American history. This literary trend was also an excellent example of integrative cultural diversity. One novel in which all of the above could be seen at work was Toni Morrison's *Song of Solomon* (1977).

Morrison's brilliant epic novel about a midwestern black middle class family clearly rivaled Ralph Ellison's *Invisible Man*. Allegorical, historically grounded, and steeped in black folklore and magical tradition, Morrison's novel took what was actually a simple story (a young man's search for his roots) and with it wove an intriguing web of myth, history, and psychological portraiture about AfroAmerica. Like any novel, it was not without its flaws, but it showed white literary critics that, especially in the hands of gifted talent, AfroAmerica was by no means finished yielding powerful insights into the nation's dialogue over race (and gender).[66]

It was the grounding in history that gave *Song of Solomon* its particular verve. Morrison traced Milkman Dead's family from Reconstruction through to the sixties and into the seventies, that is, from the first moment of emancipation, when true freedom had yet to be struggled for, to the final realization of freedom, when Milkman achieves self-determination and literally *flies*. This message—that it takes freedom from within to gain freedom from without—prefigured the political call of the black neoconservatives for the black community to revive self-help strategies to solve its problems. However, it would be a mistake to confuse Morrison's intentions with black neoconservative politics. Morrison's vision, like that of two other writers, Charles Johnson and Julius Lester, was loftier than that. She was, as were Johnson and Lester later on, deeply engaged in a meditation on the history and soul of America and AfroAmerica. Her work can be interpreted as a message to African Americans to reacquaint themselves with their history from the beginnings to the present and to seek "spiritual" rather than "material" freedom. But this means that the prevailing social and political categories and dogmas have to be questioned. This process forms the subject of Charles Johnson's tour de force, *The Oxherding Tale* (1982), and Julius Lester's multilayered and haunting novel *Do Lord Remember Me* (1985).

In Johnson's novel, a mulatto slave, Andrew Hawkins, tells the story of his birth, education, escape from slavery, and quest for self-understanding. Partly humorous, yet thoroughly serious, Johnson told the story in the form of a slave narrative. But it was not the traditional slave narrative that historians and black literary critics have debated over. As Johnson puts, he wrote from the perspective of "authentic narratives written by bondsmen who decided one afternoon to haul hips for the Mason-Dixon Line," explaining that these particular narratives were "related as distant cousins are related to the Puritan Narrative," a story which told of spiritual growth. As Johnson asserted: "In point of fact, the movement in the Slave Narrative from slavery (sin) to freedom (salvation) are identical to those of the Puritan Narrative, and *both* these genuinely American forms are the offspring of that hoary confession by the first philosophical black writer, St. Augustine."[67] Several levels of meaning and message operated in this novel's complex reconstruction of the slave narrative. Threaded throughout those layers was Johnson's own preoccupation with phenomonology as a literary form.[68] But there were also important cultural and political implications in this short novel.

There was, for one, the treatment of "passing," the main theme of the book. Johnson took a long-standing genre (often called the "tragic mulatto" genre) of both black and white writers in the late nineteenth and early twentieth centuries and turned it on its head. In the familiar form of the genre, the central character is a black who is light-skinned enough to pass for white, attempts to do so, feels guilty or is eventually exposed, and finally returns to die in or be reconciled with the black world. In somewhat similar fashion, Johnson initially gives us a character, Andrew Hawkins, who through external circumstances (his escape from slavery, his encounters with racism, and his desire for freedom) is forced to "reinvent" his identity, which he does by passing as William Harris. As Hawkins/Harris puts it, "we all rearrange our past to sweeten it a little. Memory, as the metaphysicians say, is imagination" (109).[69] But unlike the typical "tragic mulatto," Johnson's protagonist did not so much reject the black world and embrace the white world as he attempted to find a way to be free from both worlds with their constricting categories that prevented him from finding and becoming himself. Charles Johnson thus sets up, in a subtle and nuanced manner, the image of Hawkins/Harris (AfroAmerica) as an "outsider" trying to escape into the mainstream for freedom.

But this notion of AfroAmerica as outside the mainstream is subverted, along with the "tragic mulatto" genre, when Johnson introduces the character of Bannon—the Soulcatcher—a bounty hunter who captures fugitive slaves. For Bannon, the greatest challenge is capturing those who are passing for white. What is most striking, however, is that the reader is somewhat uncertain whether Bannon is black or white. What does become apparent, though, is that Bannon is an altogether different kind of bounty hunter. Bannon described his method for catching runaways (especially those passing) as "a more delicate, different hunt."

> When you *really* after a mon with a price on his head, you forgit for the hunt that you the hunter. . . . It ain't so much in overpowering him physically, when you huntin' a Negro, as it is mentally. Yo mind has to soak hup his mind. His heart. (116)

As Hawkins/Harris listens to the description, he realizes that Bannon's "Negroid speech, his black idiosyncracies, and tics" were the result of absorbing "the countless bondsmen he'd assassinated." Bannon further describes his methods, bragging that "if Ah ever meet a Negro Ah can't' catch, Ah'll quit." But Hawkins/Harris feels reassured: "Because I knew his techniques, the strategies, that poisoned my father, I could stare them down, second guess Bannon and escape destruction" (117). Hawkins/Harris is able to understand Bannon because, as a result of his obsession with catching runaway black slaves, the white man had identified with his quarry to the point that he had in effect become black. Hawkins/Harris eventually does escape from being killed by the Soulcatcher but only after acknowledging the symbiotic tie that had developed between them—a tie that symbolizes the ongoing interdependency of black and white in America.

Johnson's tale set out to redefine the received wisdom about race and freedom and AfroAmerica as the "outsider." The relationship Johnson constructed between Hawkins/Harris and the Soulcatcher allowed him to examine many of the themes that James Baldwin pursued in his essays: the need that whites have for the black presence as Other, the white need to dominate, and the white need for black love. The Soulcatcher's earnest desire to be the best bounty hunter leads him into a sort of "reverse passing" that, Johnson seems to suggest, reveals the absurdity of race. Here, the creolization of American history—the intertwining of European and African cultures—has turned the image of the outsider on its head. African Americans, given their sufferings and their struggle for freedom, dignity, and a sense of identity, are insiders; whites, revealed as an amalgam of European ideas, prejudices, and thirst for power, are outsiders. Of course, Johnson was perfectly well aware that whites have power over blacks, but he also knew that this power was not limitless.

At their best, Charles Johnson's novel and his later award-winning work *Middle Passage* (1990) expressed the essence of AfroAmerica even as they exposed the absurdities of racial categories and the damaging effects of these categories on both blacks and whites.[70] Johnson clearly embraced the more positive nationalist sentiments at work in AfroAmerica, but above all he strove toward a restructuring of American history in which AfroAmerica would be recognized as a vital life force. Whatever the unique and respectable differences of African Americans and white Americans, a true America could not exist without the mixture and cooperation of both.[71]

Julius Lester's adult fiction moved in much the same direction. He, too, dealt with the history of African Americans, their struggles with the conundrums of race and color, and their quest for freedom. And although like Johnson (and many other black writers of the late twentieth century) Lester was influenced by James Baldwin, he was forged to a large extent in the crucible of the civil rights movement.

As the son of a black Methodist minister, Lester was firmly rooted in the southern black middle class. He had no real relationships with whites until his fourteenth year. When the civil rights movement began, Lester moved to the North (and later the West) hoping to find breathing space away from the stultifying prison of segregation. But as the movement proceeded, Lester found himself drawn back, however reluctantly, to the South and to the immense changes that were taking place there. As a field secretary for the SNCC, he arrived on the scene thoroughly imbued with the initial ideals of the SNCC—the notions of a beloved community and of black and white together, and the dream of Martin Luther King, Jr. Yet by the mid-sixties, shortly after Lester's arrival, the SNCC was rapidly radicalizing itself into an angry black nationalist group that condemned white America for its racism and imperialism.[72]

While no doubt the critiques of the SNCC were to a large extent on the mark, the retreat into an angry black nationalism proved troubling for Lester. As a musical artist and a writer, Lester was concerned with the transformation of people's spiritual selves. Pursuing power solely for the sake of retribution would ultimately serve only to maintain the existing inequities of society—an insight that was clearly at odds with an angry movement that demanded FREEDOM NOW. As the movement became more radicalized (and was increasingly pushed to the margins of political and intellectual discourse), Lester found himself in the position of tactfully but incisively criticizing the movement's directions and objectives. Recognizing that black people had been cast in the role of outsiders, Lester tried to explain what ultimately had to be done (and not done):

> Perhaps this has been the peculiar mission of blacks in America. As Outsiders we were to lead the way from History. The victim is the only one who can clear the way to salvation but only by accepting the existential pain of refusing to become executioner as he ceases to be a victim. Instead of leaping into the void, blacks are jumping to the other side and, redefining ourselves as blacks, we impose

racial definitions on the rest of humanity. Murder is committed when we define others as anything except a variation of ourselves and we of them. And the greater victim of the murder is the murderer.[73]

Lester amplified on these intellectual critiques in his fiction. The short story "The Valley of the Shadow of Death," published in the early seventies after he had left the SNCC, focuses on the tensions and strains that afflicted those who had devoted their lives to the movement. David, the protagonist, had given his all to the movement; he was as close to "the people" as any of the organizers in the movement could ever have hoped to be. Perhaps too close. For when it becomes apparent that the movement has lost its direction—its soul—David realizes that he will have to make a painful choice: to accept the movement's blind embrace of black power or seek out a world that treated all human beings as human beings, with equality, dignity, trust, and respect.[74]

In *Do Lord Remember Me*, Lester's evocative novel in which a black minister comes to grips with his life on his dying day, Lester created what amounted to an historical view of the long journey on which AfroAmerica had traveled in its uneasy coexistence with America. One of the themes of the novel was whether integration was truly meaningful for African Americans. If within the confines of enforced segregation black communities had been able to build strong and nourishing institutions (principally centered around the church), then the reforms proposed by the civil rights movement, with its basically liberal, middle-class perspective, would not necessarily bode well for the poorer black masses. The black middle class that developed within the admittedly stifling atmosphere of segregation provided a bridge of accommodation to the white world, on the one hand, and a valuable role model for young blacks, on the other. Moreover, the segregated black middle class furnished an example of communal solidarity even as it espoused individual achievement and moral character. In other words, the black middle class held in balance the tension between being African and American. But the successes of integration, as envisaged by the civil rights movement, threatened to remove this vital artery from the community.

For the Reverend Joshua Smith, this potential loss of community seemed painfully real.

Reverend Smith thought about all that he had endured, all that he had done, and because it was a NEW DAY, his life had become memories for which no one would have any use as they sat in integrated schools, on buses, and lunch counter stools beside white people. And his pain as he sat there was not only the affliction of memory but the lacerating knowledge that his life in slavery's cold shadows was being ground to dust beneath the hard soles of marching demonstrators. A new song was being sung and its melody was freedom. Was he the only one who could remember the simple melody of survival.[75]

Granted, the injustices of segregation had obstructed black men and women from access to meaningful participation in the larger society and full self-determination within their own communities. However, while the legal successes of the civil rights struggles and the liberal programs of the Johnson administration's Great Society afforded opportunities for the expansion of the black middle class and for its increased participation in the society at large, it did so at the cost of fragmentation within black communities.[76]

Lester continued to be a prescient observer of AfroAmerica as it entered the post–civil rights age. And even as AfroAmerica faced new setbacks in the waning decades of the twentieth century, the enlarged black middle class was still struggling, culturally and politically, to come to grips with the victories of 1964 and 1965. Black writers of the seventies, eighties, and nineties, like their predecessors in the twenties and thirties, attempted to portray, and perhaps thereby to shape, the moral, cultural, and political terrain of an AfroAmerica existing within yet apart from American society. Collectively, their work, along with events taking place in other cultural arenas, challenged white America's perception of black people and made AfroAmerica (or at least the black bourgeoisie's image of it) more visible. But the portraits that these writers presented often conflicted. Indeed, by the mid-eighties the dubious success of integration and the tenacity with which race continued to plague American society was forcing AfroAmerica (and especially the black middle class) to reexamine their values and their place in an America whose contracting economy diminished expectations for racial harmony and hopes for a more humane society.

Nonetheless, the rebirth in literature continued, drawing on its roots in the Harlem Renaissance and the later black arts movement and striving further to elaborate the meaning of AfroAmerica to American society. More important, those producing this literature also worked their way toward a resolution of the two visions—of Africanness and of Americanness—with which AfroAmerica continued to wrestle. Now the idea of integrative cultural diversity began to deepen and acquire greater nuance. Writers such as Alice Walker, Julius Lester, Ishmael Reed, and Toni Morrison attempted to offer America a more subtly etched portrait of AfroAmerica and to suggest anew the importance of African Americans to the culture at large. Meanwhile, other cultural forms began as well to address the issues that had for so long preoccupied black writers. If somewhat uncertainly and uneasily at times, the vision of integrated cultural diversity thus began to find expression not merely in print but in music and the visual media.

CHAPTER 5

Sound and Image

The Cultural Fruits of Integration

The cultural representations of African Americans through music and visual imagery has always been a concern of the black middle class. There was, of course, the wish to celebrate the rich rhythms and creative artistic expression of African Americans. But there was also an underlying concern as to how these cultural productions would be received by a larger public accustomed to often vicious racial stereotypes. Added to this was the tension between the idea that artistic renditions of AfroAmerica should be free to depict that culture openly and completely, warts and all, and the desire of the black middle class to have art stress the positive and uplifting, a tension that persisted even as the movements for civil rights and black power swept the nation. Indeed, those movements went a long way toward reconfiguring the cultural landscape not only of AfroAmerica but of America itself. In the cultural arenas of rock music, motion pictures, and television, African Americans proceeded to demonstrate the cultural fruits of integration, presenting a rich and powerful array of musical, dramatic, and visual reflections, messages, and visions. Even though these presentations seemed at times to give expression to negative images that made many in the black middle class uncomfortable, they undeniably helped to reshape the nation's attitudes toward black people. Moreover, the cultural productions of African Americans from the 1960s onward had a profound impact on the way in which Americans viewed their culture, as it continued to undergo crucial social, economic, and political changes.

One aspect of black history and of American history generally that has often been neglected is the influence of African American culture on rock and roll. Without a doubt, rock music played a significant role in social and political movements from the late 1950s onward, and most chroniclers of this period indeed acknowledge the advent of this music. But considerations of the phenomenon of rock music tend to be subordinated to descriptions of the youth movement, the counterculture, or the fanciful trends of an affluent, suburban-oriented society.[1] While no one can seriously argue with this kind of approach, there is nonetheless much that remains to be said about the tremendous transformations in American society either brought about or encouraged by the Afro-American element in this music.

Rock music, together with protest music (which grew out of folk music), is deeply indebted to Afro-American music, especially the blues and its offshoot, rhythm and blues. Rock and roll gave expression to concrete experiences that young people were having during a decade or more of economic prosperity, social activism, and political turmoil. More specifically, the music of this period played a crucial role for young people (particularly whites) in focusing their disillusionment with and alienation from a prosperous society that had given them so much materially but so little humanly. For young whites searching for new values and ultimately, though more tentatively, for the political transformation of a segmented society, the African American roots of rock and protest music in some ways stood for the promise of social connection. Equally important, black music enabled millions of young whites to appreciate, if not fully understand, something of the African American experience as well as the need to search for a more humane and harmonious community.

The history of black-based rock music is, of course, intertwined with the overall history of the black presence in America. As various historians, rock critics, and social commentators have acknowledged, Afro-American music formed the foundation for much of American popular music, be it jazz, country, pop, or gospel. Indeed, rock music has specific connections to the rural blues music of black southerners that reach as far back as the end of the Civil War.[2]

It was in the fifties, however, that major transformations would take place, at once lifting black music to a central place in American culture and incorporating it in the endeavor to provide reflections on a tormented society and possible visions of a new one. From the fifties to the eighties black music variously gave sustenance to, benefited from, or simply coexisted with the newly evolving form of American rock music. Simultaneously, the music industry grappled with the cultural and political significance of the immersion of large numbers of American youth in the music. Taken by surprise at first, the music industry ultimately took over the production of this music, garnered immense profits—and aided in the general emasculation of the cultural and political critique that the best of this music had to offer. If, then, by some four decades later black music had effectively been absorbed into the mainstream culture, rock music, with its Afro-American roots, had nonetheless managed to build an enduring bridge over which young whites could cross over into AfroAmerica. At the same time, black music has played a crucial role in unifying and giving voice to an oppressed black populace, not only in their political struggles but also in their day-to-day lives.

To understand the significance of the Afro-American roots of rock and protest music requires a brief examination of the sources of this music. A particular musical form, the blues, itself a mixture of African rhythms, gospel music, and folk music from Europe, provided the main thrust to the later creation of rock and roll.[3] But it was the secular form of the blues, as opposed to the spirituals sung by black churchgoers, that proved most influential. The secular blues emerged from the various musical forms that developed among the former slave community during plantation life in the South after the Civil War. Some Afro-Americans, both then and later on, viewed the blues as "sinful tunes," but in actuality this music was an expression of the inner and outer life of a people who were attempting to define themselves culturally and socially in a harsh terrain and during severe times. As Carl Boggs, a black social theorist and student of the blues, has noted, "the social conditions that shaped the blues were agrarian, precapitalist, and racially defined. . . . The music existed primarily *outside* of bourgeois hegemony and was thus alien to dominant culture."[4] Because of the social conditions to which Boggs calls attention and because of a pervasive belief on the part of white society that blacks could not create their own cultural forms, the blues for the most part remained hidden from white America. If, by chance, whites did hear the music, it sounded peculiar to their ears primarily because throughout most of the nineteenth century the most popular form of black entertainment in white society was the minstrel show.

Inasmuch as it amounted essentially to a white interpretation of Afro-American life, the minstrel show could not deal with the element of rebellion, both spiritual and cultural, that especially characterized the blues. However, minstrels did provide a first glimpse of how an industrializing capitalist nation used the culture of the oppressed as commodified entertainment without upsetting the racial status quo and in some respects thereby fashioned a white identity. It later fell to the recording industry (which emerged with the invention of the phonograph in the 1880s) to reproduce the blues for consumption by a large audience: first for blacks, under the so-called "race labels," and later for whites interested in "exotica" or who had some prior experience of such music.[5]

By the end of the nineteenth century, among rural southern blacks, the blues had rapidly become the most popular music played. Indeed, different forms of the blues could already be discerned that would later provide new horizons in American music. Through its secularization, the blues enabled Afro-Americans to confront an industrialized world of work, the stringent Jim Crow caste system, and in many cases neoslavery and poverty. It was through the blues that black people expressed what Boggs (and others after him) saw as the "totality of black social reality, including religion, community, racial identity, and personal-sexual life as well as work."[6] For example, the following blues song, which incorporates a call-and-response form, expresses the harshness of work and the deprivations with which poor blacks lived:

> LEADER: All right now, boys, let me tell you
>   what I had for breakfast now
> GROUP: Little rice, little beans
>   no meat to be seen
>
> Hard work ain't easy
> Dry bread ain't greasy
> Yeah—

In the morning when you rise
Pick and shevil by yo' side

In the morning when you rise
Got a pain in yo' side.[7]

Sexual themes also frequently found expression in blues songs. From a modern vantage point, blues lyrics were unquestionably negative in their stance toward women. Yet women participated extensively in the blues, and the lyrics in their music often offered a crucial counterpoint to those of the men. Nonetheless, these songs mirrored the deep-seated tensions, the sexual exploitation, and the male dominance that pervaded AfroAmerica, as it did America generally. In fact, this tradition of misogyny continued to be prominent in much of rock music and rap music into the eighties and nineties. Consider, for example, the words to a tune by thirties' musician Robert Johnson, whose earthy lyrics (and virtuoso guitar licks) were inspirational to rock groups like Led Zepplin and the Rolling Stones, among others:

I said I flashed your light, mama, and your horn won't even
  blow
I even flashed my light, mama, this horn won't even blow
There's a short in this connection way down below.[8]

As the two examples above both demonstrate, a social reality was being expressed in the blues, whether it was the harshness of work conditions in an impoverished and caste-ridden southern region or the sexual attitudes and frustrations of men and women. The blues thus enabled rural working-class Afro-Americans to vent their feelings and somehow to bear up, sometimes painfully, sometimes joyfully.

The intolerable living conditions engendered by racism and poverty, along with the increased mechanization of southern farms, began either to encourage or to force many rural African Americans to leave the region. As black people migrated north, the blues traveled with them and, in an urban setting, underwent further and more profound transformation. While initially retaining a view of black social reality brought from the country, the blues soon began to reflect the disillusionment that blacks faced as social discrimination and economic depression engulfed them.

Undoubtedly, by migrating to the cities some Afro-Americans did manage to escape the oppressive atmosphere of the South and find happiness. But for most blacks urban life did not fulfill the promise of a better life, with jobs and freedom from the cruelties of white racism. Instead, over the years a more subtle and vicious form of racism, embedded in the industrial structure, shackled most migrant blacks to increasingly high levels of unemployment and relegated them to a marginal status in urban America. It was within the black enclaves of the cities across the nation that the blues took on a new dimension, a new rhythm that reflected at once the longings for home and the frenetic pace of the street. A new subculture was born. Its public space was the bars, nightclubs, and street corners, as opposed to the fields, ramshackle juke joints, and plantation tenant quarters of the South. Other changes came as well. The commercialization of blues music grew rapidly as the emerging record industry created "special division products," popularly called "race records," for those blacks who could afford to purchase them. During the teens and twenties, such music was also aired on radio (at special times and often on special stations) so that almost all African Americans had an opportunity to hear it.[9] Giving impetus to this commercialization were the multifaceted changes taking place in the blues.

The blues became more expansive musically, especially as a new form of black music, jazz, made its appearance in the late teens and the twenties. Concomitant with changes in rhythm, now more aggressive and hot, there appeared new forms of dance, which swept across the nation, together with the excitement and exhilaration of Afro-Americans sensing new hope for themselves at the close of World War I and the dawn of the Harlem Renaissance. It was, moreover, inevitable that American society would soon become aware of this specifically black cultural phenomenon. David L. Lewis, a well-known African American historian of the Harlem Renaissance, captured that mood vividly when he described the homecoming of the Fighting 369th Black regiment to Harlem in 1919:

> The tide of khaki and black turned west on 110th Street to Lenox Avenue, then north again into the heart of Harlem. At 125th Street . . . a field of pennants, flags, banners, and scarves thrashed about the soldiers like elephant grass in a gale, threatening to engulf them. In front of the unofficial reviewing stand at 130th Street [Big Jim] Europe's sixty-piece band broke into "Here Comes My Dad-

dy" to the extravagant delight of the crowd. At this second platform, Harlem notables and returning heroes beheld each other
with almost palpable elation and pride. No longer now in the dense
rapid-stepping formation learned from the French, ranks opened
gait and loosened.[10]

The triumphal return of Afro-American soldiers to Harlem after
the war signaled a new political spirit among Afro-Americans. The
"New Negro" was not only involved in the arts but also in the quest
for dignity and political equality. Moreover, African Americans exerted a steady push for the recognition of their culture and for their right
to participate in the life of the nation. From Du Bois's editing of the
Crisis to Garvey's mass nationalist movement to the writings of the
Harlem literati, the entire period teemed with hope and aspirations.
But it was Afro-American musical culture that swept America off its
feet. The Roaring Twenties set urban America ablaze with the hot
sounds of jazz, the frenetic gyrations of the Charleston and the Black
Bottom, and the evolving rhythms of the blues. And the focus on
music increased as both the music and radio industries developed and
grew more commercial.

In a period that also saw the rapid growth of automobile manufac-
ture and of motion pictures, the radio and music industries served
especially to bring Americans more closely in touch with the unknown or repressed segments of their society. Radio, with its need for
advertising revenues, brought a wide variety of entertainment—
music, comedies, serial dramas (later called "soaps")—to millions of
listeners nationally. The music industry, with its recordings (still
called "race records") of such cabaret blueswomen such as Mamie
Smith, Ma Rainey, and Bessie Smith and of bluesmen like Blind
Lemon Jefferson, Muddy Waters, and Tommy Johnson, made black
music newly available to whites. With the successful commercial recording of Mamie Smith's "Crazy Blues," the blues became part of the
increasingly financially successful entertainment industry, itself a significant part of the burgeoning leisure culture of twenties' America.[11]

Among the black middle class of the period there was, however, a
split over how to receive or respond to this music. The more straitlaced
among the black intelligentsia greeted it with disdain. Scholars such
as Carter G. Woodson had no use for jazz. Likewise, J. A. Rogers, the

noted black journalist and race-conscious historian, felt that jazz was demeaning. Even Du Bois, who, much like Rogers, Woodson and others, was concerned that Afro-American culture be represented in a positive light, was not entirely thrilled with the display of black rural or urban folk culture. At the same time, younger black artists, most of whom had middle-class, bourgeois backgrounds, embraced the blues and jazz. To them this was the music of the people. Whether it was Langston Hughes's celebration of black urban life and its connection to jazz or Zora Neale Hurston's explorations of black rural folk culture, the young artists and writers of the Harlem Renaissance saw music as a core component of the "New Negro" and of Afro-American culture.[12]

The music industry quickly capitalized on this untapped market and before long the music of Afro-Americans, whether in the rural South or the urban North, was being heard throughout the nation. The black music heard by most whites, however, had been significantly watered down. The music industry worked a sophisticated transformation on the gutsy and emotional music formed over the years in the Delta and on the urban streets. Passed through the ideological filter of racism and through various profit-oriented strategies of the music industry, Afro-American music was often diluted by well-known white singers and bands, suggestive lyrics were cleaned up, and racially offensive (to white ears) lines were omitted or altered. Moreover, despite a loose and, at times, even touching attempt at integration among the musicians in the industry (particularly in the jazz arena), profits rarely went to the original black composers or artists.[13]

Of course, the blues also survived undiluted. As Imamu Amiri Baraka (Leroi Jones) has pointed out in his study *Blues People*, rhythm and blues was still an "exclusive " music in that it was performed almost exclusively for, and had to satisfy, a black audience. For this reason, it could not suffer "the ultimate sterility that would have resulted from total immersion in the mainstream of American culture."[14] Because the recording industry had identified a market for such music, original compositions of many blues artists continued to be recorded and distributed throughout the black belt in the South and the black enclaves of the urban North.

Despite the continued ghettoization of African American music, its form, style, and rhythm gradually seeped into mainstream America. No one today can seriously argue that "The King of Rock and Roll," Elvis Presley, or the numerous groups that made up the "British Invasion" in the sixties, or even the host of middle-of-the road pop stars were not in some way influenced by black rhythm and blues. While there is certainly a plausible argument that much of pop music was a mélange of various styles (folk, country, jazz, rhythm and blues), there are nonetheless significant distinctions between those styles.

Country music and folk music most certainly are genres in their own right and can be identified with particular groups (mostly white) and particular regions, such as the up-country South or the South-west. Folk music has, moreover, often been a political force. Inspirational songs, originally crafted to organize workers in the early twentieth century and through to the thirties, continued to provide sustenance to the Beats in the fifties, and in the sixties helped to inspire youth in its search for an authentic self in a homogenous society. In the late eighties and early nineties, folk music began to reemerge as a forum for social commentary. In all of these musical genres there was at least a trace, a faint recognition, of the black presence in America. Many country singers, for example, knew something of the blues; their conditions of life almost demanded it.

As Simon Frith has argued, the similarities between Afro-American blues and country music were many, but there were also striking ideological differences.[15] Country music, like the blues, featured lyrics about sexuality, the harsh conditions of work, and struggles in the face of adversity. It could even be considered an early form of populist music when it spoke of racism and other injustices. Nonetheless, country music was in the end rooted in the essentially conservative beliefs of the traditional American family, in fundamentalist religion, and in rugged individualism. Injustices could be alluded to (in modern commercial country music such allusions have all but vanished— only to be replaced, in some cases, by patriotic fervor), but the country musician still typically maintained an underlying belief in the social separation of the races. Its opposition to this "musical segregation" was one of the things that made rock music particularly threatening. When Elvis Presley bridged the gap between white country music and the black blues, he was pointing the way toward a "social intermingling" of the races.

With so many lower- and middle-class white youth identifying with this music and its new integrative potential, it was not surprising that parents turned out in force against the emerging rock culture of the fifties. Rock and roll's most potent danger was its supposed appeal to immorality: its seductiveness to young people, its call to sensual abandon. Given their adolescent inexperience, America's young people would not be able to cope. The raw rhythms of the music would purportedly titillate youth, loosen their inhibitions, and finally unleash a destructive delinquency that would shatter the peaceful calm and traditional mores of the suburbs. However, while the fears of most parents were generated by the putative immorality of rock and roll, underneath there was a current of racism. After all, where did this music originally come from? Were not blacks the ones who sang and danced to these sounds? Did not Elvis Presley seem to be imitating Negro gyrations and sullen sultry mannerisms?[16] In the South, the meaning was especially clear to white parents: rock was subversive music designed to shred the social fabric; it would lead to race mixing and ultimately to the mongrelization of society. In the rest of the nation, parents may have shied away from such open imputations of racial prejudice, but they were nonetheless concerned.

In the larger historical framework, there were other events of even greater concern to Americans, events that fed into the anxieties over this new form of music. Although the period was one of relative peace, there was a postwar recession. Added to this was the advent of the Cold War and the subsequent obsessive display of fear and distrust (if not outright hatred) of the Soviet Union and others of a left bent who might undermine the nation's democracy or overtake it militarily. Fearing their archrivals, the Soviets, Americans felt a gnawing unease, bordering at times on paranoia, that an international Communist conspiracy would engulf them, destroy their freedoms, and displace their leadership in world affairs. The Soviets, moreover, had the bomb, which raised the specter of nuclear holocaust.

As if to compound these fears, on the domestic scene there were loud rumblings of change: Afro-Americans were moving steadily toward achieving legal equality. In *Brown vs. Board of Education, Topeka,*

Kansas (1954), the Supreme Court unanimously called for the desegregation of schools. Although this landmark decision is often regarded as the beginning of the civil rights movement in AfroAmerica,
that movement had a long history of fits and starts. As momentous an
occasion as *Brown* was, it only added to a build-up of changes that
threatened the very core of the ideology and society that many held so
dear. In a peculiar way, rock and roll became the connection, in many
minds, between the rise of black people to equality through civil
rights and the undermining of the social fabric through youth. It
could also be said that rock and roll was the first musical form that
harbored the vision of a culturally integrative diversity that recognized and respected the importance of the black experience in American society.

Not surprisingly, young people resisted the opinions of their parents regarding rock and roll, laughing at their anxieties and condemning the older generation for stodginess and opacity. Rock and roll was
exciting music for youth, a chance to escape the perceived drabness of
their lives. In other words, rock and roll provided a means through
which the young in the fifties could explore the world beyond the
suburb and distance themselves from the seemingly rigid values of
their parents. And, although they were undoubtedly unaware of the
visionary potential for integration that rock and roll held out, it also,
if indirectly at first, provided them with a look at another crucial part
of the nation: AfroAmerica.

Those who listened to late-night radio heard such black singers as
Little Richard, Fats Domino, and Bo Diddley. These singers were
well known in AfroAmerica, along with many others that whites had
never heard of. But with the rhythm and blues of a Fats Domino or
Bo Diddley playing in the late evenings, the fears of middle-class
white (and black) parents were underscored. Little Richard wore
lipstick and rouge and flaunted his homosexuality; Fats Domino sang
about finding his girl on Blueberry Hill; Bo Diddley elicited much
worry with his rocking tune about hand-jive. While the sexuality in
most of these songs was implicit—it was an extension of the preoccupation of the blues with sexual matters—this sexuality was clearly
threatening to a middle-class morality that valued the nuclear family
and heterosexual monogamy. For the young people caught in an age
of conformity, however, the music sparked new life and presented

new opportunities for forming bonds of adolescent group identification and separation from the straitlaced world of adults.[17]

Most fifties' rock and roll songs sublimated the rawness of the blues
even as they borrowed from it. "Cover songs" by white artists such as
Pat Boone, Patti Page, Teresa Brewer, and Johnny Ray, as well as
romantic moon-in-June songs by these and other artists, blunted the
primal force of black blues–based rock. To some extent, such music
eased the anxieties of concerned parents and provided relief to harried
radio station managers, while still appealing to millions of young
listeners. Moreover, some Afro-American artists made hit records
within this romantic, balladeering mode. The popularity of Johnny
Mathis, the Platters, and the Coasters, for example, cut across racial
lines. But there could be no getting around the sensuousness of their
music or the messages it contained that spoke directly to the sentiments of young people. Sam Cooke, whose music had deep roots in
the gospel tradition, sang wonderful love songs that were, for example, cast in terms of the pointlessness of schooling ("Don't know
nothin' about geometry, don't know nothin' about history . . . but I
do know that I love you") or the grind of the working world ("Another Saturday night and I ain't got nobody"). Even when Cooke sang
about the grimness of working on a chain gang, which clearly made
particular reference to the trials of African Americans, his message
resonated with the experience of young whites who groaned under
the restrictive chains of conformity.[18]

It was, however, in the realm of folk music that more explicitly
political concerns were addressed. Groups such as the Weavers had
members (notably Pete Seeger) whose roots reached as far back as the
activism of the thirties.[19] Such music was to some extent muted by
the McCarthyism of the fifties. Nonetheless, despite blacklisting, political folk music held on to its existence and provided a crucial meeting point for progressive traditions in the black and white communities. This conjunction strengthened in the sixties, fueled by the
political struggle over civil rights in the South, by the fears attending
the threat of nuclear disaster, and by the hopes engendered in young
people by a youthful president and his seemingly vibrant administration's attempts to address their concerns and to provide the nation
with a new vision.

The most significant black influence on political folk music arose in the South in connection with the campaign to register black people to vote. In 1962, two years after the lunch counter sit-ins in Greensboro, North Carolina, and the formation of the Student Non-Violent Co-ordinating Committee, four black SNCC field secretaries who had met and worked together in the Albany, Georgia, demonstrations in 1961 and 1962 formed a quartet called the Freedom Singers. The group sought to raise money for the fledgling SNCC organization and, perhaps more important, to tell the story of the movement through the music it was producing.[20]

The Freedom Singers reached their goals, bringing in much-needed revenue and acquainting many people, mostly college students, with the music of the civil rights struggle. Songs such as "Ain't Gonna Let Segregation Turn Me Around," "Over My Head," and "Woke Up This Morning" became familiar anthems in the North as well as the South. The original group disbanded shortly after the 1963 Newport Folk Festival. In 1964 a new group of Freedom Singers was formed, this time consisting of six black men. While they, too, were SNCC field secretaries, they brought with them a diversity of experience gained during the civil rights movement throughout the South. They also had among them a former jazz musician, Matthew Jones, who wrote prolifically and provided most of the group's music. When the new group was sharply criticized for departing from the gospel-oriented style of the original Freedom Singers, Jones was said to have replied that the freedom movement reflected more than the Negro's tradition in gospel and that, in the end, Negroes were not the only ones involved in the freedom movement.[21]

Two aspects here are noteworthy with regard to the influence of Afro-American culture on rock: the deep-seated base of rock and roll in black music (traceable through the blues) and the political notion that freedom was not just a black concern but a matter that affected all Americans. These two ideas would weave together in an uneasy dialectic throughout the music of the sixties, reinforced on the one hand by an explicit Afro-American presence in music, and on the other by the exploration of themes that would have at their core the idea of freedom, whether personal or political. Bob Dylan, for example, a young Minnesotan who had been much influenced by the blues, wrote prolifically around the notion of personal freedom and the frustration of being hemmed in by an unfeeling conformist society. Peter, Paul, and Mary sang out of an older folk tradition, but their songs quickly took on a new force as they participated in the civil rights struggles for freedom. Their appearance at the Selma, Alabama, rally in 1965 singing "If I Had a Hammer" clearly illustrated their hope for the successful struggle for freedom for everyone.

As folk music asserted its political message, rock and roll in the early sixties languished. Much of the music was commercially bland and featured a preoccupation with teenage romance, high school hops, and fast automobiles.[22] Originating on the West Coast, the music served more to establish the mythology of California as the land of sun, fun, and surf. But the early sixties also saw the birth of the "soul sound," a popular black middle class appropriation of black folk music. The commercialization of soul music rested firmly on what was called by its founder, Berry Gordy, the "Motown sound," a music played, written, and produced by upward-striving young blacks, in part for white consumption. Motown resonated with an urban black verve ("soul") and was thus easily acceptable to those Afro-Americans who resided in the many urban housing projects throughout the nation. But it was also sufficiently mainstream to be equally palatable to a mass audience of young whites. Motown was an Afro-American announcement of a belief in the central values of America, a demonstration that black people could swing and be proper citizens simultaneously. Motown was an attempt to show that African Americans understood the rags-to-riches legend of Horatio Alger and could join the lessons of that legend with Afro-American folk cultural traditions and still meet white standards of acceptability. Motown met with amazing success, well beyond the fondest dreams of its early practitioners.[23]

But "black middle class soul" had another side, a side that did not relinquish its roots in the black community so readily. It too was commercialized, but, as has often been the case with black music, this particular brand of soul music was marginalized into that category of rhythm and blues called "race music." This raw sound of soul came from the South, and its star performers indirectly shared the struggles that all southern blacks were engaged in at that time. Thus it was not surprising that while civil rights workers and most youth in general listened to Motown, with its implicit and soothing message of inte-

gration, black civil rights workers and their young white allies also
unwound to Otis Redding, Rufus Thomas, Aretha Franklin, Wilson
Pickett, Sam and Dave, Joe Tex, and Carla Thomas. These singers and
many others were the embodiment of the black blues musical tradition: sensuous, sexual, visceral, soulful.

Granted, in many ways the Motown singers were no less soulful—
and no less black—than those of the Stax-Volt, Atlantic, and King
Records crowd. But listeners detected a difference in style and presentation. Motown performers such as Smokey Robinson and the Miracles, Martha and the Vandellas, the Supremes, the Four Tops, and the
Temptations were polished, slick, and wholesome; they masked their
anger (or hatred) under a heavy gloss of sharp dance routines, sentimental lyrics, and thoroughly professional performance. Although
these performers were mostly from working-class backgrounds, their
music was oriented toward the middle class and embodied a relatively
unthreatening image of blackness that most young white youth could
respond to, which allowed them to pull away from the racism of their
parents' world. Not only that, it was entertaining music, and perfect
for dancing.

The increasing attraction of Afro-American music was not generated solely by the black artists of Motown or Stax-Volt but came as
well from a wholly unexpected source: Great Britain. In 1964, one
year after the idealism of the Kennedy administration was shattered
by an assassin's bullet, four working-class boys from Liverpool appeared on Ed Sullivan's Sunday night variety show. The Beatles' initial
appearance was certainly preceded by a significant amount of hype,
but adults and the media were still unprepared for the enormous
popular response. For young whites, the Beatles filled in a musical
gap in a period when not much exciting was happening musically. In
pulling rock and roll out of its doldrums, their music also overshadowed Afro-American music, which was still, for the most part,
relegated to clubs in black urban enclaves or to late-night radio airplay. Nonetheless, the Beatles and the other British rock groups to
follow would provide solid proof of the centrality of the African
American roots in their music.[24]

The basic appeal of the Beatles was simple: the music was both
rough and gentle, it spoke to adolescent sexual yearnings, and it had a
strong flavor of insouciant behavior. Their music also, as John Len-

non would later proudly admit, had origins in black music. These young musicians had gone directly to the roots of rock and roll in order to create their own music. Blues, and rhythm and blues, had long been admired by many British working-class youth, and notably by that other immensely popular British group, the Rolling Stones. Many Afro-American artists such as Bo Diddley, Chuck Berry, and Howling Wolf were heroes to British young people and musicians. Indeed, in 1966 it was in Britain that an American-born superstar was made and then transported back to his homeland: Jimi Hendrix.[25]

The reign of the Beatles in the United States began in the midst of a period of rapid social change and contributed to the creation of an integrated youthful counterculture. By 1965 the British invasion (so labeled by the recording industry and the media) marched side-by-side with the accelerated explosions in the nation's black urban communities. America watched in dazed bewilderment the outpouring of pent-up black anger and the movement of young whites further and further from the traditional values of home, family, and bourgeois sexual morality. The Beatles signaled such a departure in early 1964 when they met Bob Dylan and smoked marijuana. By 1967, when their landmark album *Sgt. Pepper's Lonely Hearts Club Band* appeared, rock music had become a significant part of virtually every young American's life.

Among Afro-American youth, however, there was seemingly little interest in the Beatles or the British invasion. Instead, young blacks, especially those of the middle class, were discovering the sounds of Stax-Volt and Motown, both of which espoused subtle integrationist messages. Young whites were at the same time being exposed to what had long been existent in black musical circles—not only soul music or rhythm and blues but also a striving for genuine humanity. This musical cross-pollination reinforced the notion that a transformation in the direction of integrative cultural diversity was taking place. Julius Lester, perhaps the most important black social critic of the period, commented on this transformation and its rationale among white youth: "To be white in America is to be buried in a compost of meaning that means nothing because it isn't lived. . . . With their music, they slapped America continuously."[26] Music was no longer something to dance to or to make out to; it was something to be listened to, analyzed, and, above all, to be experienced. Granted, there was a potentially dark side to this new attitude in that this age of "psychedelic music" accompanied a meteoric rise in the use of drugs, often rationalized on artistic grounds. One had to raise one's consciousness, confront the repressions of a smothered existence, and ultimately tap into inner resources. Bourgeois American youth accepted drugs as a useful way to escape the more painful and enduring realities of American society—to "tune in, turn on, and drop out."

These painful realities included the decisive shift in the civil rights movement from the fight for integration to increasingly open dissatisfaction with piecemeal reforms and anger over power politics, economic oppression, and entrenched racism. Loyal and sincere young whites were dismissed from the SNCC and told that they must exterminate racism in their own communities.[27] At the same time, there was a recognition that America's domestic problems were in complex ways entwined with those of the world at large. By 1969 over a half a million young men were fighting in the rice paddies and tropical forests of Vietnam, purportedly to preserve democracy among the South Vietnamese. It soon became all too clear to many Americans, however, that this military intervention was not in the best interests of either the Vietnamese or the American people. Vietnam was a painful reality for those young people who believed that social ills could be corrected by working within the system, and it led many to conclude that it was the system itself that caused the problem. For them, and for other young people who were not as politically aware (quite possibly the majority), rock music held out the hopeful prospect of a new world. If it sometimes encouraged a dangerous escapism, this music also provided the basis for a youth community.

In the increasingly surreal world of rock, black music remained an important presence, as white singers and song writers continued to tap into the blues. But, perhaps more than any other, it was one individual who bridged the gap between black and white. When James Marshall (Jimi) Hendrix released his first album, its title captured the question of the moment: *Are You Experienced?* The songs were an odd mixture of rock and roll, psychedelia, and the blues, and the album became an instant classic.[28] Hendrix's greatest achievement, artistically, was his ability to make the electric guitar sound almost human and use it to express anguish, joy, and liberation. The guitar was, of course, an established fixture in rock and roll, and many of the chord progressions used in rock guitar could be traced directly back to the bluesmen.[29] But Hendrix innovated on this old tradition to create new musical forms with the electric guitar. At the same time, he constantly let people know who his heroes were: the black blues singers of yesteryear, along with such iconoclastic white artists as Bob Dylan.

At the Monterey Pop Festival in 1967, Hendrix made his grand debut. His set was bracketed by two separate but parallel cultural expressions of American pop, both deeply rooted in black music. First there was Otis Redding, a powerful Afro-American blues and soul singer from Georgia; following Hendrix's performance there was Janis Joplin, a young white woman from Texas, who borrowed amply from blues singers Mama Thorton and Ma Rainey. Redding represented Afro-American soul music and culture at its best, while Joplin embodied an emerging integrative counterculture. But it was Hendrix who most successfully merged the two cultures, singing the pop song "Wild Thing" with an electrifying sensuality and sexuality and a Bob Dylan song, "Like a Rolling Stone," in pointed rhetorical fashion.[30]

Jimi Hendrix moved further and further into America's white counterculture, providing it with an integrative cultural diversity that kept older forms of Afro-American music in full view of the white listeners. In doing so, Hendrix paid a certain price, as many socially active young blacks found Hendrix's move dismaying, even traitorous. Nonetheless, Hendrix's presence in the counterculture's musical world remained an important reminder to young whites of where much of the music came from. Moreover, it was Jimi Hendrix who, so to speak, turned millions of young whites on to black music, especially the blues. Indeed, future guitar players such as Eric Clapton, Stephen Stills, and Johnny Winters, to name only a few, would draw on his legacy in shaping their own music. Hendrix's influence ultimately extended beyond the sixties and seventies and into the eighties, where his mastery of the guitar inspired a number of black rock and rollers, in particular the group In Living Color. The direct legatee of Hendrix in the eighties, however, was the immensely successful, and controversial, singer/composer/performer Prince.

Jimi Hendrix never really lost sight of his Afro-American musical roots. Toward the end of his life, he increasingly plunged into that background, using his guitar to forge links between the blues and jazz—all, of course, within the rock idiom. His music sometimes took an overtly political turn, especially on the live album recorded in Harlem, *Hendrix* (1970), and at Woodstock, where, in the early morning hours of the final day, he played the "Star-Spangled Banner." His striking rendition was, as Julius Lester put it, "like a history of America in sound." In November of 1970, Jimi Hendrix died in England of a drug overdose.[31]

The latter part of the sixties, then, saw rock music form a critical part of the foundation of a would-be integrated youth community, a counterculture. Young people sought, and found, relief and release from the painful constraints of their traditional social life. Likewise, they searched for political wisdom, new values, and a new style of living. Most of all, they wanted to feel good and to experience joy. They wanted a new world, and they wanted it now.

In every region of the country (but particularly on the East and West coasts) rock music drew people together. On the West Coast, which had drifted musically since the decline of sun-and-surf music, a rock mecca formed in and around San Francisco. During the fifties, San Francisco's North Beach had been a haven for the Beats; by the late sixties the Haight-Ashbury district had become the same for the counterculture. A whole assortment of influential groups emerged: the Byrds, Country Joe and the Fish, the Grateful Dead, Jefferson Airplane, Buffalo Springfield, Poco, and, in the early seventies, Crosby, Stills, and Nash, and the Eagles. Likewise, individual artists such as Neil Young, Joni Mitchell (a Canadian who, with Gordon Lightfoot, would carry on the emotionally reflective and romantic folk tradition of the counterculture), and Jim Morrison (of the Los Angeles–based Doors) took on personal meaning for many young people.

Many of these artists were influenced by black music and in many cases black bluesmen played on the same bill with them.[32] Later in their careers some, such as Joni Mitchell, would increasingly use jazz in their music, thus demonstrating how much of the counter-culture's artistic forms were integrated into black art forms. Meanwhile, Afro-American youth continued to listen to the sounds of James Brown, Marvin Gaye, Smokey Robinson and the Miracles, and a psychedelized Temptations, but young whites, particularly in the East, listened as well. Even in the South there were groups forming that clearly revealed the cultural integration of black and white musical styles. A pertinent example was the Allman Brothers, whose success extended throughout the seventies.

Still, the political climate was turbulent. Anti-Vietnam war demonstrations, student revolt on campuses, and annual long hot summers in urban AfroAmerica forced young people to question the validity of many facets of American society. Without a doubt, the majority were not especially politically active, but they could hardly avoid becoming socially and politically sensitized by the music. Thus, for example, mainstream young white Americans still watched (as their older brothers and sisters had) Dick Clark's "American Bandstand," where they heard commercially popular, and often clichéd, rock and roll music. But even "Bandstand" had to keep up with the times, and that meant there were more African American couples on the floor, dancing to the pulsating, blues-derived rhythms of the Rolling Stones, the mind-expanding (and blues-oriented) music of Cream, and the earthy and soulful songs of Janis Joplin and Big Brother and the Holding Company.

Thus, by the late sixties and early seventies, the integrative influence of black music in all areas was pervasive. The sounds may have meant different things to young blacks and whites, just as the political movements did. However, to a large extent, everyone was listening to the same music and the same lyrics, and, most of all, watching the same artists on television. It has been argued that television did much to break down the racial barriers of the past through the presentation of Afro-American singers and groups on variety shows such as "American Bandstand" and other teen-oriented programs. But whatever the merits of this argument, at the very least, political sensitivities were certainly raised, as millions of Americans viewed the coverage of struggle for equality by Afro-Americans, the fighting of American soldiers (black and white) in Vietnam, and the lighthearted, but incisive, political satire of the Smothers Brothers.[33] As for rock music, while it may not have directly encouraged young people to be politically active, it did open their eyes to the diverse world around them.

At the same time, within the African American community (and its neighbor, the Latino community) a different set of sounds were emerging. The political winds were beginning to shift in the wake of "white backlash" to the long hot summers, while the talk of violent rebellion heightened the fears of the white populace, threatening to slow the momentum of the movement toward equality that Afro-Americans had built throughout much of the sixties. Having witnessed the steady repression of black political organizations such as the Black Panthers, young black musicians began to create sounds that spoke on the one hand of survival, yet, on the other, seemed to urge the black community to "get with" the increasingly self-indulgent atmosphere of the larger society. Songs such as Van Mc-Coy's "The Hustle" (1973) and Isaac Hayes's "Shaft" (1974) embodied this ambivalence. This music seemed clearly aimed at that first generation of African Americans who were entering into middle-class status and yet were still imbued with the inner-city values of the working class and the poor.

The stresses and strains and the political tragedies that left most of those who had lived through the vibrant years of the sixties weary, confused, and in some cases, cynical proved to be fertile ground for the creation of an introspective, personal kind of music. Astute political observers of the sixties' youth movement had long recognized the need for self-examination and criticism, an inventory as it were of where the movement had come from and where it was heading.[34] While this was a sensible tactic, it was never massively pursued. Instead of engaging in self-examination, many wallowed in self-indulgence or self-flagellation. Black music certainly reflected those concerns, whether it was pleading for love ("If You Don't Know Me by Now," Harold Melvin and the Blue Notes, 1973), or arguing for simple survival ("Superfly," Curtis Mayfield, 1973). These songs also reflected the mixed emotions of the new and expanding black middle class that still had one foot in the urbanized Afro-American cultural world but with the other foot was moving forward into mainstream white America.

By now, black music was predominately an urban music, and even though it drew on certain blues traditions (especially in its love ballads), its connection to its roots had weakened. If anything, important currents within white rock drew more heavily on traditional blues, while retaining a certain flavor of the sixties, although as "heavy metal" evolved from the blues-oriented Led Zepplin to more raucous sounds it frequently became more cynical. In the end, of course, both kinds of music were worth listening to, but Afro-American music was more buoyant, more urgent in its appeal to have a good time, to party, or to get down. It was no accident that during the early seventies the most popular black group among both blacks and whites was probably Earth, Wind, and Fire, musicians who presaged much of what would develop among groups, black and white, in the late seventies and eighties: a heavy reliance on Afro-Caribbean rhythms and the blues, to produce an eminently "danceable" music. Politically, Earth, Wind, and Fire was more of a black middle class reassurance to their audience that all was right with humanity as long as listeners knew, trusted, and loved themselves and each other. The music of Earth, Wind, and Fire did carry an "Afrocentric" message, but, in retrospect, theirs was an Afrocentricity that could be considered "soft" compared with the "hard" Afrocentric style of Public Enemy or Brand Nubian.[35] Their music, as well as that of Kool and the Gang, was uplifting for young blacks but at the same time soothing for other listeners.

By the end of the seventies, however, American society and culture had come under heavy criticism for being self-absorbed and apolitical—in a word, narcissistic.[36] Such censure may have had a point, particularly when directed at the modus operandi of a mature corporate capitalism that encouraged a breakdown of the idea of deferred gratification in favor of rampant consumerism. As even the most superficial glance reveals, popular music could certainly be used to document the narcissistic thesis. The commodification of race was also evident in this music, as the stereotype of "black rhythm" deeply embedded in American racialist ideology was exploited by the media and disseminated throughout the culture. However, rock music and Afro-American music in particular were not totally devoid of political concern or feeling.

While young Americans of the sixties had not, in general, embraced the counterculture or New Left political ideas, there were plenty of musicians around in the seventies who still believed in the possibility of social change and who remained commercially viable. Indeed, throughout the seventies and eighties, Americans reared in the sixties, along with a new generation of young people, listened to performers like the Who, the Rolling Stones, David Bowie, Neil Young, and Joni Mitchell. The force of integrative cultural diversity was deepened as whites of the previous generation waxed nostalgic over the Motown sound and listened enthusiastically to black artists such as Marvin Gaye, Diana Ross and the Supremes, or the Jackson Five. Aretha Franklin, Earth, Wind, and Fire, and Isaac Hayes continued to be popular, as did James Brown, long a recording hero in AfroAmerica and newly discovered by young whites in the eighties. But possibly the most innovative and popular black artist to emerge from the sixties was Stevie Wonder.

Stevie Wonder could almost be credited with being the only artist to maintain a consistent political thrust while at the same time producing commercially successful music. It was Stevie Wonder, for example, who could tell of the anguish and pain of street life through the eyes of a young black newly arrived from the country to the big city ("Living for the City," 1975). It was also Stevie Wonder who wrote a birthday ode to Martin Luther King, Jr., which served as a rallying cry for the successful lobby for a national holiday in King's honor. Perhaps above all, it was Stevie Wonder who introduced millions of young whites to at least a mild version of the sensuous and highly political Afro-Caribbean sounds of reggae.[37]

Reggae music was well known in certain areas of the black community. Its origins were in the Jamaican city slums, where it had drawn inspiration from Afro-American rhythm and blues and soul sounds, often heard on radio stations broadcasting from Florida. Fused as it was with the Caribbean religious and political sect of Rastafarianism, it was never much promoted on American radio stations. In England, however, which saw among other things an increase in Caribbean immigration during the eighties, the music quickly caught on among young British whites. Reggae's revolutionary spiritual and political message gained strength in opposition to the stringent conservatism that guided Britain's economic and political fortunes under the Thatcher government. Groups like the Police and UB40 assimilated many of reggae's musical impulses and some of its messages. More than any other, though, it was Bob Marley—a national hero in his native Jamaica—who popularized reggae in England and subsequently among African Americans in America, particularly when he played with Stevie Wonder on concert tours nationwide. By the time Marley died (of cancer), his music had finally made its impact in America, and the Police were pushing its assimilated version to new popular heights.[38]

In short, the political element in popular rock music had not totally receded, and its black roots remained visible. Indeed, by the mid-eighties, rock music critics, many of whom had come of age during the fifties and sixties, were unanimous in their agreement that the roots of rock and roll lay principally in Afro-American blues and culture.[39] Moreover, many rock musicians were more than willing during the eighties to extend recognition and praise to Afro-American music as well as gratitude to Afro-American musicians for helping them develop their craft. On the surface, such openness was (and continues to be) a striking change from the fifties, when white musicians performed black music but typically failed to acknowledge the black musician's talent and originality.

At the same time, the controversial values that rock music and Afro-American music had once espoused were all too often diluted or deflected. In the advanced capitalist America of the eighties, which was bent on enticing its citizenry into unreflective consumption, almost any new artistic endeavor stood vulnerable to having to compromise its value and meaning in order to succeed commercially. Throughout the sixties, the recording industry had been willing to package and promote the innovative ventures and statements of many rock groups, even as it continued to produce records that were derisively labeled by critics (and by many listeners) as "bubble gum music" or "teenybopper songs." By the mid-seventies, however, the record industry in America was no longer so apt to be artistically quixotic. It had merged with corporate capital's cultural sensibilities, resulting in something that might be called "corporate rock," designed to appeal to—and indeed to shape—the musical tastes of a huge public. If the corporate ethic threatened the spontaneous creativity of rock music generally, for Afro-American music it also foreshadowed a resegregation.

In the mid-seventies, with the rise of disco music, American music seemed finally to reveal the fruits of integration. Young whites and blacks alike danced to a heavy beat that emanated directly from the music of the black community, added to which were the sounds of a culturally diverse Latino community. With the appearance of the Bee Gee's soundtrack recording of *Saturday Night Fever*, an immensely popular 1978 movie, disco became the hottest rage since the twist.

There were, moreover, other indications of integration in American music. On the one hand, young Afro-Americans often shunned the blues and much of sixties' soul music, embracing instead a multiracial, electronically produced rock. Meanwhile, young whites not only took avidly to disco but also "discovered" the blues and jazz, both of which went through various incarnations electronically. Nonetheless, despite all this apparently healthy assimilation, the most significant (and perhaps the most insidious) development was the absorption of rock music into corporate consumer capitalism.

By the seventies, rock music had become big business. Demographic statistics clearly showed that the preponderance of young people had large amounts of discretionary income; rock was a market ripe for profit. As in any corporate consumer venture, the accent in the record industry was placed heavily on product, packaging, and profit, aided in this case by rapid advances in technology. By the eighties, electronically sophisticated stereo systems and cassette players, together with the advent of compact discs, not only produced clearer sound but provided an ideal opportunity to lure youth into the consumer culture. Unfortunately for the record industry, however, the instability of the economy during the eighties led simultaneously to increases in the prices of records, cassettes, and CDs and to a shrinking discretionary income among the young. These economic factors caused the record industry numerous headaches.

In an attempt to maintain, and ideally to increase, their profits, the industry embarked on an all-out effort to develop intricate marketing procedures that would permit them to tap into (and ultimately to shape) the public's musical tastes. The aggressive marketing of rock music had a long history, of course. During the late seventies and throughout the eighties, however, new factors came into play: the political advances achieved by Afro-Americans, women, and other dispossessed minorities, increasingly advanced technologies, and the gradual absorption of certain "revolutionary" cultural values of the sixties. These factors, in combination with the dictates of the economy, encouraged a new sophistication in marketing strategies to be conceived.

The transformation began first in the area of radio broadcasting. For decades, AM radio, with its "Top 40" programming, had been the main means for radio advertisers to tap into the youth market.

Disc jockeys played music to large, faceless audiences of young people, thereby exerting a significant influence in shaping their tastes and musical habits. Bound by the often rigid demands of advertising agencies and the need to avoid controversial material, and often tempted to feature certain records in exchange for cash on the side (accusations regarding "payola" were sometimes confirmed), radio disc jockeys walked a tightrope between their felt obligation to open up young ears and minds to new music and their bosses' mandate to maintain the ratings and profit margins of their respective stations.[40]

In such an atmosphere, Afro-American music rarely got heavy play. Originally labeled "race music" and confined to a late-night format, or else played on minor black AM stations in select urban areas, black music and its artists rarely made it to the top of the hit record charts in white America's land of AM radio. The recording industry and its trade publications never really abandoned their racist division of musical forms, even though political and cultural changes wrought by African Americans and their white allies were gradually changing the musical tastes of white America.[41] But, quite apart from the effect of cultural and political developments, there was the proliferation of FM radio signals allowed by the Federal Communications Commission in the mid-seventies.

Early FM radio had been relentlessly highbrow, consisting of long hours devoted to classical music, to intellectual talk shows, and, in some urban enclaves, to "better" jazz. But by the mid-sixties FM stations in major metropolitan areas had begun playing "experimental music," mostly the increasingly popular psychedelic rock music. Some stations also played extended sets of blues and soul music, thus paving the way for white listeners to gain some exposure to little known blues singers and the newer souls artists. Taking advantage of the increase in the number of FM stations, the music industry was able to play longer cuts from a record or even whole albums at a time, which tended to enhance record sales. Likewise, FM radio listenership grew as more FM stations went on the air and as their programming became more diverse.

As AM radio listenership declined during the seventies, more advertisers switched to FM radio. To make certain that they would not lose out in the competition, FM stations developed new and more sophisticated programming strategies, which turned on a peculiar compartmentalization of music. Thus, in the seventies and eighties FM became firmly locked into particular programming categories such as "AOR" (Album Oriented Rock) and "Easy Listening." By the eighties even black music had acquired a new category. No longer labeled race music (if only because African American music was now played on almost every mainstream radio station in the country), it now became "Urban Contemporary," signaling a superficially liberal but nonetheless suspect definition of black music that appealed to a rapidly expanding creation of late-twentieth-century capitalism: the black underclass. These particular categories came out of the marketing techniques devised by a new entrepreneur who took the place of the deejay: the radio programmer.

The radio programmer used his market research abilities, often in concert with a company of researchers trained in the latest computer technology, to determine the demographic structure of a particular station's listening audience. The programmer's profile, which was intended to measure the station's chances of making a profit in a particular area, included his audience's age level, income status, and listening habits, as well as the size of the local area. The information gathered by the radio programmers would be given uncritically to the stations, along with "objective" market recommendations for featuring particular kinds of music or programs that would build listenership. For example, the demographic projections of radio programmers in the 1980s revealed a decline in the teenage market—perhaps not surprising, in view of the popularity of portable cassette players— and a preference among the post-sixties generation for "mellower" music. Among teenagers who still listened regularly to radio, there was a decided demand for the latest in black music (rap) and rock (heavy metal).

The recording industry, ever alert to new trends, would then begin to feed the programmed radio stations with that music suitable to a given station's market. The end result came to be known as "narrowcasting." On the surface, "narrowcasting" seemed to hark back to the old AM radio days when the ubiquitous disc jockey was the main force in shaping the music and tastes of the listeners. But by the late seventies American society was in the grips of significant external forces, notably a shrinking economy, that changed the nature of the recording industry and radio. The period also saw the introduction of the youth of the 1960s into the work force and the simultaneous expansion of the black middle class. One result of these new demographics was corporate rock. Purveyed by the radio programmer, corporate rock consciously and deliberately recycled modified forms of sixties' music to the aging sixties' generation, as well as to a new generation of young people.[42] The increasingly conservative political and economic atmosphere of America in general, however, had as much to do with the rise of corporate rock as did the rise of new entrepreneurs like the radio programmer. Perhaps the most significant event was the bottoming out of the record market owing to the deep recession of 1977–80.

Much has been written to explain the slump in record sales.[43] Among the reasons given are: the oil crisis; high inflation; unemployment, which depleted the young's disposable income; the exorbitantly high cost of albums; the proliferation of cassette tapes and video games; the reluctance of rock stars to cut new records; the declining number of rock concerts; the rise of fundamentalist (and anti-rock) religious groups; and America's failure to produce a new generation of consumption-oriented youth who would take the place of those baby boomers who came of age in the sixties.[44] Taken separately, no one of these reasons suffices as an explanation, although doubtless there is some truth in all of them. But a more satisfying understanding of the situation requires a consideration of how corporate rock assimilated and reshaped the major political advances of the sixties and seventies for mass consumption.

For one thing, the capture of FM radio by advertising and corporate rock's front people (the programming consultants) had limited opportunities for young people to hear new music or to realize the political and cultural potential of the old. This development was perfectly in keeping with the immensely conservative atmosphere of the times, which encouraged the entertainment industry's conscious attempts to sanitize the music of the sixties and/or induce social amnesia about that period. Corporate rock contributed to this obliteration through the proliferation of AOR stations, which played bland, noncontroversial music by performers such as Styx, Journey, REO Speedwagon, an early eighties Sheena Easton, Kenny Rogers, a "mellower" Neil Diamond, and the occasional black artist (one of the most popular during the eighties was Lionel Richie). As a result, narrowcasting tended to lock out, or at least to marginalize, significant achievements by Afro-American artists and newer young white musicians. The contrast between two examples, both pertaining to television, serves to illustrate this development.

MTV (Music Television) was started in 1981 to serve as an advertising conduit for corporate rock in order to sell records and to allow advertisers in a wide range of industries to zero in on America's teenagers. The key idea was to present, twenty-four hours a day, music video clips (initially furnished by the major record producers) and punctuate those clips with a string of glitzy fast-paced commercials for teen products ranging from clothes and footwear to acne medicine. MTV was immensely successful. As its cable subscriptions grew, more and more established rock groups began to have videos made. Whereas those who had grown up in the fifties and sixties had to imagine what songs were about, the MTV generation saw the songs acted out in a series of fast cuts that could at times be dizzying. MTV did much to revive rock and certainly created a whole new manner of perceiving the music. But the bottom line was that it was a way of ensuring the recording industry profits. While the network did create new stars who had a measurable impact on the American culture (the two who immediately stood out and had a continuing impact were Madonna and Prince), it did so within the confines of the corporate rock programming mentality. Moreover, a furor was raised over the lack of video recordings by black artists.

Confronted with the charge of racism, the creator of MTV, Bob Pittman, responded that market research had predicted that young whites in the suburbs would be alienated by black artists and black music. As Pittman himself angrily pointed out: "Our definition is not speculation. There's a million dollars worth of research there."[45] Thus, even on MTV, whose programs ostensibly were designed to highlight all the varieties of rock and roll—Afro-American roots and all—demographics and programmed narrowcasting ultimately dictated what got aired. Some Afro-American artists, however, refused to be rendered musically invisible and sought to change MTV's format. But, more important, the black middle class had already begun a move to gain some control over the airwaves.

In 1979 Charles Johnson, a young African American entrepreneur, started BET—Black Entertainment Television—in Washington, D.C. At a time when cable television was rapidly growing, Johnson seized upon the growth of the black middle class and the fact that there was a need for entertainment features that African Americans could relate to. BET featured videos of black artists and later would add series that had been canceled by the networks ("Frank's Place" being an example). The success of BET was a clear demonstration that African Americans, especially those newly arrived to middle-class status, would watch a cable network that spoke to their interests. From its inception in 1979 BET grew so rapidly that by 1985 it posted its first year of profit. By 1991 the cable service had 29 million subscribers and had expanded its company to include two magazines aimed at the young blacks of the middle class and at middle-class black professionals : *YSB* (Young Sisters and Brothers) and *Emerge*.[46]

In the meanwhile, MTV expanded its range and began to show some black videos, mostly those of the newest superstar in the nation during the eighties, Michael Jackson. In 1983 Jackson produced the country's largest selling album, *Thriller*, from which six singles climbed high in the Top 40. Jackson, however, appealed to whites as well as blacks (he was in the industry jargon a "crossover"), so MTV's airing of Jackson videos did not necessarily mean that the network had changed its basic attitude. Again, it was Bob Pittman who demonstrated where corporate rock stood in relation to rock's Afro-American roots and to rock music itself:

> They [black artists] don't realize that this is a business. Bloomingdale's wouldn't work if it carried every kind of clothing ever made. MTV is a phenomenon of the youth culture. . . . I don't know who the fuck these people are to tell people what they should like. They sound like little Hitlers or people from Eastern-bloc communist countries. The good thing about America is that the people rule. That's the essence of America![47]

In Bob Pittman's commercial world, rock music that contained messages reminiscent of the sixties was studiously avoided, although this is not to say that the network was committed to "wholesome" entertainment. MTV came under a lot of fire from parents and feminist groups for its titillating videos. In other areas, they did exercise censorial restraint, usually for equally commercial reasons. In short,

MTV was guided by what would sell—or what the network decided would sell.

MTV played very few of the black videos that BET played, thus closing off an opportunity for young whites of the post–civil rights generation to see integrative cultural diversity in action. The major exceptions were in the case of Madonna and Prince, two rock super-stars who rivaled Michael Jackson throughout the eighties and were prime examples of how a visionary integration could work.[48]

Veronique Madonna Ciccone, who grew up in a working-class Italian American home in Flint, Michigan, surrounded by African Americans and other working-class whites, went to New York City, hung out in the dance clubs populated by African Americans and Latinos, and worked her way up to being a singer/songwriter and dancer. Her development as a musical superstar can be directly traced to her immersion in the African American musical culture and her exposure to the Latin community. Her first best-selling single, "Bor-derline," was a big success in the black community. As far as the record industry was concerned, Madonna was thought to be another "crossover," able to expand her appeal to a larger audience as opposed to marginal groups such as blacks, Latins, or gays. But Madonna went on to display that she was an artist of genuine substance, and she continued to draw on African American culture, her own Italian background, and her understanding of Latino culture.

In 1989 Madonna recorded "Like a Prayer" and made two videos based on the song: one for MTV and one a commercial for Pepsi-Cola. Never one to flinch from controversy, Madonna produced in both videos stunning portrayals. In the Pepsi commercial she was a young woman reminiscing about her childhood and adolescence in Michigan. In the other, a richly layered story, Madonna played a young woman who witnesses a rape by white men and a miscarriage of justice when a black man is arrested for the crime. Pepsi did not like the commercial, arguing that it was too "sensitive" for young viewers, and it was shown only once. The MTV video, however, excited a wide range of people from feminists to parents to ministers to avowed white racists. Religious people were upset over Madonna's kissing of a black saint (presumably St. Martin De Porres, the Roman Catholic patron saint of race relations, who was canonized in the early sixties) in a dream sequence. Feminists were disturbed by the messages conveyed by the image of Madonna in a subordinate role to a man. And many were upset over the scene where Madonna sung the refrain to the song in a field at night, surrounded by burning crosses.

It clearly was a provocative video. But, what with all the competing voices clamoring to express distress or anger over various part of it, the most important theme(s) of the video tended to be overlooked. If anything, this was Madonna's artistic vision of how a multiracial society should work. Within the video is a mosaic of many different cultures—African American, Italian American, Latino, European—as well as a deep appreciation of the various cultures that make up America. But perhaps the most important role was given to African American culture. In what could only be seen as a masterful piece of art, Madonna, asleep and dreaming in a Catholic church with its ornate Italian frescoes but housing a black saint, awakens to a black gospel choir, which inspires her with the courage to go to the police station and reverse the miscarriage of justice, the arrest of a black man for a crime committed by whites.

In much the same manner, Prince Rogers Nelson, a young African American of mixed heritage from Minneapolis, Minnesota, set about to provide the rock world with a thoroughly integrated view of society. Prince, however, adhered closely to black music of the sixties: his music was deeply influenced by James Brown, Jimi Hendrix, and the rhythm and blues singers associated with Stax-Volt. Nonetheless, Prince, like Madonna, showed himself to be a highly versatile musically and shrewd in matters of business. But the key to the success of both Prince and Madonna was their unwillingness to be pigeonholed. Both continued to confound the critics, to stir up controversy throughout the society, and to present their vision of what America could be, a vision that rested firmly on a belief in integrative cultural diversity, with the acceptance and inclusion of Afro-American culture at its core. Moreover, the inclusiveness of both Prince and Madonna's worldview went beyond race to challenge people's perceptions and received notions regarding gender and sexuality as well.

In the early nineties, MTV introduced a new program called "Yo! MTV Raps." Shown at a later hour on the weekends, this show was intended to give exposure to the hip-hop culture of the eighties' biggest rage in black music, rap. One result was to legitimate rap music as the mainstream music of Afro-America. Actually, black music had enjoyed a variety of musical resurgences during the eighties in almost every one of its forms, from jazz (Wynton Marsalis) to the reemergence of sixties' stars such as Aretha Franklin, Stevie Wonder, Marvin Gaye, and Smokey Robinson to the rise of Afro-Americans in rock and roll (Living Color). Much of this music retained deep-seated African American cultural forms and dispensed messages of political and social import. Nonetheless, it was rap music, which reflected the frustrations of inner-city Afro-American youth caught in devastating cycle of unemployment, drugs, and murderous gang violence, that moved to the forefront of black popular music.

One only had to listen to Grandmaster Flash and the Furious Five's "The Message" in order to learn about the harsh reality of black urban life in the eighties and the anger born of alienation, joblessness, and racism. Part of the refrain to "The Message" could have served as a warning to American society: "Don't push me! Cos I'm close to the edge, I'm trying not to lose my head." The song also addressed many problems facing young black males in the inner city, from the despair over ever realizing any fruitful potential from education ("My son said Daddy I don't want to go to school cuz the teacher's a jerk he thinks I'm a fool") to the supposedly lucrative and attractive underworld of pimps, hustlers, drug pushers, and bookmakers. "The Message" was a forceful urban Afro-American missive to all Americans, who, as Richard Wright once pointed out, were creating in their cities an army of Bigger Thomases. In the eighties that army continued to grow, and the political protests became ever more harsher. Rap songs addressed the issue of police brutality, as in the controversial 1988 song from the West Coast group Niggaz With Attitudes, "The Police" ("Some police think they have the authority to kill a minority"). Rap groups like NWA proliferated throughout the Los Angeles and San Francisco areas in the late eighties, sending musical messages that spoke of pain and anger at having been cut off from the rest of the society.

Other groups used the rap style to encourage young black youth to be aware of their racial heritage, to promote community solidarity, and to invoke a sense of empowerment. Prominent here was the group Public Enemy, who reworked much of the rhetoric and doctrines of the Nation of Islam in their songs. At its best, Public Enemy's music was a source of inspiration, opening the door to a new view of Malcolm X for many young blacks who were born after his death. Public Enemy's music also had a middle-class edge to it, probably owing to the Nation of Islam's bourgeois stance. But that was in some ways a plus, as it provided necessary lessons in civility and self-respect. Where Public Enemy went seriously astray was in their pandering to anti-Semitic stereotyping, as in the song "Welcome to the Terrordome." During the eighties, tensions between blacks and Jews, which had their roots in the late sixties, became especially enflamed in the Eighties, owing in part to the rightward shift of many Jewish intellectuals and organizations on issues of critical importance to African Americans, in particular the issue of affirmative action. Anti-Semitism was not peculiar to rap groups or even those Afro-Americans living in the inner city; it seemed to have emanated as well from the newly expanded black middle class. That rap music featured anti-Semitism was once again an indication that the music reflected the fears and feelings of African Americans, be they members of the inner-city underclass or of more affluent segments of AfroAmerica.[49]

Equally alarming was the intense misogyny in much of rap music. However, while this objectification of and brutal disregard for women was certainly not an admirable attitude, once again it mirrored some painful realities of AfroAmerica. Fortunately, there was also some counterpoint to this attitude, as women rappers, notably Queen Latifah and Salt 'n' Pepa, answered back with songs that stated that women should resist violent overtures from men. Indeed, much of the more bourgeois-oriented rap music often came from the women, although male rappers like Fresh Prince and Jazzy Jeff, Kid 'n' Play, and the popular Hammer also addressed middle-class themes—self-respect, civility, morality, and the importance of getting an education.

Finally, there were also white groups who immersed themselves in African American culture and Afro-Latin culture, so as to produce music that was not only great for dancing but lyrically important to young people. Borrowing from a tradition that extended back to the psychedelic days of the sixties, these musicians seemed to say that the road to freedom and integration, so often traveled separately by black and white youth, could be merged.[50] Again, the themes were clear: education, war, love, and sex. As Talking Heads, one of the more interesting groups that drew on Afro-American and Afro-Latin cultures, sang in "Life during Wartime":

> This ain't no party
> This ain't no disco
> This ain't no fooling around . . .
> I stand tight, I go to night school.

Taking a cue from the Delta bluesmen, Talking Heads evolved from a new wave group into a band that consciously drew on the deep reservoir of black rhythm and blues. Their song "Swamp," however, from the *King of Comedy* soundtrack, was an example of what happened when white rock musicians drew directly on black roots. The song was rarely played on FM stations, simply because corporate rock did not want a repetition of the sixties, when musicians spoke and young people listened and learned of a new and better world.[51]

In short, by the early nineties the signals were mixed. In purely musical terms, integration had certainly been achieved. Mainstream rock and roll was by now so heavily imbued with black musical traditions that it could not properly be regarded as "white" music. Popular white musicians—from Madonna to Talking Heads to Paul Simon—continued to draw openly on African and Caribbean sounds, while many black performers had achieved massive commercial success in the rock music industry. A distinctly black musical form—rap—was now enormously popular among both blacks and whites. But the social and political significance of this musical version of integrative cultural diversity remained an open question. Although white youth was listening to rap, for example, it was by no means clear whether its political messages were really rubbing off—whether this exposure was contributing to a heightened consciousness of the problems of inner-city blacks, say, or whether, for middle-class kids, rap was simply "cool." Nor was it clear that this musical integration implied a corresponding social integration, the ideal of black and white together that had characterized the early days of the civil rights movement and had found expression in its music.

But perhaps this is asking too much. The fact remains that, even if much of the music young people listened to in the eighties was shaped by the corporate concerns of the music business, corporate rock had succeeded neither in stifling the voices of performers engaged in social and political commentary nor in permanently dulling the public appetite for "message" music—as the renewed popularity of sixties' songs attests. Moreover, black musical artists—along with black filmmakers and television performers—had achieved an unprecedented visibility that could not but have its consequences for the society at large. In their concern over the situation of AfroAmerica—and the role of African Americans in guiding the nation toward a new vision of itself—these artists continued to express ever more complex definitions of integrative cultural diversity.

CHAPTER 6

Changing the Guard
AfroAmerica's New Guardians of Culture

As if exhausted by the tumult of the sixties, the post–World War II baby boom generation turned inward during the seventies and eighties, settling into careers and raising families. Apparently turning their backs on the radical idealism of their youth, a vast number of these people voted for Ronald Reagan, although it was by no means clear that their political ideology matched his. In all likelihood, Reagan's appeal lay more in his promise to make them feel good about themselves amid economic stagnation and in a fragmented, postmodern world. In keeping with the postmodern ethic—the denial of reliable meaning, coupled with an emphasis on quick stimulation and easy gratification—white Americans increasingly concentrated on the attainment of self-fulfillment, whether through material wealth, leisure activities, new age spirituality, or fitness. The postmodern worldview had, moreover, the ability to level historical consciousness and to induce a political apathy born of disenchantment with political institutions and processes. By the eighties, then, white Americans generally had little interest in the notion of community, much less political community, which was not surprising in a generation so self-concerned and consumption-oriented. Given such an indifference to political issues, these Americans were all too willing to allow the "experts" to assume the burden of running the country, thereby leaving them free to indulge in their own individual pursuits of happiness.[1]

But the cultural and political legacy of the sixties had not entirely evaporated. During the eight-year tenure of the Reagan administration, many Americans refused to support the right-wing agenda of increased military activity in Central America, blatant attacks on the Soviet Union, or attempts to undermine Supreme Court decisions regarding the reproductive rights of women. Reagan's notion of a "color-blind" society was, however, more troublesome. The color line ran deep, deeper than most people, black or white, were able to fathom. Prone to the lack of a long view of history, most white Americans were easily manipulated into conceiving a whole new set of fears regarding black people.

As we saw in chapter 3, most of these new fears arose in reaction to the results of affirmative action. Although Afro-Americans had never intended affirmative action to be the centerpiece in the struggle for civil rights (just as miscegenation was never intended to be the centerpiece of Reconstruction), in the minds of many whites affirmative action was quickly linked with "special preference," "quotas," and "reverse racism." The accomplishments of African Americans, some argued, had come about through a lowering of standards and had resulted in a violation of fairness.

The mean-spiritedness of the Reagan administration's attitude toward affirmative action put veterans of the civil rights movement, specifically established organizations such as the NAACP and the National Urban League, on the defensive. Following the passage of civil rights legislation, black leadership had shifted their focus to securing political positions at the state and local level and in Congress, and with considerable success: many major cities had black mayors; state legislatures saw increasing numbers of blacks, and Douglas Wilder of Virginia had become the first black governor since Reconstruction. There were African American representatives to Congress, and there seemed to be little doubt that before the end of the century there would again be black senators as well (as indeed there were).[2] But when the black leadership tried to shift the focus to economic rights—an area in which the black masses lagged severely behind—matters were different. It was not only the African American masses who were suffering economically. The early years of the eighties saw recession, a rapid decline in industrial jobs, and the continuing shrinkage of the family farm, all of which affected vast numbers of whites. Economic injustice was as color-blind as the Reagan administration hoped their civil rights policies would be. If white Americans were reasonably willing to share political power with their black brethren, they tended to draw the line when it came to competition for scarce resources.

What seemed to elude the traditional civil rights organizations was the ability to battle for economic justice on their own terms. Their inability to do so left them at risk of looking like a caricature of their predecessors who, whatever ideological criticisms could be made of them, had mounted and sustained forceful moral, legal, and political justifications for civil rights. In contrast, the civil rights leadership under Joseph Lowery (SCLC), Vernon Jordan and John Jacob (NUL), and Benjamin Hooks (NAACP) spent more energy on defending the claim that Martin Luther King, Jr., should be recognized as a national hero than on expanding creatively on his ideas. All too frequently, these leaders ended up in the role of angry supplicants to a Reagan administration that consistently ignored them.

Indeed, within the media and the arena of conventional politics, the traditional civil rights leaders were made to look like ungrateful children. In a bitter twist, Ronald Reagan refused to meet publicly with the established civil rights leadership, seeking out instead Afro-Americans who not only believed in his conservative policies but also adhered to the early civil rights movement's notion of a color-blind society. Thus Clarence Pendleton, armed with credentials that included a former position as Urban League director in San Diego, California, was appointed head of the Civil Rights Commission, where he could unleash his intentions of drastically cutting back its functions if not eliminating it altogether. Later in the eighties Reagan appointed another African American, Clarence Thomas, a member of the Equal Opportunity Employment Commission, to a federal judgeship. Judge Thomas was subsequently nominated by President George Bush in 1991 to replace Thurgood Marshall on the Supreme Court.

As is well known, the confirmation hearings that followed Clarence Thomas's nomination proved extremely controversial, given the allegations of sexual harassment from one of Thomas's former aides,

Anita Hill. In the course of these highly visible and volatile Senate hearings, America was shown one sector of the black middle class that had emerged over the last thirty years. The first generation of post–civil rights African Americans who went before the nine white male senators on the Senate Judiciary Committee to argue the case for or against Thomas were educated, articulate, and serious black women and men. However much anyone watching the hearings may have agreed or disagreed with certain individuals or their statements, claims about unqualified African Americans getting "preferential treatment" over the years and thus bringing down standards of quality and excellence were quickly rendered suspect. At the same time, the fact that the center of the controversy revolved around the issue of sexual harassment threatened to reinforce the deep-seated, lurid attitudes that many white Americans had about race and sexuality.[3] The situation was, at best, ironic: a "politically correct" appointment but of a possibly "sexually incorrect" black man who was, moreover, known for the conservatism of his opinions.

What was also ironic about both Thomas and Pendleton (and even Anita Hill) was how closely they in fact all held to many of the same bourgeois values promoted by the black leadership in the NAACP and NUL. The main difference was that they were willing to be part of the Reagan-Bush government. The defensiveness of the civil rights leadership to threats against civil rights legislation, however, prevented them from granting a respectful hearing to those black conservatives or to the basic positions that the neoconservatives and the right, in general, supported. Again, the reasons were not hard to find or understand. The traditional civil rights establishment (as well as many conservative black nationalists) accepted the traditional ideological terrain. They accepted the economic reality of liberal capitalism (and they had little choice, given the collapse of socialist economies in the early 1990s) and demanded only that Afro-Americans be given a fair share of opportunities, jobs, and political power. That the established civil rights leadership wore the badge of liberalism, even as white liberals shrank from the label, and promoted New Deal–Great Society programs only provided further testimony to Afro-American leadership's overall embrace of the system's political economy and their inability to put forward innovative alternatives. But if the forces of traditional civil rights leadership were in disarray,

AfroAmerica was making its presence felt in other ways, notably in film and television.

Any understanding of the success of Afro-American films and the impact of black actors and actresses on both the big and small screen has to take account of the situation of the black middle class in the seventies and eighties. As we have noted, the fruits of civil rights legislation were initially most apparent in politics. Major cities such as Los Angeles, Philadelphia, Atlanta, and Chicago had black mayors for one or more terms; the House of Representatives had an active Black Caucus; Jesse Jackson ran for the presidency in 1984 and 1988; and Ron Brown became the Democratic party's national chairperson. All of these confirmed the impact of the legislative battles won during the days of the civil rights–black power movements. The black middle class was also visible in the corporate structure, although black professionals continued to face a corporate culture entrenched in racist notions about the ability of African Americans to perform. Nonetheless, black managers were branching out on their own in the late eighties and nineties. In institutions of higher education, Afro-Americans were also present in increased numbers, although, as in the corporate world, entrenched institutional racism found fewer blacks as teachers and more located in lower-level administrative positions.[4]

Despite these successes, the new visibility of the black middle class and the media coverage accorded it revealed some disturbing trends. In 1985 the *New York Times* conducted a citywide poll, which found that racial divisions persisted, most blacks and whites living in neighborhoods populated mainly by their own race. Afro-Americans often expressed the opinion that companies were not serious about hiring minorities and that, when they did hire them, it was only a token gesture. The social divisions between the two races were also glaring. The masses of Afro-Americans and white Americans rarely socialized together, at least not in New York City. At the end of a workday or on weekends the two groups retreated to their own neighborhoods where they socialized among themselves. So strictly delimited were these communities that, at times, black or white Americans who happened to be in the wrong neighborhood found themselves beaten or even murdered. These divisions, coupled with a legacy of police harassment and brutality in the nation's black urban areas, only added to the ever increasing tension and polarization not only between the races but also within the Afro-American class structure. In a weird turnabout, New York City, possibly the most ethnically diverse city in the North, was becoming as segregated as the South had been twenty-five years earlier, while in the South the most ethnically diverse city, Atlanta, was the most integrated in the nation.[5]

Moreover, in contrast to the migration of Afro-Americans from the South to the North during the fifties and sixties, a large number of blacks were now returning to the South: in 1990, 53 percent of the total African American population lived there. It thus appeared that, even as some among the expanded black middle class were becoming suburbanized, many working-class Afro-Americans were going to places where the economy was relatively robust, as indeed were many whites. Most members of the black middle class, however, continued to reside in the Northeast and Midwest. (The West had the lowest proportion of Afro-Americans in the nation—8.5 percent—but interestingly enough the median family income was highest there.) Throughout the United States, moreover, African Americans tended to be clustered in urban areas. Black middle class professionals earned the sobriquet "buppie," which stood for "black urban professional," as opposed to the white "yuppies." And although black middle class families were to some extent moving into the suburbs, these suburban enclaves were not necessarily integrated.[6]

At the same time, despite the persistence of social segregation, the 1980s witnessed a steady increase in the integration of Afro-Americans into American culture at large. Whether in sports such as basketball, which showcased the grace and finesse of Magic Johnson, Kareem Abdul Jabbar, Michael Jordan, James Worthy, and Isiah Thomas, or in popular music with the revival of soft soul ballads (dubbed "retronuevo" by black music critic Nelson George) and the innovations of rap and hip-hop, African Americans demonstrated physical talent and creative energy. Perhaps the most telling advances, however, were to be found in television and motion pictures. In these areas of popular mass culture Afro-American activity not only pursued the goal of true integrative cultural diversity but also displayed a positive race consciousness that raised exciting questions about the future of the American nation in the next century.[7]

American popular culture had traditionally been deeply arrogant with regards to race. Black people, when not ignored, were generally portrayed in woefully stereotypical form, at once the result of and serving further to reinforce the preconceived image that whites had developed of blacks. Even as late as the 1980s the stereotypes persisted. That Robert Townsend could devote an entire movie, *Hollywood Shuffle*, to the struggle of African Americans in Hollywood, with the obstacles posed by derogatory stereotypes as the movie's underlying theme, illustrated that these racial attitudes remained ingrained. Not very surprisingly, Townsend had to make his movie on a shoestring budget, using his own credit cards as a means of financing.

The economics of Hollywood (and of most media-produced mass culture) has generally militated against controversial social commentary or daring artistic innovation. As the economy worsened during the late twentieth century, studio heads more than ever paid attention to demographics and cost effectiveness, often blatantly repeating winning formulas (the ubiquitous sequels) in an effort to ensure profits. Always conscious of what they perceived would appeal to the largest possible audience, the studios ended up producing "safe" films that reflected social values at their lowest common denominator. In this respect, Hollywood emulated its long-time archrival, television, in terms of reaching for a mass audience.[8]

Given the prevailing economic and artistic climate, it was remarkable that there were a number of commercially successful motion pictures about Afro-Americans. There had, of course, been black movie stars in the past; actors such as Sidney Poitier, Ethel Waters, Harry Belafonte, and Dorothy Dandridge were featured in highly acclaimed movies. But in most respects, these industry stars were confined within the cultural boundaries drawn by the general society and by white producers, writers, and studio heads, boundaries that reflected predominant cultural attitudes. Granted, Hollywood may be credited with showing off its liberalism in the 1967 movie *Guess Who's Coming to Dinner?* starring Sidney Poitier. There was also Steven Spielberg's 1985 adaptation of Alice Walker's *The Color Purple*. But the long tradition of either presenting negative images of black people or positive images as imagined in liberal white minds obscured what black filmmakers and artists might have thought or wished to present (as the differences between Walker's book and Spielberg's film amply illustrate).

But by the late eighties, black filmmakers and performers were challenging this tradition. Consider, for example, the work of Spike Lee (of which more below). Films such as *She's Gotta Have It* (1986), *School Daze* (1988), *Do the Right Thing* (1989), *Mo' Better Blues* (1990), and *Jungle Fever* (1991) were provocative yet sensitive cinematic explorations of black relationships and of AfroAmerica that far exceeded the understanding of mainstream Hollywood directors. In some sense, such films might seem reminiscent of those made for exclusively black audiences in the thirties and forties.[9] But Lee's themes and content would have been too controversial in that period, given the black bourgeoisie's attempt to present themselves as a reflection of the white middle class. Indeed, films such as Lee's doubtless could not have been made prior to the expansion of the black middle class in the seventies and eighties. For one thing, many of those newly arrived to the middle class well remembered the civil rights struggles and race consciousness of the sixties; for younger middle-class blacks there was a revival of racial consciousness owing to the conservative turn in national political culture. Furthermore, there was now an attempt to present "universal themes" but through a particular black perspective in such a way as to suggest, not simply that Afro-Americans were equal to white Americans, but that they also embodied values that were or could be consonant with the best in the American tradition. Such a formulation reflected a convergence of the early civil rights movement's integrationist concerns with the later black nationalist preoccupation with the beauty and importance of all things black.[10]

The success of artists such as Spike Lee enabled other African Americans to create and to produce television programs and films that presented the Afro-American perspective to white audiences, who were unused to such images of black people. For example, Henry Hampton's brilliant and award-winning "Eyes on the Prize," made for PBS, was a striking visual history of the civil rights movement, while Julia Dash undertook a cinematic project on the Gullah blacks of the Sea Islands off the coast of South Carolina.[11] What the growing number of African American cultural productions had in common was a basis in the ideological shift in the expanded black middle class toward an inversion of the integrationist ethic. This inverted integrationist ethic was deeply influenced by the black nationalist sensibilities that arose during the black power movement of the late sixties and seventies. The absorption by the black middle class of cultural nationalism and black pride coexisted reasonably comfortably with America's increased awareness of and willingness to accept ethnic cultures. Thus, throughout the eighties and into the nineties, on the cultural level black Americans celebrated themselves as African Americans or Afro-Americans, unmindful perhaps that a subtle but important ideological battle was being played out before the nation's eyes, whether in the movies or on television. That battle was over a view of integration that also emphasized a reverent upholding of the national qualities of AfroAmerica. The themes, statements, and suggested direction of those cultural productions provided some arresting clues for what the fruits of integration and the idea of integrative cultural diversity really were.

"The Cosby Show," which ran from 1984 to 1992, was by far the most popular network television program in an era when video technology—cable, VCRs, and satellite dishes—caused a steady decline in viewership among the "big three," NBC, CBS, and ABC. Indeed, "The Cosby Show" pulled NBC out of third-place position in the ratings, where it had long been mired. At first glance the program's themes were not all that original. "The Cosby Show" stuck very close to the tried and true formula of a family-based situation comedy. Even the fact that its characters were black was not all that innovative. In the 1960s Diahann Carroll had played a single mother and working nurse in "Julia"; by the early eighties there were several programs about blacks, such as "The Jeffersons" (with its theme song "Moving on Up," which pretty much told the program's story); and "Good Times," which was about a southside Chicago family living in the projects—and featured more stereotypes than anyone needed to see. These programs were popular with both black and white audiences, but none of them garnered the success that the Cosby program enjoyed.

Why this was so had more to do with the shrewd calculations of Bill Cosby and the conservative political climate than with any demonstrable shifts in audience taste. Cosby was a longtime comedian and television performer; his 1960s' program "I Spy" was the first dramatic series to feature an Afro-American in a costarring role, albeit often as comic relief. He created "The Cosby Show" ostensibly as a corrective to the heavy tide of cops-and-robbers, car-chase serials that were flooding the viewing screen. But whatever his initial motivation, using a time-honored TV format Bill Cosby was able to represent Afro-Americans in a more positive light than ever before and inject a view of integrative cultural diversity, while not radically departing from the conservative cultural agenda of the Reagan administration, with its concerns about traditional family values.[12]

The Huxtable family was the classic black bourgeoisie family of E. Franklin Frazier's time, but with one important difference: they were so comfortable with their blackness that they had no need to flaunt it or feel anxious about it. The family was the quintessential mirror image of an upper-middle-class white professional family: there was Dr. Huxtable, an obstetrician; Mrs. Huxtable, a career woman in law; two daughters in college; a son and daughter in high school; and a cute little girl just entering school. All of the problems facing families in the eighties, from unwed mothers to drug usage to a career woman's problems, were explored in a humorously entertaining but conscientiously educational manner.

Perhaps more than anything, it was Cosby's humor that buoyed the show. The audience, of course, was already familiar with Bill Cosby. As a young man who had grown up in Philadelphia and dropped out of Temple University to pursue show business (he later returned to school and in 1982 received his doctorate in education from the University of Massachusetts), Cosby became one of the first widely successful black comedians. Although he used his life experiences as a background for his comedy routines, there was a subtle form of masking in the way Cosby represented himself. In his routines about his family, his peers, or his personal experiences with everyday concerns, he seldom made open reference to his race. White audiences could thus identify with Cosby, laughing at traits they saw in themselves, but without ever truly understanding the experiences of Afro-Americans. Cosby's comedy was nonthreatening and universal. Black audiences understood the world he joked about, but they also laughed, perhaps finding relief from the pressures (and at times the oppressiveness) of urban living. Cosby's humor, so adored by liberals of every color, came to resonate with the true meaning of integration:

that humor knew no color and life's basic experiences were shared by all.

Cosby's successors built on his platform but stripped off the mask. In the tense and turbulent years of the late sixties and early seventies, comedians such as Richard Pryor, Scoey Mitchell, and Paul Mooney began to talk about AfroAmerica and white America in a raw, harsh, and often profane manner. The master of this new comedy of AfroAmerica was Richard Pryor.

Pryor, born in the Midwest of working-class parents, not only operated out of his own experiences in shaping his comedy routines but was able in his detailed vignettes, presented through the medium of television and later motion pictures, to unveil facets of Afro-America that white America had never seen. He never flinched from using the vernacular of the urban street scene or presenting graphic descriptions of contemporary black city life. His portraits—of the Old Wino, the Oilman, and the Reverend, among others—were at once humorous and filled with a pathos that in earlier years might have been found in the poetry of Langston Hughes or the detective novels of Chester Himes. African American audiences immediately identified and laughed (many to keep from crying) at the characters and situations. White audiences laughed as well, but often uncomfortably. Even for whites who truly admired Richard Pryor (and later Eddie Murphy and Arsenio Hall, both protégés of Pryor), it was not easy to take his humor whole. Embedded in that humor was a telling commentary and criticism that refused to victimize Afro-Americans or let whites off the hook for their racism. But just when the comedy routine threatened to get too serious, Pryor would pull the audience back to his side with clever one-liners or a broad-based humorous sketch.[13]

The movies in which Pryor appeared tended to follow his line of comedic discourse. What was interesting here, though, was the way in which Hollywood reacted to many of the more serious themes Pryor tried to pursue. So long as he stayed within the "minstrelsy" confines to which white Hollywood had consigned black comedy, Pryor's films were easy to market, and at least minimally successful. The moment he stepped beyond those boundaries, however, script changes were introduced and unnecessary comedy thrown in, and the resulting films (if ever completed, that is) were not promoted vigorously.[14] In short, Hollywood producers were still not eager to play their part in stripping off the mask.

The peak of Richard Pryor's achievement came during the late seventies and early eighties. The incredible tension in his work, which in many ways reflected his personal life, at times threatened to overwhelm him. Pryor was a master of self-creation, but his personal self-indulgences (a series of wives and a dangerous habit of using the trendiest drugs, some lethal) caused his equilibrium to collapse. After he nearly burned himself to death while free-basing cocaine, he emerged a chastened man. Moreover, following the accident, the drive and tension that had got him to the top were noticeably softened. Then, in the early nineties, Pryor underwent heart surgery, after which it was revealed that he was suffering from multiple sclerosis. His career came to a halt—but it was nonetheless clear that his talent and gifts were abundant. Perhaps most important, Pryor had laid the foundation for a new generation of black comedians. Among these younger comedians, Eddie Murphy and Arsenio Hall stood out.

Eddie Murphy, popular black comic and television/motion picture star, was arguably both the best representative of the success of the post–civil rights black middle class and the best example of its confusion over the question of how to retain a black identity while also entering into the mainstream of American life. Where Richard Pryor's humor was drawn from an AfroAmerica unknown to most white Americans, Murphy focused on a black middle class grappling with the legacies of integration. Eddie Murphy grew up a resident of a working-class Afro-American neighborhood in New Jersey that could be said to have benefited, at least to a degree, from the civil rights movement, and Murphy clearly operated in an integrated world. His early stand-up routines were presented to white audiences; his rise to television fame was on "Saturday Night Live," which played before white audiences; and of course his motion pictures such as *Beverly Hills Cop* were also aimed at a broad audience. It was equally clear, however, that he put forth a persona that was essentially Afro-American, however mediated by the assimilative effects of integration. "Right now, I'm your worst nightmare: a black man with a badge," Murphy menacingly (yet comically) intoned to a white man in a redneck bar in his first movie, *48 Hours*. It was a telling line.

If white audiences were initially uneasy with Richard Pryor, Eddie

Murphy quickly became an idol for younger white Americans who had grown up with integration and were attracted by the "entrepreneurial spirit" of Murphy's brashness. Adults may have deplored Murphy's language and sexual references, but Murphy did display a feature of the black neonationalist spirit that made him nonthreatening to whites: he was not after white women. As he told Oprah Winfrey (the black female version of this entrepreneurial spirit), he preferred black women over white women and could not readily imagine marrying anyone who was not black. Not that he did not date white women; he did. But his affirmation of the endogamous nature of African Americans served not only to exalt Afro-American women but to demolish a worrisome racial myth that successful black men only wanted to marry white women. Murphy claimed the right to date anyone he chose but in the end would only marry another black. This stance, while reassuring to whites, in fact betrayed an uneasy tension between enjoying the fruits of integration, on the one hand, and retaining one's racial identity and resisting assimilation, on the other. Nor was this stance peculiar to Murphy; it was a hallmark of postmodern black culture.[15]

More troubling for Murphy, his pal Arsenio Hall, and others of the fabled "Black Pack" was their easy embrace of given gender constructions and the decidedly homophobic cast to their humor. At a time when so many artists, both black and white, were contesting the vicious resurgence of misogyny and homophobia, it seemed unfortunate that Eddie Murphy, Arsenio Hall, and Robert Townsend pandered to those very trends. Playing off the political backlash against the women's movement and the cultural hysteria caused by AIDS, these artists incurred the justifiable wrath of more socially conscious artists. Yet, perhaps inevitably in a consumption-oriented and commercialized mass culture, it boiled down to a trade-off. By appealing to "popular" sentiments, however unappetizing, Murphy and others were able to achieve commercial success, which in turn allowed them to continue to present new images of AfroAmerica to a broad audience.

Nonetheless, what was troublesome here was the accommodationist ethic that underlay many of the younger black artists' efforts. In an age when Ronald Reagan's neoracist (and neosexist) Hollywood version of a new morning in America was being played out, African

American cultural efforts were at once on the defensive and the offensive. Determined to act on and thus to preserve the rights gained nearly a generation previously, artists like Spike Lee, Eddie Murphy, Robert Townsend, and Oprah Winfrey defensively drew on the existing mechanisms of commercial production (and their values), accepting at least minimally the dictum of black neoconservatives to come back to the community and be of service. However, the resulting productions of certain of these artists departed from the prescriptions of black neoconservatives and managed to shake loose the constraints of commercialization.

For example, Spike Lee's films offered sharp criticisms of Afro-American intraracial class stratification (*School Daze*), the double standard of gender relations (*She's Gotta Have It*), and color consciousness within the black middle class (*Jungle Fever*). However daring his subject matter, Lee worked in a tradition that harked back to the documentary films of early black filmmakers of the sixties, films that, while not unsympathetic to the notion of an interracial society, were made in the heat of the black power movement and reflected the intense racial pride and consciousness of the era. The nationalist sentiment was retained in the work of Spike Lee. To the charge that he made films for black audiences, Lee retorted, in a manner of speaking, Why not?

St. Clair Bourne, one of the early black independent filmmakers, agreed with Spike Lee's assertion that the new generation of black filmmakers were "children of the nationalist 1960s," but noted that there was a noticeable difference in how that ideology was displayed: "For example, unlike their predecessors, they have no hesitation in dealing with mainstream production and distribution sources, primarily because of their desire for distribution to wide audiences."[16] In reaching for that audience, Lee demonstrated that he was unafraid to display before America the warts and blemishes of AfroAmerica. Even his criticisms, however, were in keeping with the nationalist sentiment, as they were intended to alert the black middle class to the dangers of uncontrolled assimilation into white society. He also aimed to defang white racist notions about the lack of dramatic quality within African American culture. It was a bold venture, and for the most part Lee succeeded. He was certainly not above doing Nike sneaker commercials with Michael Jordan or ads for 501 jeans, especially since these were in themselves somewhat subversive, deconstructing the white world of advertising in an attempt to reach the black masses while also promoting images of cultural pluralism.[17]

Nor did Lee, or many other black entertainment artists and filmmakers, shrink from social and political responsibilities. Spike Lee produced a political advertisement for Jesse Jackson in 1988.[18] Arsenio Hall devoted several of his late-night programs to a dialogue between gang members and city officials and the audience in the aftermath of the 1992 Los Angeles riots. Robert Townsend, in his first comedy special for HBO, used a comic vignette to warn against the dangers of AIDS. It was disarmingly funny but also a serious and commendable statement. The superstar athlete Magic Johnson resigned from professional basketball after announcing that he had AIDS, forcing the black middle class and white America to confront, once again, the fact that this a crisis was coursing through not only the underclass but the middle class, too.[19] Finally, both Bill Cosby and the singer Whitney Houston gave large sums of money to historically black colleges, Cosby donating $20 million to Spelman College in Atlanta and Houston $10 million to Meharry Medical College in Nashville.

Such individual gestures of social and political commitment were clearly laudable and consequential. Doubtless more important, though, was the cumulative effect of the various cultural productions of these artists on their audience, black and white. Overwhelmingly received and widely debated, Spike Lee's films managed to rejuvenate, and in a more positive way, critical self-reflection as to AfroAmerica's present situation and the role it saw for itself in the re-creation of America. As the films of Spike Lee, Robert Townsend, and Julia Dash made apparent, there was a firm finger pointed in the direction of a multicultural, multiracial America. No longer could America be designated a "white man's country," nor could questions of race be divorced from class and gender. Moreover, as long as Hollywood persisted in either avoiding or treating only superficially crucial matters with regards to race, history, and gender, these films, their individual flaws notwithstanding, offered an essential alternative.

It remained to be seen, however, whether the rich activities of African American cultural production would have a decisive impact on American popular culture. The immediate signs were somewhat confusing.

As academics and the media argued over Afrocentricity, "political correctness," and the need for a "national community,"[20] much of African American cultural effort was directed toward giving a voice to the many within AfroAmerica who were often not heard. But such efforts were not always welcomed. For example, despite the critical acclaim accorded to his 1986 TV documentary, "Eyes on the Prize," Henry Hampton had to struggle to bring out the sequel, which would cover the years from 1965 to 1980 and continue Hampton's painful but necessary retelling of the Second Reconstruction. Several corporate sponsors of the first program, fearing representations of an oppositional politics that might tarnish their image, nervously withdrew their support for "Eyes on the Prize II." Fortunately, Hampton's efforts galvanized black entertainers such as Bill Cosby and black business leaders such as Earl Greaves, the publisher of *Black Enterprise*, who organized benefit functions to raise money to complete the production. Likewise, other attempts to get at the reality of AfroAmerica often encountered difficulty in getting their message heard. John Singleton's *Boyz 'n' the Hood* (1991) aimed to portray middle-class virtues struggling to survive in the midst of the economic deprivation, drug use, and gang warfare of south central Los Angeles. Yet the positive messages of the movie (and there were many) were easily drowned out, since the press made so much noise—no small amount of it sensationalistic—over the real violence that occurred outside of the theater as well as the violence on the screen.

Inspired to cash in on the baby boomers' memories of the events of the sixties, Hollywood conceived a new fascination with topics such as the civil rights movement, but with predictable results. Indeed, *Mississippi Burning* (1988) was harshly criticized in the mainstream press for its grossly distorted portrayal of the FBI and for conspicuously downplaying black civil rights activity, which in turn raised the hope that enough change had taken place in the society that such films, which relied on old formulas, would in the future be totally reconceived. But this thinking proved deceptive. For one thing, few Hollywood films about the civil rights era were written, produced, or directed by African Americans, who arguably might have been more apt to bring a fresh perspective to bear. Moreover, having to compete with television—notably VCRs, movies produced for cable networks, and regular broadcast movies—Hollywood once again was caught in a catch-up game, which discouraged innovation. Added to this was the inherently conservative nature of an industry that tried to appeal to a mass market, and thus aimed at the lowest common denominator. It rapidly became clear, then, that there was little likelihood that Hollywood would ever be a leader in shaping a multicultural and multiracial America.

At the same time, the fragmentation of American life (which touched the middle class of AfroAmerica) to some extent provided the necessary opening through which African American cultural productions could contribute to a re-creation of America even as they preserved a distinct racial heritage. Comedians Eddie Murphy, Arsenio Hall, and Whoopi Goldberg, filmmakers Julia Dash, Spike Lee, Robert Townsend, and John Singleton, and musicians such as Prince, Living Color, Public Enemy, and Whitney Houston presented AfroAmerica not as monolithic but as a widely diverse, sometimes volatile, sometimes confused, but always creative nation within a nation, striving to formulate a new vision of America. Granted, attitudes toward class and gender, which were often a reflection of external forces within the larger society, at times caused debilitating lapses, but this only suggested how extensively AfroAmerica was intertwined with America. The new black middle class, moreover, took their cue from these cultural activities. As America entered the nineties, there seemed to be a strange sense of déjà vu. In the twenties and early thirties, when AfroAmerica enjoyed a renaissance artistically and a reemergence of nationalism politically, there was a struggle to control and direct those activities. The same might be said of the closing days of the twentieth century, with the crucial exception that, legally, racial integration had taken place.

Albeit with varying degress of sincerity, the majority of white people had taken to heart the dream of Martin Luther King, Jr. Given this, the black middle class seemed in a prime position to further that dream along the lines of an integrative cultural diversity that would not only include the dispossessed (the black masses, poor whites, and others excluded because of gender, sexual preference, or ethnicity) but also create the necessary space in which collective identities could be protected and even nurtured. The new guardians of the black middle class—the African American culture brokers—seemed, moreover, to be the best hope for that possibility.[21]

Indeed, the black middle class, when polled by *Ebony* magazine in 1985, was optimistic about the year 2000: 49 percent felt that race relations would improve; 55 percent felt conditions generally would improve; and 80 percent felt that a child growing up in 1985 would have a better life in the year 2000 than his or her parents had at that moment. Still, there was an anxious realization that real problems loomed ahead. Some 45 percent of those polled point to unemployment as the major concern at that time, overshadowing both racial discrimination and drug abuse. The African American middle class was also concerned about violence in the inner cities, police brutality, and the need for a multicultural approach to education.[22]

But overall the black middle class seemed poised to enter the twenty-first century more hopeful and more certain that the fruits of integration would not only continue but also increase, to the point that America would finally begin to realize its true identity as an integrated but culturally diverse nation.

A cogent reminder of how inevitable the movement toward integrative cultural diversity was can again be found in the annals of history. In 1944 the University of North Carolina Press at Chapel Hill produced a volume of essays, *What the Negro Wants*, edited by the learned Afro-American historian, Rayford W. Logan. The idea was to examine what African American intellectuals at that time felt about Gunnar Myrdal's massive study of black Americans, *An American Dilemma* (1944) and, more important, to discover why racial tensions were so high during the war years.[23] What was most remarkable with regard to the black middle class and the notion of integrative cultural diversity was the prescience of the work as a whole. From the opening sentence in Rayford Logan's short preface—"Race Relations in the United States are more strained than they have been in many years"— to the startling and revelatory publisher's introduction to the essays themselves, one could hardly fail to recognize that not only had the seeds of integration been sown but that the idea of integrative cultural diversity was very much in vogue among black intellectuals during the height of World War II.[24] The Press had stipulated that the volume represent a broad spectrum of views. Logan accordingly stated in his preface that he had selected contributors "four of whom might be called conservatives, five liberals, five radicals," but that he had nevertheless found there was a "surprising unanimity with respect to what the Negro wants" (vii). It must be remembered that this una-

nimity has to be seen within the context of rigid Jim Crow segregation in the South and somewhat less virulent, but still blatant, forms
of segregation—that, for example, disallowed blacks and whites to
marry or buy homes because of "covenant clauses" or prevented
blacks from serving in the armed forces or in fire departments—
throughout the rest of the nation.

Nonetheless, the essays by Afro-American intellectuals contained
in the volume demonstrated that integrative cultural diversity was
already an emerging force. Thus we find the radical Doxey Wilkerson
claiming that the "Negro freedom movement must forge the closest
possible unity among the Negro people themselves, and between the
Negro people and their natural allies in the progressive white population and the organized labor movement" (213). Further on, we encounter the freshly minted conservative George Schuyler stating that
in the future "the words 'Negro,' 'white,' 'Caucasian,' 'Nordic,'" and
'Aryan' would have to be permanently taken out of circulation except
among scholars and scientists. There would have to be an end of
gathering population statistics by so-called race" (298). And finally,
there was Langston Hughes proclaiming:

> This is my land, America. Naturally I love it—it is home—and I am
> vitally concerned about its *mores*, its democracy, and its well-
> being. . . . My ancestry goes back at least four generations on
> American soil and, through Indian blood, many centuries more.
> My background and training is purely American—the schools of
> Kansas, Ohio, and the East. I am old stock as opposed to recent
> immigrant blood. (299)

Integration, in the legal sense, has been won and will not be rolled
back. America has come too far. In the next century, despite the
reintensified discussions of race and identity among black middle class
intellectuals, the main concern will be to grapple with the ideas put
forth by those black middle class intellectuals represented in Logan's
collection, who lay the foundation for integrative cultural diversity. In
the postintegration era, we must find new ways to give life to those
ideas such that America truly begins to realize how diverse it always
has been and how vital the African American presence has been to the
creation of an American identity.

NOTES

INTRODUCTION: The Ambiguity of Nomenclature

1. The scenario in which these events were played out is described in the *New York Times*, December 10, 1988. The use of the term *African American* was proposed by Ramona Edlin, president of the National Urban Coalition. For an interview with Edlin, see *USA Today*, April 20, 1989.

2. For example, the term *African American* was used in 1980 by Stanley Crouch, the *Village Voice*'s resident jazz critic and observer/essayist of AfroAmerica, who was considered by some in the eighties to be a black neoconservative. For more of Crouch's thought, see his *Notes of a Hanging Judge: Essays and Reviews, 1979–1989* (New York: Oxford University Press, 1990).

3. The historical literature on slavery has seen enormous growth. But as far as nomenclature is concerned, one detects a certain resistance on the part of the historical profession to surrender yet again to the social sciences. Thus historians have long held to the term *Afro-American*, which they consider an accurate reflection of the fact that, over time, Africans adjusted to their new home and became an indigenous population. This "hybridization," as Peter Kolchin refers to it, is without doubt ideologically charged, but it does call attention to an important element in the general search for an appropriate name for black Americans. See Peter Kolchin, *Free and Unfree Labor* (Cambridge, Mass.: Harvard University Press, 1987), chap. 2. See also Sterling Stuckey's fine work, *Slave Culture: Nationalist Theory and the Foundations of Black America* (New York: Oxford University Press, 1987), especially his discussion of "naming ceremonies."

4. Of course, even in the nineteenth century black nationalism began to emerge as a coherent ideology among northern free blacks, whose knowledge of Africa was laced with ideas drawn from the ongoing "invention" of Africa by Western European scholars. Thus, black nationalists such as Alexander Crummell and Martin Delany, among others, were as concerned with bringing Africa up to Western standards of civilization as they were with seeing Africa as the homeland of all black people. On the "invention" of Africa,

philosophically and historically, see Kwame Anthony Appiah, *In My Father's House: Africa in the Philosophy of Culture* (New York: Oxford University Press, 1992). On black nationalist conceptions of Africa and Western civilization, see Wilson Jeremiah Moses, *Alexander Crummell: A Study of Civilization and Discontent* (New York: Oxford University Press, 1989).

5. On this score, see the detailed examination of naming in Michael Mullin, *Africa in America: Slave Acculturation and Resistance in the American South and the British Caribbean, 1736–1831* (Urbana: Univeristy of Illinois Press, 1992), chaps. 1–3.

6. On the reemergence of identity and multiculturalism, see Hazel V. Carby, "The Multi-cultural Wars," in Michele Wallace, *Black Popular Culture: A Project by Michele Wallace*, ed. Gina Dent (New York and Seattle: Dia Center for the Arts and Bay Press, 1992), 187–200.

7. Throughout this book I will use the terms *Afro-American* and *African American* as well as *black*. I intend no ideological purpose here other than to demonstrate the wide range of names by which black Americans call themselves. From a historical point of view, however, I do tend to see "Afro-American" as being more accurate. Like "African American," it calls attention to black people's place of origin while also denoting their identity as Americans, but unlike that term, "Afro-American" underscores the fact that blacks are not just another immigrant group but deserve at this point to be regarded as part of the indigenous population. In other words, I do not see "Afro" as having anything to do with hairstyles. Rather, I see it as a reminder of the role that people of African descent have played in making American history and constituting what it is to be an American. Finally, I use the term *AfroAmerica* throughout this book to desginate the black community as a "nation within a nation." Some prefer the appellation *AfricanAmerica*, which is in keeping with the currently popular "African American." I refrained from using it here only because I find it unwieldy. Again, no offense, ideological or otherwise, is intended.

8. See Edward Pessen, "Status and Social Class in America," in Luther S. Luedtke, ed., *Making America: The Society and Culture of the United States* (Chapel Hill: University of North Carolina Press, 1992), 362–75, but especially pp. 363–66 and 371–73. My own materialism is more akin to that of Barbara Jeanne Fields. See her "Slavery, Race, and Ideology in the United States of America," *New Left Review* 181 (1990): 95–118, especially the discussion on pp. 109–11 of ideology as it relates to class and race.

9. The African American summit that took place in New Orleans on April 21–23, 1989, offered a somewhat dismaying example of the difficulties facing the black bourgeois leadership when it came to defining how to proceed in order to address the crucial realities confronting AfroAmerica. Tellingly,

well-known black organizations such as the NNACP were not represented at these meetings; the most visible persons included Coretta King, Jesse Jackson, and Louis Farrakhan, along with several black Congressmen. See "Blacks Discussing Routes to Power," *New York Times*, April 24, 1989. This conference was an outgrowth of the first meeting held in Chicago in December, 1988, which was the first conference of the "black leadership" since Gary Hatcher held a meeting in Gary, Indiana, in 1972.

10. A good summary of this development can be found in the *New York Times*, February 21, 1989. See also Salim Muwakkil, For More Blacks, Islam Is "the Old Religion," *In These Times*, April 5, 1989; and George E. Curry, "The Remaking of Louis Farrakhan," *Emerge*, August 1990.

11. There were, to be sure, some brilliant socialist theoreticians who developed penetrating analyses and prescriptions. Cornel West and Manning Marable spring immediately to mind. See West's *Prophetic Fragments* (Grand Rapids, Mich., and Trenton, N.J.: Erdmanns Publishing and Africa World Press, 1988); and Manning Marable, *Black American Politics*, 2d ed. (London and New York: Verso, 1987). Other black leftist intellectuals whose analyses were tied more to the mainstream were Martin Kilson, who wrote regularly for Irving Howe's democratic socialist journal *Dissent*, and William Julius Wilson, author of *The Declining Significance of Race* (Chicago: University of Chicago Press, 1978) and *The Truly Disadvantaged* (Chicago: University of Chicago Press, 1987). See also Manning Marable's valiant effort to resuscitate a socialist politics that can promote multiculturalism and egalitarianism in "The New American Socialism," *The Progressive* 57, no. 2 (February 1993): 20–25. Granted, Marable's essay reveals a turn toward democratic socialism that was a recurring feature of leftist opinion during the eighties. Under the new Clinton administration, however, a good deal of what Marable calls for may well be attempted. Yet it remains for the left to come to grips with the issue of how much sacrifice Americans are going to have to make or, more important for ethnic politics and African-descended people, how to develop strategies for eradicating the effects of racism once and for all.

CHAPTER 1: Leaders of Thought, Missionaries of Culture

1. Pendleton spoke at Olin Hall on April 4, 1984. The author was in attendance.

2. Julian Bond, former SNCC activist and Congressional representative from Georgia, was the month's opening speaker. Hooks spoke on February 23, 1986 at Strong Auditorium. The author was in attendance.

3. Afrocentricity, which arrived on the scene at the same moment that educators were calling on campuses to become more culturally diverse,

sought to present the viewpoint of African Americans through an under-standing of African values, African history, and African philosophy, as a corrective to the traditional Eurocentric viewpoint. Afrocentricity was thus the eighties' version of the Pan-Africanism of the sixties and the earlier idea of "Negritude." The chief proponent of Afrocentricity, Molefi Kete Asante, was an activist during the sixties who entered the academic world with a degree in communications and went on to head Temple University's (and the nation's) first doctoral program in African American Studies. His ideas are presented in *The Afrocentric Idea* (Philadelphia: Temple University Press, 1987) and his earlier *Afrocentricity: A Theory of Social Change* (Buffalo: Amulefi, 1980).

4. The most often quoted of these references was Farrakhan's comment that Judaism was a "gutter religion." Farrakhan spent many an interview, in print and on screen, explaining that he really meant to attack the "puppet state of Israel," which had abused the holy tenets of Judaism. In most in-stances, however, what started out as a reasonable explanation lapsed into incoherence or yielded more inflammatory rhetoric. See George E. Curry, "The Remaking of Louis Farrakhan," *Emerge*, August 1990.

5. The following description of Farrakhan's talk at Madison Square Garden is drawn from the reportage and analyses of Julius Lester, "The Time Has Come," *New Republic*, October 28, 1985, 11–12; Stanley Crouch, "Nationalism of Fools," in his *Notes of a Hanging Judge: Essays and Reviews, 1979–1989* (New York: Oxford University Press, 1990), 165–75. See also Adolph Reed's fine analyses of Farrakhan's ideology in "The Rise of Louis Farrakhan," *The Nation*, January 21, 1991, and "All for One and None for All," *The Nation*, January 28, 1991.

6. Crouch, "Nationalism of Fools," 170; Lester, "The Time Has Come," 11.

7. Crouch, "Nationalism of Fools," 171, 173; Lester, "The Time Has Come," 12.

8. Lester, "The Time Has Come," 12; see also Crouch, "Nationalism of Fools," 173–74. For observations on Farrakhan by other Afro-American intel-lectuals, see Playthell Benjamin, "The Cosmology of Louis Farrakhan," *Emerge*, February 1990.

9. Eric Foner's *Reconstruction, 1863–1877: America's Unfinished Revolution* (New York: Harper & Row, 1988) provides ample evidence for this "superfi-cial" comparison.

10. Charles P. Henry, *Culture and African American Politics* (Bloomington: Indiana University Press, 1990), 94. Henry is referring to a general tendency in African American mass politics. But traditionally it has been the "represen-tative colored men and women" who have elaborated and carried out the political messages. See also August Meier, *Negro Thought in America, 1880–1915* (Ann Arbor: University of Michigan Press, 1990), pt. 5.

11. On the nationalistic tendency, see Wilson Jeremiah Moses's excellent discussion in *The Golden Age of Black Mationalism, 1850–1925* (New York: Oxford University Press, 1988), especially pt. 2.

12. The best biographical treatment of Washington is Louis Harlan's *Booker T. Washington*, vol. 1, *The Making of a Black Leader, 1856–1901*, and vol. 2, *The Wizard of Tuskegee, 1901–1915* (New York: Oxford University Press, 1972 and 1983). On Du Bois, there are numerous works. An excellent introduction, however, is Julius Lester, ed., *The Seventh Son: The Thought and Writings of W. E. B. Du Bois*, 2 vols. (New York: Random House, 1971), which includes a biographical account. More recently, Du Bois's work has been collected and annotated by Nathan I. Huggins in *Du Bois: Writings* (New York: Viking Press, 1986). General scholarship in which the ideas of these two men, among others, are analyzed includes Meier, *Negro Thought in America, 1880–1915*, and Moses, *Golden Age of Black Nationalism, 1850–1925*.

13. See William Toll, *The Resurgence of Race: Black Social Theory from Reconstruction to the Pan-African Conferences* (Philadelphia: Temple University Press, 1979), chaps. 2 and 4; Moses, *Golden Age of Black Nationalism*, 97–99.

14. Moses, *Golden Age of Black Nationalism*, 132–45, offers a penetrating analysis of Du Bois's black nationalist roots and his journey toward socialism (which Du Bois based on African patterns). On the mature result of Du Bois's cultural pluralism during the thirties, see "The Negro and Social Reconstruction," in *Against Racism: Unpublished Essays, Papers, Addresses, 1887–1961, W. E. B. Du Bois*, ed. Herbert Aptheker (Amherst: University of Massachusetts Press, 1985), 143–57. See also Thomas Holt, "The Political Uses of Alienation: W. E. B. Du Bois on Politics, Race, and Culture, 1903–1940," *American Quarterly* 42, no. 2 (June 1990), 301–23.

15. See Moses, *Golden Age of Black Nationalism*, 97; Harlan, *Booker T. Washington*, vol. 1, chaps. 2–4; Toll, *Resurgence of Race*, chap. 2.

16. See Toll, *Resurgence of Race*, 69; Harlan, *Booker T. Washington*, vol. 2, chaps. 1 and 2. On Du Bois's New England background, see Arnold Rampersad, *The Art and Imagination of W. E. B. Du Bois* (New York: Schocken, 1990), chap. 1; and W. E. B. Du Bois, *Dusk of Dawn*, chap. 2, in *Du Bois: Writings*. The elitist views of Du Bois are examined in Moses, *Golden Age of Black Nationalism*, 137, 139–40. See also Du Bois's essay "The Talented Tenth," in *Du Bois: Writings*, 842–61.

17. See Toll, *Resurgence of Race*, chap. 4; Moses, *Golden Age of Black Nationalism*, 98–99; Harlan, *Booker T. Washington*, vol. 2, chap. 6. On the role of philanthropy in educating and creating a black work force, see James D. Anderson's perceptive analysis, *The Education of Black Folks in the South, 1860–1935* (Chapel Hill: University of North Carolina Press, 1989).

18. For a useful overview, see Paula Giddings, *Where and When I Enter: The Impact of Black Women on Race and Sex* (New York: William Morrow,

1984). See also Moses, *Golden Age of Black Nationalism*, 103–31, for instructive and persuasive analyses of black women's clubs and their relation to black middle class ideology.

19. Giddings, *Where and When I Enter*, 77. See also Moses, *Golden Age of Black Nationalism*, 106–10.

20. See, for example, George Washington Williams, *A History of the Negro Race in America, 1619–1880* (New York, 1883); and Carter G. Woodson, *The Mis-Education of the Negro* (Washington, 1933). The role of literature in encouraging race pride will be discussed in chap. 4. See, however, Rampersad, *Art and Imagination of W. E. B. Du Bois*; Moses, *Golden Age of Black Nationalism*, chaps. 7–9; Eugene Terry, "Charles W. Chestnutt: Victim of the Color Line," *Contributions to Black Studies: A Journal of African and Afro-American Studies* 1 (1977): 15–44.

21. There remains a real need for a comprehensive study of Afro-Americans' role in the Progressive movement. See John Dittmer's *Black Georgia in the Progressive Era, 1900–1920)* (Urbana: University of Illinois Press, 1977) for an example of a fine study of one state.

22. See E. Franklin Frazier, *Black Bourgeoisie* (Glencoe, Ill.: Free Press, 1957), chaps. 2, 4, and 7; Bart Landry, *The New Black Middle Class* (Berkeley: University of California Press, 1987), 23–43.

23. Landry, *New Black Middle Class*, 28–29. See also Frazier, *Black Bourgeoisie*, chap. 5. Gunnar Myrdal's *An American Dilemma: The Negro Problem and Modern Democracy* (New York: Pantheon, 1972 [1944]), 2:695–700 and 704–5, contains a useful overview of the impact of color within the black community as well a sound discussion of the black middle class. See also Willard Gatewood, *Aristocrats of Color: The Black Elite, 1880–1920* (Bloomington: Indiana University Press, 1991), chaps. 1 and 6.

24. Gerald David Jaynes, *Branches without Roots: Genesis of the Black Working Class in the American South, 1862–1882* (New York: Oxford University Press, 1986), 267.

25. Booker T. Washington and W. E. B. Du Bois, *The Negro in the South* (New York, 1907; repr. 1970).

26. Washington, "The Economic Development of the Negro after Emancipation," in Washing and Du Bois, *Negro in the South*, 55; Du Bois, "The Economic Revolution in the South," in ibid., 111.

27. Du Bois, "The Economic Revolution in the South," in ibid., 99.

28. Quoted in Harlan, *Booker T. Washington*, 2:299. Harlan's depiction of the Atlanta riot is also illuminating; see pp. 295–300. The best short account of the riot can be found in Dittmer, *Black Georgia in the Progressive Era*, 123–31. For Du Bois's actions, see his *Dusk of Dawn*, in *Du Bois: Writings*, 616.

29. See Dittmer, *Black Georgia of the Progressive Era*, 130; Du Bois, *Dusk of Dawn*, in *Du Bois: Writings*, 594.

30. Quoted in Harlan, *Booker T. Washington*, 2:299.

31. Du Bois, *Dusk of Dawn*, in *Du Bois: Writings*, 616; see also Dittmer, *Black Georgia of the Progressive Era*, 130–31.

32. Du Bois, *Dusk of Dawn*, in *Du Bois: Writings*, 623. On Trotter's assimilationism, see Stephen Fox, *The Guardian of Boston: William Monroe Trotter* (New York: Atheneum, 1971), chap. 8; and Moses, *Golden Age of Black Nationalism*, 132–33.

33. There are numerous studies on the great migration. The standard treatment is Florette Henri's *Black Migration: Movement North, 1900–1920* (Garden City, N.Y.: Anchor/Doubleday, 1975). But see also the recent work by Carole Marks, *Farewell—We're Good and Gone: The Great Black Migration* (Bloomington: Indiana University Press, 1989). On the migration and the tensions it created for the black middle class, see the excellent discussion in James Grossman's examination of Chicago and the black migration, *Land of Hope: Chicago, Black Southerners, and the Great Migration* (Chicago: University of Chicago, 1989), chap. 5.

34. Du Bois, *Against Racism*, 110. E. Franklin Frazier was also distressed at the inability of the new black middle class to help the majority of African Americans. See Anthony M. Platt, *E. Franklin Frazier Reconsidered* (New Brunswick, N.J.: Rutgers University Press, 1991), chap. 14. See also Frazier's *Black Bourgeoisie*, as well as his textbook *The Negro in the United States*, rev. ed. (New York: Macmillan, 1957). On the growth of the black middle class in the twenties, see Landry, *New Black Middle Class*, 43–66.

35. See James O. Young, *Black Writers of the Thirties* (Baton Rouge: Louisiana State University Press, 1973), chap. 2. See also David Levering Lewis, *When Harlem Was in Vogue* (New York: Alfred A. Knopf, 1982), 83; Arnold Rampersad, *The Life of Langston Hughes*, vol. 1, *1902–1941: I, Too, Sing America* (New York: Oxford University Press, 1986), chap. 4; Cary D. Wintz, *Black Culture and the Harlem Renaissance* (Houston: Rice University Press, 1988), 147–52. Wintz demonstrates persuasively that Garvey was not all that fond of the younger writers of the Harlem Renaissance.

36. For George Schuyler, see his *Black and Conservative* (New Rochelle, N.Y.: Arlington House, 1966), chap. 3. See also Young, *Black Writers of the Thirties*, 85–93; Lewis, *When Harlem Was in Vogue*, 252–54. E. Franklin Frazier, though not dismissive of Garvey, was nonetheless critical of his particular brand of cultural nationalism; see Platt, *E. Franklin Frazier Reconsidered*, 177–78.

37. For one of the better studies of African Americans and the left, see Mark Naison, *Communists in Harlem during the Great Depression* (New York: Grove Press, 1984). Harold Cruse, *The Crisis of the Negro Intellectual: An Historical Analysis of the Failure of Black Leadership* (New York: William Morrow, 1967), contains some highly critical analyses of the relationship between

African Americans and the communists in the thirties; see especially pp. 171–80. The standard treatment of blacks in the Communist party is Wilson Record, *The Negro and the Communist Party* (New York: Atheneum, 1971 [1956]). See also Robin D. G. Kelley, *Hammer and Hoe: Alabama Communists during the Depression* (Chapel Hill: University of North Carolina Press, 1990).

38. See John B. Kirby, *Black Americans in the Roosevelt Era: Liberalism and Race* (Knoxville: University of Tennessee Press, 1980), 125–26.

39. See ibid., chaps. 1 and 2.

40. See Holt, "Political Uses of Alienation," 308–16.

41. See Young, *Black Writers of the Thirties*, 47–49; Platt, *E. Franklin Frazier Reconsidered*, 188–89.

42. Young, *Black Writers*, Chapter I; Du Bois, "The Negro and Social Reconstruction," Chapter XI in Herbert Aptheker, ed., *Against Racism* (Amherst: University of Massachusetts Press, 1985.

43. See Du Bois, "The Negro and Social Reconstruction," in *Against Racism*. See also Young, *Black Writers of the Thirties*, chap. 1.

44. See Platt, *E. Franklin Frazier Reconsidered*, 186–93. See also Young, *Black Writers of the Thirties*, 47.

45. Quoted in Young, *Black Writers of the Thirties*, 48. See also Platt, *E. Franklin Frazier Reconsidered*, 189–90.

46. See Platt, *E. Franklin Frazier Reconsidered*, 183. For further discussion, see Naison, *Communists in Harlem*, chaps. 1–3; and Maurice Isserman, *Which Side Were You On? The Communist Party during the Second World War* (Middleton, Conn.: Wesleyan University Press, 1982), chaps. 1–3.

47. See Young, *Black Writers of the Thirties*, 48–49; Platt, *E. Franklin Frazier Reconsidered*, 167–69. But Frazier was skeptical of Park's notion of "assimilation." He favored economic and political integration and an eventual changeover in American society from capitalism to socialism.

48. Young, *Black Writers of the Thirties*, 53.

49. E. Franklin Frazier, "The Negro Slave Family," *Journal of Negro History* 15 (April 1930): 203. Anthony Platt correctly notes that this analysis, along with Frazier's belief that slavery had a damaging effect on the Afro-American personality, predates the controversial argument of Stanley Elkins in *Slavery: A Problem in American Institutional and Intellectual Life*, 3d ed., rev. (Chicago: University of Chicago Press, 1976 [1959]).

50. Quoted in Platt, *E. Franklin Frazier Reconsidered*, 121. Melville Herskovits, *The Myth of the Negro Past* (Boston: Beacon Press, 1958 [1941]) is still used in courses. For an in-depth examination of the Frazier-Herskovits debate, see Frazier, *The Negro in the United States*, pt. 1; see also Albert J. Raboteau, *Slave Religion: The "Invisible Institution" in the Antebellum South* (New York: Oxford University Press, 1978), 48–55. Frazier's article, "La Noire Bourgeoisie," appeared in *Modern Quarterly* 5 (November 1928): 84.

51. Frazier, *The Negro in the United States*, xi, xii.
52. See Kirby, *Black Americans in the Roosevelt Era*, chap. 6.

CHAPTER 2: From the Hollow to the High Ground and Back

1. On these issues, see Harold Cruse, *The Crisis of the Negro Intellectual: An Historical Analysis of Black Leadership* (New York: William Morrow, 1967), 402–19; and Peter Clecak, *America's Quest for the Ideal Self: Dissent and Fulfillment in the 60s and 70s* (New York: Oxford University Press, 1983), 162–71, 173.

2. See E. Franklin Frazier, *Black Bourgeoisie* (Glencoe, Ill.: Free Press, 1957), 213–16. There is a whole body of literature devoted to this topic. For some in-depth reconstructions of the period, see Peter Novick, *That Noble Dream: The "Objectivity Question" and the American Historical Profession* (New York: Cambridge University Press, 1988), 472–91; and August Meier and Elliott Rudwick, *Black History and the Historical Profession, 1915–1980* (Urbana: University of Illinois Press, 1985), chap. 13. Older, more contemporary examples include Nathan Glazer and Daniel P. Moynihan, *Beyond the Melting Pot*, 2d ed. (Cambridge, Mass.: MIT Press, 1970); Herbert Gutman, *The Black Family in Slavery and Freedom, 1725–1925* (New York: Pantheon, 1976). For the most comprehensive study of Afro-American slavery that has yet to appear, see Eugene D. Genovese, *Roll, Jordan, Roll: The World the Slaves Made* (New York: Pantheon, 1974).

3. The major exposition on the historical impact of slavery on the black personality is Stanley Elkins, *Slavery: A Problem in American Institutional and Intellectual Life*, 3d ed., rev. (Chicago: University of Chicago Press, 1976 [1959]).

4. Daniel P. Moynihan, *The Negro Family: The Case for National Action* (Washington, D.C.: Government Printing Office, 1965). Anthony M. Platt correctly observes that Moynihan misread Frazier; see his *E. Franklin Frazier Reconsidered* (New Brunswick, N.J.: Rutgers University Press, 1991), chap. 11.

5. Frazier, *Black Bourgeoisie*, 176.

6. On Frazier's change of heart, see James O. Young, *Black Writers of the Thirties* (Baton Rouge: Louisiana State University Press, 1973), chap. 2; Frazier, *Black Bourgeoisie*, chap. 2; and Platt, *E. Franklin Frazier Reconsidered*, chap. 14. Frazier himself was born into a working-class black family that aspired toward the petite bourgeoisie. He married into the middle class but never really felt himself part of it. In this sense he was not unlike many of the "new middle class" of the twenties and thirties. See Platt, *E. Franklin Frazier Reconsidered*, 11–20; and Bart Landry, *The New Black Middle Class* (Berkeley: University of California Press, 1987), chap. 1. The middle class to which Landry refers was the one Frazier criticized as being the "old middle class."

7. See Frazier, *Black Bourgeoisie*, 209–11. On the involvement of individualism in institutional religion, see Robert Bellah et al., *Habits of the Heart: Individualism and Commitment in American Life* (Berkeley: University of California Press, 1985), 248–49, 250–52. Albert J. Raboteau, *Slave Religion: The "Invisible Institution" in the Antebellum South* (New York: Oxford University Press, 1978), traces the historical roots of Afro-American religion.

8. See Frazier, *Black Bourgeoisie*, chap. 2. See also Frazier's discussion in *The Negro Family in America* ((New York: Macmillan, 1957).

9. See the introduction to George Davis and Glegg Watson, *Black Life in Corporate America: Swimming in the Mainstream* (Garden City, N.Y.: Anchor/Doubleday, 1982); Gerald David Jaynes and Robin M. Williams, Jr., eds., *A Common Destiny: Blacks and American Society* (Washington, D.C.: National Academy Press, 1989), 272.

10. Quoted in Julius Lester, "Morality and Education," *Democracy* 2, no. 2 (April 1982): 30–31. The historical summary here is drawn from Frederick F. Siegel, *Troubled Journey: From Pearl Harbor to Ronald Reagan* (New York: Hill and Wang, 1984). See also Richard Kluger, *Simple Justice* (New York: Viking Press, 1977).

11. An interesting and persuasive discussion of these matters can be found in Stephen L. Carter's essay "The Logic of Racial Preferences," *Transitions 51* (1991), 121–52. Affirmative action will be discussed in chap. 3.

12. On the participation of the black masses in these protests, see Aldon Morris, *The Origins of the Civil Rights Movement* (New York: Free Press, 1984); Martin Luther King, Jr., *Stride toward Freedom: The Montgomery Story* (New York: Harper & Row, 1958); Taylor Branch, *Parting the Waters: America in the King Years, 1954–63* (New York: Simon & Schuster, 1988).

13. See Siegel, *Troubled Journey*, 141–51. Allen Matusow, *The Unraveling of America: A History of Liberalism in the 1960s* (New York: Harper & Row, 1984), is a solid source on liberals during the sixties. See also Richard Pells, *The Liberal Mind in a Conservative Age: American Intellectuals in the 1940s and 1950s* (New York: Harper & Row, 1985), chap. 6, especially pp. 387–90.

14. Quoted in Bellah et al., *Habits of the Heart*, 249. The best intellectual biography of Frederick Douglass is E. Waldo Martin, *The Mind of Frederick Douglass* (Chapel Hill: University of North Carolina Press, 1985); see also the recent biography by William McFeely, *Frederick Douglass* (New York: W. W. Norton, 1991). The phrase "representative colored man" comes from Nell Irvin Painter, *Exodusters: Black Migration to Kansas after Reconstruction* (New York: Alfred A. Knopf, 1976).

15. Examined closely, the "I Have a Dream" speech presents the view of a unified, multicultural nation as one that will release America from the harmful effects of racist ideology. Ironically, in the eighties and nineties this cultur-

ally diverse view has been used by black middle class conservatives to justify moving away from government intervention on behalf of Afro-American rights. See, for example, Shelby Steele, *The Content of Our Character: A New Vision of Race in America* (New York: St Martin's Press, 1990). King's message was very much integrationist, but he was not an assimilationist to the degree that Douglass was. See Martin Luther King, Jr. *Where Do We Go from Here: Chaos or Community?* (Boston: Beacon Press, 1968); Martin, *The Mind of Frederick Douglass*, chap. 8.

16 Jaynes and Williams, eds., *A Common Destiny*, 272. For comparison, see Gunnar Myrdal, *An American Dilemma: The Negro Problem and Modern Democracy* (New York: Pantheon, 1972 [1944]), 183. Looking at the years between 1915 and 1940, Myrdal found that 90 percent of the blacks who had migrated to the North and West lived in urban areas. For more recent, and suggestive, analyses, see Joe Trotter, ed., *The Great Migration in Historical Perspective: New Dimensions of Race, Class, and Gender* (Bloomington: Indiana University Press, 1991); and Alferdteen Harrison, ed., *Black Exodus: The Great Migration from the American South* (Jackson: University Press of Mississippi, 1991).

17. The plight of the civil rights workers was richly documented in Henry Hampton's excellent PBS series "Eyes on the Prize" (Blackside Productions, Boston, 1987). The historical literature is vast. Some very good general surveys are Branch, *Parting the Waters*; Harvard Sitkoff, *The Struggle for Black Equality, 1954–1992*, rev. ed. (New York: Hill and Wang, 1993); and Robert Weisbrot, *Freedom Bound: A History of America's Civil Rights Movement* (New York: W. W. Norton, 1990).

18. Julius Lester, "On Becoming American: Reflections on the Black Middle Class," *Race Relations Reporter* (September 1974), 13; Davis and Watson, *Black Life in Corporate America*, 33.

19. The best sources for the history of the Nation of Islam remain E. U. Essien Udom, *Black Nationalism: A Search for Identity in America* (Chicago: University of Chicago Press, 1962); and C. Eric Lincoln, *The Black Muslims in America* (Boston: Beacon Press, 1961). Recent analyses of the Nation's antecedents can be found in Wilson Jeremiah Moses, *The Golden Age of Black Nationalism, 1850–1925* (New York: Oxford University Press, 1988).

20. Lester, "On Becoming American," 13; Cornel West, "The Paradox of the Afro-American Rebellion," in Fredric Jameson et al., eds., *The 60's without Apology* (Minneapolis: University of Minnesota Press, 1984), 53.

21. See, for example, Herbert Hyman and Paul Sheatsley, "Attitudes toward Desegregation," *Scientific American* 211 (July 1964), 16–23. The best survey of these issues can be found in Jaynes and Williams, eds., *A Common Destiny*, chap. 3. For Afro-American attitudes, see Lee Sigelman and Susan

Welch, *Black Americans' Views of Racial Inequality: The Dream Deferred* (New York: Cambridge University Press, 1991).

22. See Jaynes and Williams, eds., *A Common Destiny*, 168–71; Davis and Watson, *Black Life in Corporate America*, chaps. 1–3.

23. Jaynes and Williams, eds., *A Common Destiny*, 169. The figures in Myrdal, *An American Dilemma*, vol. 1., chaps. 15 and 16, reflect the impact of the Depression on the blacks in general and the relative effectiveness of the New Deal in providing relief. What can be inferred from these figures is that the black middle class, as small as it was, managed to survive, but no real growth took place.

24. See Nathan I. Huggins, *Afro-American Studies: A Report to the Ford Foundation* (New York: Ford Foundation, Office of Reports, 1985). On the issue of objectivity, see Novick, *That Noble Dream*, especially pp. 469–92; Meier and Rudwick, *Black History and the Historical Profession*, chap. 6. The best attack on relativism can be found in Allan Bloom, *The Closing of the American Mind* (New York: Simon & Schuster, 1987). On the impact and influence of the black power movement, see William L. Van Deburg, *New Day in Babylon: The Black Power Movement and American Culture, 1965–1975* (Chicago: University of Chicago Press, 1992).

25. Davis and Watson, *Black Life in Corporate America*, 2–3.

26. For an assessment of the doubts raised in the minds of blacks, see Steele, *Content of Our Character*, chap. 3.

27. These figures are drawn from Jaynes and Williams, eds., *A Common Destiny*, tables 6.6 and 6.7.

28. Ibid., 419. But even though nearly half of the victims of homicide were black, this did nothing to ease the fearful perception among whites about black crime. Indeed, historically Afro-Americans have been imprisoned in disproportion to whites for all manner of offenses. When the overwhelming majority of Afro-Americans lived in the South, chain-gang labor and lynching were frequent modes of punishment, serving variously to provide cheap labor and for brutal intimidation. The disproportion of black inmates in prison was not just confined to the South; it occurred throughout the nation and has continued through to the present. In 1985, for example, 46 percent of the prison population in the United States was Afro-American. See ibid., 455–56; see also Pete Daniel, *The Shadow of Slavery: Peonage in the South, 1901–1969* (Urbana: University of Illinois Press, 1972).

29. Jaynes and Williams, eds., *A Common Destiny*, 412. It was also found that because of the disproportionately high rate of pregnancy among black teenagers, the abortion rate for Afro-American women was double that of white women (ibid.).

30. Ibid., table 8.1.

31. For an analysis of black elected officials by region, see ibid., table 5.10; table 5.11 traces the growth of black elected officials in selected offices. As of 1985 there were twenty black representatives in the Congress; that figure had increased to 35 by 1990.

32. William Chafe, "The End of One Struggle, The Beginning of Another," in Charles Eagles, ed., *The Civil Rights Movement in America*, (Jackson: University Press of Mississippi, 1986), 146.

33. J. Mills Thornton III, "Comment on William Chafe," in Eagles, ed., *Civil Rights Movement in America*, 155.

34. Nathan Glazer, *Disaffirmative Action* (New York: Free Press, 1974). See also George Gilder, *Wealth and Poverty* (New York: Basic Books, 1981).

35. In 1965 the average African American had 9 years of education, the average white 12. By 1990 the average number of years African Americans attended school had increased to 12.4 but still lagged slightly behind the average of 12.7 years for whites. See *U.S. News and World Report*, July 22, 1991, 20–21. For the overall summary, I have relied on Jaynes and Williams, eds., *A Common Destiny*, 369–79.

36. "Student Leaders Are Optimistic about the Future: They See Gains in the Job Market and in Politics," *Ebony*, August 1985, 69–74; the quote is from p. 74. This was a special issue devoted to exploring what the situation of African Americans would be in the year 2000.

37. *U.S. Bureau of Labor Statistics: Annual Reports for 1980–1984*. See also Jaynes and Williams, eds., *A Common Destiny*, chap. 6.

38. Since 1968 conservatives had tried to limit the force of the voting rights legislation but were in the end unable to do so. See Weisbrot, *Freedom Bound*, 280–82, for a discussion of that struggle. See also Hugh Davis Graham, *The Civil Rights Era: Origins and Development of National Policy, 1960–1972* (New York: Oxford University Press, 1990), 377–81.

39. See Matusow, *The Unraveling of America*; Siegel, *Troubled Journey*, especially chap. 7; and West, "Paradox of the Afro-American Rebellion," 43–55.

40. Nicholas Lemann, "The Origins of the Black Underclass," pt. 1, *Atlantic Monthly*, June 1986, 35; pt. 2 appeared in the July 1986 issue. Lemann's subsequent book, *The Promised Land: The Great Black Migration and How It Changed America* (New York: Alfred A. Knopf, 1991), built on the thesis I am analyzing. Although his book was praised by many black and white liberals, I continue to stand by my criticisms.

41. Lemann, "Origins of the Black Underclass," pt. 1, 36, 38. Lemann expands on this point in *The Promised Land*, chap. 1.

42. Lemann, "Origins of the Black Underclass," pt. 1, 36–38. See also *The Promised Land*, chap. 3.

43. Lemann, *The Promised Land*, 281–91.

44. Lemann, "Origins of the Black Underclass," pt. 2, 68.

45. Mickey Kaus, "The Work Ethic State," *New Republic*, July 7, 1986. For further elaboration, see Kaus's book *The End of Equality* (New York: Basic Books, 1992).

46. Kaus, "Work Ethic State," 23.

47. William Julius Wilson, *The Declining Significance of Race* (Chicago: University of Chicago Press, 1978). Wilson later wrote a more detailed work, *The Truly Disadvantaged: The Inner City, the Underclass, and Public Policy* (Chicago: University of Chicago Press, 1987).

48. Wilson, *Declining Significance of Race*, 153–54.

49. Manning Marable, *Blackwater: Historical Studies in Race, Class Consciousness, and Revolution* (Dayton, Ohio: Black Praxis Press, 1981), 115, 121. Marable, one of the more prolific writers on the black left, extended his analysis of the progressive black nationalist position in two later works, *Black American Politics* (London and New York: Verso, 1986) and *From Rebellion to Revolution: Afro-American Politics from Civil Rights to Black Nationalism, 1954–1985* (Jackson: University Press of Mississippi, 1987; rev. ed., 1991).

50. Julius Lester, "The Mark of Race," *Civil Liberties Review*, January/February 1979, 116, 117.

51. See Wilson, *The Truly Disadvantaged*, 153–64. Wilson's critics from among the progressive nationalists include Manning Marable and Cornel West. West is more generous than Marable and acknowledges Wilson's left-liberal perspective. See his *Prophesy Deliverance! An Afro-American Revolutionary Christianity* (Philadelphia: Westminster Press, 1982), as well as his *Prophetic Fragments* (Grand Rapids, Mich., and Trenton, N.J.: Erdmanns Publishing Company and Africa World Press, 1988), 50–52.

52. For further discussion, see West, *Prophetic Fragments*, pt. 1. Marable, *Black American Politics*, chap. 3, examines the same topic from a left nationalist perspective, while Thomas Sowell, *Race and Economics* (New York: William Morrow, 1975), presents a forceful conservative critique.

53. See Harold Cruse, *Plural but Equal: Blacks and Minorities in America's Plural Society* (New York: William Morrow, 1987), especially pt. 1.

54. John Dittmer, "The Politics of the Mississippi Movement, 1954–1964," in Eagles, ed., *Civil Rights Movement in America*, 67.

55. Cruse, *Plural but Equal*, 386.

56. Ibid., 389. Cruse also asserted that this contemporary black middle class was even more "nonnationalistic" than its predecessors in the thirties and fifties (see pp. 388–89), a point with which I cannot agree.

57. Wilson, *The Truly Disadvantaged*, 155.

CHAPTER 3: To Preserve the Dignity of the Race

1. Arguably, Reagan was attempting to atone for his past affiliation with the Democrats and the New Deal. See Michael Rogin's interesting analysis, "Ronald Reagan's American Gothic," *Democracy* 1, no. 4: 51–60. For a good overview the Reagan administration's attempt to roll back civil rights, see Robert Weisbrot, *Freedom Bound: A History of America's Civil Rights Movement* (New York: W. W. Norton, 1990), 298–312.

2. The claim that affirmative action principally benefited the middle class has been made many times. See, for example, Cornel West, "The Paradox of the Afro-American Rebellion," in Fredric Jameson et al., eds., *The 60's without Apology* (Minneapolis: University of Minnesota Press, 1984), 44–58; Charles V. Hamilton, "The Future and the Civil Rights of Minorities," in Stephen C. Halpern, ed., *The Future of Our Liberties* (Westport, Conn: Greenwood Press, 1982), 233–40; and Harold Cruse, *Plural but Equal: Blacks and Minorities in America's Plural Society* (New York: William Morrow, 1987).

3. The two major works that stress these arguments are Nathan Glazer, *Affirmative Discrimination* (New York: Basic Books, 1975), and George Gilder, *Wealth and Poverty* (New York: Basic Books, 1981).

4. See Hamilton, "The Future and Civil Rights of Minorities," 233–36, for an example.

5. For further discussion, see Barry L. Goldstein, "The Historical Case for Goals and Timetables," *New Perspectives* (Summer 1984): 24–25; John B. Kirby, *Black Americans in the Roosevelt Era: Liberalism and Race* (Knoxville: University of Tennessee Press, 1980), chaps. 2 and 3; Harvard Sitkoff, *A New Deal for Blacks: The Emergence of Civil Rights as a National Issue*, vol. 1, *The Depression Decade* (New York: Oxford University Press, 1978), chaps. 1–3; Charles Pete T. Banner-Haley, *To Do Good and To Do Well: Middle Class Blacks and the Depression, Philadelphia, 1929–1941* (New York: Garland Publishing, 1993), chap. 2.

6. See William H. Harris, *The Harder We Run: Black Workers since the Civil War* (New York: Oxford University Press, 1982), chap. 5.

7. See ibid., chap. 5. For an excellent analysis of labor union struggles in the late twentieth century, see Mike Davis, *Prisoners of the American Dream: Politics and Economy in the History of the U.S. Working Class* (London and New York: Verso, 1986).

8. Quoted in Harris, *The Harder We Run*, 114. See also John Dowser, *War without Mercy* (New York: Pantheon, 1986).

9. The Honorable Elijah Muhammad (Leroy Poole) went to jail as a conscientious objector to the war against the Japanese; see John Blassingame and

Mary Frances Berry, *Long Memory: The Black Experience in America* (New York: Oxford University Press, 1982), 323. On the reaction of the black press, see the *Philadelphia Tribune* and the *Philadelphia Independent*, December 13, 1941. See also Andrew Buni, *Robert L. Vann of the Pittsburgh Courier* (Pittsburgh: University of Pittsburgh Press, 1974), chap. 10.

10. Harris, *The Harder We Run*, 122. Harris found that there were "approximately 1,000,000 black workers . . . added to the industrial work force during the war, 60 percent of whom were women" (ibid.).

11. See ibid., chap. 6. See also Davis, *Prisoners of the American Dream*, chap. 2; Gerald David Jaynes and Robin M. Williams, eds., *A Common Destiny: Blacks and American Society* (Washington, D.C.: National Academy Press, 1989), 275, 302–4.

12. See Cruse, *Plural but Equal*, chap. 1.

13. See Hugh Davis Graham, *The Civil Rights Era: Origins and Development of National Policy, 1960–1972* (New York: Oxford University Press, 1990), 171–73.

14. Clayborne Carson, "Civil Rights Reforms and the Black Freedom Struggle," in Charles Eagles, ed., *The Civil Rights Movement in America* (Jackson: University Press of Mississippi, 1986), 27. See also Clayborne Carson, *In Struggle: SNCC and the Black Awakening in the Sixties* (Cambridge, Mass.: Harvard University Press, 1981); and Howard Zinn, *The New Abolitionists* (Boston: Beacon Press, 1965).

15. Julius Lester, "Memoir of the Movement," *New Republic*, April 1, 1985, 34, 36. Lester refers here to civil rights workers who gave their lives to the cause. Viola Liuzzo was murdered by the Ku Klux Klan in 1965 as she drove demonstrators back to Birmingham after the rally in Selma; Jonathan Daniels, a white minster and activist, was killed by a shotgun blast as he helped black women register to vote; William Moore was a member of the SNCC who was also killed while helping black voters to register; likewise, Andrew Goodman, Michael Schwerner, and James Chaney were brutally murdered. See also Michael Thewell, *Duties, Pleasures, and Conflicts: Essays in Struggle* (Amherst: University of Massachusetts Press, 1987), pt. 1; Carson, *In Struggle*, chaps. 1 and 2.

16. See Goldstein, "The Historical Case for Goals and Timetables," 20. See also Graham, *Civil Rights Era*, 28, 41–43. Graham attributes the term *affirmative action* to language first found in the Wagner Act of 1935 (p. 4). But that act concerned labor relations and was not specifically about race relations.

17. Goldstein, "The Historical Case for Goals and Timetables," 20; see also Graham, *Civil Rights Era*, 282–87. Graham points out that Sylvester,

who was an Afro-American, also wanted affirmative action to be policy of "results" as well as action (p. 286).

18. Frederick S. Siegel, *Troubled Journey: From Pearl Harbor to Ronald Reagan* (New York: Hill and Wang, 1984), chap. 8; Allen Matusow, *The Unraveling of America: A History of Liberalism in the 1960s* (New York: Harper & Row, 1984), chap. 7; Alonzo Hamby, *Liberalism and Its Challengers* (New York: Oxford University Press, 1984), chaps. 5 and 6. Detailed, behind-the-scenes descriptions of the development of affirmative action plans can be found in Graham, *Civil Rights Era*, chaps. 7–9.

19. Two influential studies that pursued this line of thought were Stanley Elkins, *Slavery: A Problem in American Institutional and Intellectual Life*, 3d ed., rev. (Chicago: University of Chicago Press, 1976 [1959]); and Daniel P. Moynihan, *The Negro Family: The Case for National Action* (Washington: Government Printing Office, 1965). Moynihan was deeply influenced by E. Franklin Frazier's *The Negro Family in the United States* (Chicago: University of Chicago Press, 1939).

20. See August Meier and Elliot Rudwick, *Black History and the Historical Profession, 1915–1980* (Urbana: University of Illinois Press, 1986), chap. 1 and especially chap. 4. For the recollections of black historians, see Earl Thorpe, *Black Historians* (New York: William Morrow, 1972).

21. In Kenneth Stampp's original words, "I have assumed that the slaves were merely ordinary human beings, that innately Negroes *are*, after all, only white men with black skins, nothing more, nothing less." See his time-honored history *The Peculiar Institution: Slavery in the Ante-Bellum South* (New York: Vintage Press, 1956), vii–viii.

22. Quoted in Hamby, *Liberalism and Its Challengers*, 212.

23. Quoted in Hamilton, "The Future and Civil Rights of Minorities," 233.

24. For Johnson's remarks, see Hamby, *Liberalism and Its Challengers*, 212.

25. See Nancy Weiss, "Creative Tensions in the Leadership of the Civil Rights Movement," in Eagles, ed., *The Civil Rights Movement in America*, 39–55.

26. This theme is developed in Cruse, *Plural but Equal*. See also Thelwell, *Duties, Pleasures, and Conflicts*, chap. 2; Alan B. Anderson and George W. Pickering, *Confronting the Color Line: The Broken Promise of the Civil Rights Movement in Chicago* (Athens: University of Georgia Press, 1986); Manning Marable, "The Contradictory Contours of Black Political Culture," in Mike Davis et al., eds., *The Year Left 2: Towards Rainbow Socialism. Essays on Race, Ethnicity, Class, and Gender* (London and New York: Verso, 1987), 1–18.

27. See Carson, *In Struggle*, chaps. 1 and 2. For a recent examination of the SNCC's vision that traces the organization's roots, see Vincent Harding, "Beyond Amnesia: Martin Luther King, Jr., and the Future of America," *Journal of American History* 74, no. 2, (September 1987): 468–76.

28. See Carson, *In Struggle*, chaps. 4 and 5; John Dittmer, "The Politics of the Mississippi Movement, 1954–1964," in Eagles, ed., *The Civil Rights Movement in America*, 65–93; Thelwell, *Duties, Pleasures, and Conflicts*, chap. 5; Matusow, *The Unraveling of America*, chap. 7; and Weisbrot, *Freedom Bound*, 92–123.

29. For further discussion, see Carson, *In Struggle*, chaps. 8 and 9. See, however, Manning Marable, *Black American Politics* (London and New York: Verso, 1986), 18–19, 165–67, for a different view that stresses a progressive nationalist and class-based analysis.

30. This alienation of young whites was commented upon at the time by Julius Lester; see his *Revolutionary Notes* (New York: Grove Press, 1969), 44–48, 124–28, and 185–90. The rise of the New Left has been ably described and analyzed by Kirkpatrick Sale, *SDS* (New York: Bantam, 1975); James Miller, *"Democracy in the Streets": From Port Huron to the Siege of Chicago* (New York: Simon & Schuster, 1987); and Maurice Isserman, *"If I Had a Hammer": The Death of the Old Left and the Birth of the New Left* (New York: Basic Books, 1987).

31. See Weiss, "Creative Tensions in the Leadership of the Civil Rights Movement," in Eagles, ed., *The Civil Rights Movement in America*, 52–53; Harding, "Beyond Amnesia," 469–70; Nancy Weiss, *Whitney M. Young, Jr., and the Struggle for Civil Rights* (Princeton: Princeton University Press, 1989), 127–28, and chaps. 10 and 12.

32. See Weiss, *Whitney M. Young, Jr.*, 154–55. Moynihan was one of the speech writers for Johnson's address, which drew heavily on Young's ideas as expressed in his book *To Be Equal* (New York: AT & T, 1965).

33. Robert L. Allen, *Black Awakening in Capitalist America* (New York: Doubleday, 1972) remains an indispensable treatment of this subject. See also Weiss, *Whitney M. Young, Jr.*, chap. 9.

34. On the expansion of the black middle class, see Bart Landry, *The New Black Middle Class* (Berkeley: University of California Press, 1987), 67–93; Jaynes and Williams, eds., *A Common Destiny*, 164–65, 272–74; Huggins, *Afro-American Studies: A Report to the Ford Foundation* (New York: Ford Foundation, Office of Reports, 1985).

35. On this point, see Cruse, *Plural but Equal*, chap. 1.

36. See, for example, Lois Banner, *Women in Modern America* (New York: Harcourt, Brace, Jovanovich, 1977). For the specific concerns of black women, see Julianne Malveaux, "The Political Economy of Black Women," in

Davis et al., eds., *The Year Left 2*, 52–73, as well as Jaynes and Williams, eds., *A Common Destiny*, chap. 6.

37. The quote is from Julius Lester (conversation with the author, April 2, 1987). See also Donald G. Nieman, *Promises to Keep: African Americans and the Constitutional Order, 1776 to the Present* (New York: Oxford University Press, 1991), 200–212.

38. For a helpful analysis, see Davis, *Prisoners of the American Dream*.

39. See Elizabeth Fox-Genovese, "Women's Rights, Affirmative Action, and the Myth of Individualism," *George Washington Law Review*, 54, nos. 2 and 3, (January and March 1986), 338–74; the quote appears on p. 339. Fox-Genovese expands on the idea of individualism in her recent book, *Feminism without Illusions: A Critique of Individualism* (Chapel Hill: University of North Carolina, 1991). I am greatly indebted to Fox-Genovese's work in this area as she has brought much clarity to an often muddled concept.

40. Fox-Genovese explores this tendency in "Women's Rights, Affirmative Action," 340–45; see also Nieman, *Promises to Keep*, 210–12.

41. See Nieman, *Promises to Keep*, 216–25.

42. Derrick Bell, *And We Are Not Saved: The Elusive Quest for Racial Justice* (New York: Basic Books, 1987), chap. 5. Bell continues his allegory in a somewhat different vein in his book *Faces at the Bottom of the Well: The Permanence of Racism* (New York: Basic Books, 1992), chap. 4. A recent examination of the hiring of black faculty under affirmative action procedures can found in the essay by G. Kindrow, "The Candidate," *Lingua Franca: The Review of Academic Life* 1, no. 4 (April 1991): 21–25.

43. Bell, *And We Are Not Saved*, 154.

44. The *American Council of Education Report 1988* contains the figures for black faculty hiring; see also Jaynes and Williams, eds., *A Common Destiny*, 375–77. On the difficulty of hiring, see Kindrow, "The Candidate."

45. For the New Left, see the sources cited in note 30. On the women's movement, see Sara Evans, *Personal Politics: The Roots of Women's Liberation in the Civil Rights Movement and the New Left* (New York: Alfred A. Knopf, 1979); Alice Echols, *Daring to Be Bad: Radical Feminism in America, 1969–1975* (Minneapolis: University of Minnesota Press, 1989); Elizabeth Fox-Genovese, *Feminism without Illusions*, especially chap. 6., "The Struggle for Women's History," which makes cogent comparisons to black history.

46. See Ellen Willis, "Sisters Underneath the Skin," *Voice Literary Supplement*, April 1983. For samples of the work of African American feminists, see Michele Wallace, *Black Macho and the Myth of the Superwoman* (New York: William Morrow, 1978); bell hooks, *Arn't I a Woman? Black Women and Feminism* (Boston: South End Press, 1981), and *Talking Back: Thinking Feminist, Thinking Black* (Boston: South End Press, 1989).

47. See Fox-Genovese, "Women's Rights, Affirmative Action," 340–50.

48. See Jaynes and Williams, eds., *A Common Destiny*, 307–8, 397–99, and 535–37.

49. See Fox-Genovese, "Women's Rights, Affirmative Action," 340–50; and George Gilder, *Wealth and Poverty*, chap. 10.

50. Pendleton publicly made this remark often, and it seldom failed to create quite a stir. I heard him repeat it during his address at Cornell University, April 10, 1984.

51. See Fox-Genovese, *Feminism without Illusions*, 75–80, for an excellent discussion of comparable worth.

52. See Kirby, *Black Americans in the Roosevelt Era*, 87.

53. Much of my information about the black neoconservatives is drawn from journalistic portraits. See, for example, Lee A. Daniels, "The New Black Conservatives," *New York Times Magazine*, October 4, 1981. Also useful is Thomas D. Boston, *Race, Class and Conservatism* (Winchester, Mass.: Unwin Hyman, 1988).

54. George Schuyler, *Black and Conservative* (New Rochelle, N.Y.: Arlington House, 1966), 135, 192. This work, Scuyler's autobiography—a fascinating, if troubling, account—remains the best source of evidence for his opinions. For Schuyler's ultraconservative views, see especially chap. 19.

55. George Schuyler, "Views and Reviews," *Pittsburgh Courier* September 15, 1934. Schuyler's column was very popular within the black community. See also James O. Young, *Black Writers of the Thirties* (Baton Rouge: Louisiana State University Press, 1973) 84–93, for a good summary of Schuyler's writings during the thirties. For a more recent appreciation of Schuyler, see Henry Louis Gates, Jr., "A Fragmented Man: George Schuyler and the Claims of Race," *New York Times Book Review*, September 30, 1992.

56. George Schuyler, "A Negro Looks Ahead," *American Mercury* 19 (February 1930), 217.

57. Quoted in Daniels, "The New Black Conservatives," 23. The rediscovery of Booker T. Washington by progressive black scholars most probably had its origins in his being classified as an "economic nationalist" in the early 1970s. See John Bracey, Jr., August Meier, and Elliot Rudwick, eds., *Black Nationalism in America* (New York: Bobbs-Merrill, 1970), xxvii–xxviii, xli, and documents 34 and 35. An excellent source that situates Washington within a nationalist context is Wilson Jeremiah Moses, *The Golden Age of Black Nationalism, 1850–1925* (New York: Oxford University Press, 1988).

58. Sowell was and continues to be very prolific. The most pertinent of his works are *Ethnic Minorities: A History* (New York: William Morrow, 1982), *Civil Rights: Myth or Reality?* (New York: William Morrow, 1983), and *Preferential Policies: An International Perspective* (New York: William Morrow,

1990). An excellent discussion of Sowell's work can be found in Stephen L. Carter, "The Logic of Racial Preferences," *Transitions 51* (1991), 158–82.

59. For Sowell's argument, see his *Civil Rights: Myth or Reality?*

60. The data on the African American attitude toward the need for government help are immense. Examples can be found in the 1980 *New York Times* poll on affirmative action, the 1987 Gallup poll on Supreme Court decisions that backed affirmative action, and the 1978 Louis Harris poll regarding the fairness of such programs. See Sigelman and Welch, *Black Americans' Views of Racial Inequality: The Dream Deferred* (New York: Cambridge University Press, 1991), table 7.1.

61. Carter, "The Logic of Racial Preferences," 176. See also Allen, *Black Awakening in Capitalist America*. Manning Marable posits this notion in several of his essays in *Blackwater: Historical Studies in Race, Class Consciousness, and Revolution* (Dayton, Ohio: Black Praxis Press, 1981). The democratic socialism of Cornel West in *Prophetic Fragments* (Grand Rapids, Mich., and Trenton, N.J.: Erdmanns Publishing and Africa World Press, 1988), though deriving from a left viewpoint, comes even closer to the young black neoconservatives. Finally, William Julius Wilson's position, so often mistaken for a neoconservative one, also emanates from the liberal-left end of the spectrum. See his *The Truly Disadvantaged: The Inner City, the Underclass, and Public Policy* (Chicago: University of Chicago Press, 1987).

62. Glenn Loury, "Beyond Civil Rights," *New Republic*, October 7, 1985. See also Jeff Howard and Ray Hammond, "Rumors of Inferiority," *New Republic*, September 9, 1985.

63. Loury, "Beyond Civil Rights," 22.

64. Ibid., 22.

65. Ibid.

66. Ibid., 25. An example of this strategy as it was used by black middle class intellectuals during the age of segregation can be seen in the journals of the Afro-American historian Lorenzo Greene, who worked with Carter G. Woodson. Called upon to speak at a Baptist church in the Georgetown area of Washington, D.C., he started out by "*shocking* the audience," telling them that "of twelve million Negroes in the United States, there is not one that is not diseased." That disease, which he proclaimed was worse than "cancer or consumption," was "an inferiority complex." Greene then proceeded to give his rather small audience a lesson in the positive contributions of blacks, downplaying slavery and demonstrating the importance of Africa to civilization and Afro-Americans to American history. See *Working with Carter G. Woodson, the Father of Black History: A Diary, 1928–1930* (Baton Rouge: Louisiana State University Press, 1989), 421 (diary entry for Sunday, December 15, 1929).

67. William P. O'Hare et al., eds., *African Americans in the Nineties* (Washington: Population Reference Bureau, 1991). The comments are those of William Welch, Associated Press writer, August 8, 1991. While I have not been able to examine the report in full, I suspect that it relied heavily on Jaynes and Williams, eds., *A Common Destiny* (1989), which was the most massive study on race and race relations in the United States since Myrdal's *An American Dilemma* appeared in 1944.

68. Loury, "Beyond Civil Rights," 25.

69. Shelby Steele, *The Content of Our Character: A New Vision of Race in America* (New York: St Martin's Press, 1990), 49. Steele has often been identified with the black neoconservatives, but in my view he fits more into the mold of E. Franklin Frazier, which is to say that he is more of a radical integrationist.

70. Ibid., 109.

71. Howard and Hammond, "Rumors of Inferiority," 17.

CHAPTER 4: Integrating the Many Voices

1. The best historical studies of the Harlem Renaissance are Nathan I. Huggins, *Harlem Renaissance* (New York: William Morrow, 1972); and David Levering Lewis, *When Harlem Was in Vogue* (New York: Alfred A. Knopf, 1981). See also Jervis Anderson, *This Was Harlem* (New York: Bantam, 1982); and Bruce Kellner, *The Harlem Renaissance: An Historical Dictionary for the Era* (New York: Metheun, 1987).

2. The term "vicious modernism" comes from an insightful analysis of the Harlem Renaissance that not only reveals its integrative cultural diversity but also situates it within other developments in the Western hemisphere. See James de Jongh, *Vicious Modernism: Black Harlem and the Literary Imagination* (New York: Cambridge University Press, 1990). The most provocative and interesting work regarding the influence of Booker T. Washington is Houston A. Baker, Jr., *Modernism and the Harlem Renaissance* (Chicago: University of Chicago Press, 1987). Baker argues cogently that modernism in Afro-American literature began with Washington's deft manipulation of the "mask." He provides many interesting and, in most cases, convincing examples and analyses of pre–Harlem Renaissance writers to support this view. Historically, however, he continues to stress the traditional dichotomous interpretation of the Washington versus Du Bois debate (see chaps. 4–6), an interpretation that has elsewhere been called seriously into question. For a discussion of the Du Bois-Washington controversy, see my essay "Tuskegee's Wizard of Oz: Booker T. Washington and Teaching History," *Teaching History: A Journal of Methods* (Autumn 1984): 81–87. On the use of slave narratives

as a strong cultural force, see Henry Louis Gates, Jr., and Charles Davis, eds., *The Slave's Narrative* (New York: Oxford University Press, 1985), especially the introduction by Gates. Important also are Henry Louis Gates, Jr., *Figures in Black: Words, Signs, and the Racial Self* (New York: Oxford University Press, 1987), and *The Signifying Monkey* (New York: Oxford University Press, 1988); Elizabeth Fox-Genovese, "To Write Myself: The Autobiographies of Afro-American Women," in Shari Benstock, ed., *Feminist Issues in Literary Scholarship* (Bloomington: Indiana University Press, 1987), 161–81; and Hortense Spillers, "A Hateful Passion, A Lost Love," also in Benstock, ed., 181–208.

3. See Baker, *Modernism and the Harlem Renaissance*, chaps 4 and 5. For a fuller treatment of Washington's deft manipulation of whites, see Louis Harlan, *Booker T. Washington*, vol. 2, *The Wizard of Tuskegee, 1901–1915* (New York: Oxford University Press, 1983).

4. For examples of the black middle class in urban areas, see W. E. B. Du Bois, *The Philadelphia Negro* (1899); John Blassingame, *Black New Orleans* (Chicago: University of Chicago Press, 1972); and St. Clair Drake and Horace Cayton, *Black Metropolis*, rev. ed. (New York: Harcourt, Brace, and Co., 1962 [1945]). See also Willard B. Gatewood, *Aristocrats of Color: The Black Elite, 1880–1920* (Bloomington: Indiana University Press, 1991). Caution should be excercised, however, in approaching Gatewood's work. While his book is otherwise splendidly researched, he confuses the issue of what constitutes the black middle class. What Gatewood calls the "black elite" is in actuality the "old black middle class," whose members could be identified by their light complexion and who attempted to bridge the gap between AfroAmerica and white America. On the creation of all-black towns, see, for example, Nell Irvin Painter, *Exodusters: Black Migration to Kansas after Reconstruction* (New York: Alfred A. Knopf, 1976); and Kenneth Hamilton, "The Origins and Development of Langston, Oklahoma," *Journal of Negro History* 62 (Summer 1977): 275–95. Hamilton has now published a book-length study, which unfortunately I was unable to consult before the present work was completed.

5. W. E. B. Du Bois, *Dusk of Dawn*, in *Du Bois: Writings*, ed. Nathan I. Huggins (New York: Viking Press, 1986), 560–61.

6. Ibid., 569–70. This passage is striking in that, in the course of my research among African Americans in upstate New York, I often encountered similar recollections and feelings. See Charles T. Banner-Haley, "Sketches of Afro-American Family and Culture in Upstate New York's Southern Tier, 1890–1980," *Afro-Americans in New York Life and History* 13, no. 1 (January 1989): 5–18.

7. Questions of political strategy and of who should lead the masses, and

in what direction, have proved divisive in AfroAmerica, with a variety of voices attempting to offer guidance. There has been a virtual explosion of commentary on this matter during the early nineties. See, for example, Shelby Steele, *The Content of Our Character: A New Vision of Race in America* (New York: St. Martin's Press, 1990); Roy L. Brooks, *Rethinking the American Race Problem* (Berkeley: University of California Press, 1990); and Stephen L. Carter, *Reflections of an Affirmative Action Baby* (New York: Basic Books, 1991). A volume of essays that will both describe and prescribe directions for AfroAmerica is Erroll McDonald, ed., *Whatever Happened to Black America? Towards the Millennium: A Reader* (New York: Pantheon, forthcoming).

8. See Arnold Rampersad, *The Life of Langston Hughes*, vol. 1, *1902–1941: I, Too, Sing America* (New York: Oxford University Press, 1986), chaps. 1 and 2. See also vol. 2, *1941–1967: I Dream a World* (New York: Oxford University Press, 1988). Rampersad's detailed and elegantly written biography is the definitive work on Hughes. See also Faith Berry, *Langston Hughes: Before and Beyond Harlem* (Westport, Conn.: Lawrence Hill, 1983).

9. See Berry, *Langston Hughes*, chaps. 1 and 2; Rampersad, *The Life of Langston Hughes*, vol. 1, chaps. 1–3. Both authors consider the merits of the rebellion theory. Berry tends more toward the psychological explanation, while Rampersad considers it one among many.

10. Quoted from Rampersad, Vol. I, 316.

11. See Robert Hemenway, *Zora Neale Hurston: A Literary Biography* (Urbana: University of Illinois Press, 1981); and Zora Neale Hurston, *Dust Tracks on the Road: An Autobiography*, 2d ed., ed. Robert Hemenway (Urbana: University of Illinois Press, 1984). This new edition, prepared by Hurston's principal biographer, contains several previously unpublished chapters.

12. Fox-Genovese, "To Write Myself," 172–76, offers an illuminating analysis of Hurston's re-creation as well as the importance of that writing in confronting gender realities. See also Spillers, "A Hateful Love, A Lost Passion," 191–96. The outpouring of writing by and about African American women signaled at long last the rightful recognition of black women's impact on the Afro-American cultural terrain. Useful summaries of their importance can be found in Fox-Genovese and Spillers, and in Henry Louis Gates, Jr., "Reclaiming Their Tradition," *New York Times Book Review*, October 8, 1987; Calvin C. Hernton, *The Sexual Mountain and Black Women Writers* (Garden City, N.Y.: Doubleday, 1987), especially chap. 2; and Charles Johnson, *Being and Race: Black Writing since 1970* (Bloomington: Indiana University Press, 1988), 94–118.

13. Nella Larsen was a mulatto whose writings might easily have been misinterpreted by whites. Deborah E. McDowell has done much to remedy

that situation in her introductions to the reprints of Nella Larsen's novels *Passing* and *Quicksand* (New Brunswick, N.J.: Rutgers University Press, 1986). Jesse Redmon Fauset was a member in good standing of the black bourgeoisie in Philadelphia and throughout her works offered a detailed study of that particular sector of AfroAmerica. It should be noted that Fauset wished her novels to be understood as stressing the commonalities of blacks and whites in America, thereby adding an important aspect to the idea of integrative cultural diversity. See Marion G. Starkey, "Jesse Fauset: An Interview," *Southern Workman* 61 (May 1932): 217–20.

14. See Hurston, *Dust Tracks on the Road*, chaps. 12, 15, and the appendix, "My People, My People"; Hernton, *The Sexual Mountain*, chap. 1.

15. As Dernoral Davis, a student of the great migration and its impact on both AfroAmerica and America, has told us, the great migration and the subsequent migration of the 1940s and 1950s would result by 1970 in African Americans being "more geographically diffused across the landscape than ever before. In general, they were less rural and southern." By 1970, African Americans were, in fact, an overwhelmingly urban populace. See Dernoral Davis, "Toward a Socio-Historical and Demographic Portrait of Twentieth Century African-Americans," in Alferdteen Harrison, ed., *Black Exodus: The Great Migration from the South* (Jackson: University Press of Mississippi, 1991), 13. See also Joe Trotter, ed., *The Great Migration in Historical Perspective: New Dimensions of Class, Race, and Gender* (Bloomington: Indiana University Press, 1991), for engaging and fresh approaches to the great migration. Davis's approach, however, takes us a long way toward beginning to understand how the urban culture so highly regarded as providing new forms of African American culture also becomes a deleterious haven for the "underclass" of the eighties and nineties in the wake of the departure of the black middle class. For a suggestive look at this occurrence, see Nicholas Lemann, *The Promised Land: The Great Black Migration and How It Changed America* (New York: Alfred A. Knopf, 1991).

16. David Levering Lewis, *When Harlem Was in Vogue*, 41–45, succinctly describes Garvey's career and the clash of his vision with the more integrative position preferred by many members of the black middle class. See also Wilson Jeremiah Moses, *The Golden Age of Black Nationalism, 1850–1925* (New York: Oxford University Press, 1988), 262–67. Moses's insightful analysis explains how Garvey bridged traditional black nationalism with a new black nationalism that saw its rise with the increasing urbanization of African Americans.

17. Hurston, *Dust Tracks on the Road*, chap. 10, details her explorations of black folklore. See also Hemenway, *Zora Neale Hurston*, chaps. 7–10.

18. Quoted in Lewis, *When Harlem Was in Vogue*, 69.

19. Granted, middle-class African Americans of the eighties and nineties still harbor an integrationist spirit. But they seem increasingly energized by the fear of losing a vital connection to their past and their racial identity. See Thomas Morgan, "The World Ahead: Black Parents Prepare Their Children for Pride and Prejudice," *New York Times Magazine*, October 27, 1985; "Black and White: How Integrated Is America?" *Newsweek*, March 7, 1988; and "Black Like Who?" *Village Voice*, special supplement, September 17, 1991.

20. In all of the novels that sketched the world of AfroAmerica this seemed to be the case. For examples, see Claude McKay, *Home to Harlem* (1925); Zora Neale Hurston, *Of Mules and Men* (1927); Jean Toomer, *Cane* (1923); and Langston Hughes, *Not without Laughter* (1930).

21. See Rampersad, *The Life of Langston Hughes*, vol. 1, chap. 1; Berry, *Langston Hughes*, chap. 1. For an analysis of the impact of black women on Hughes's life and his subsequent treatment of them in his writings, see Hernton, *The Sexual Mountain*, chap. 4.

22. See Hernton, *The Sexual Mountain*, 98–99.

23. Hurston, *Dust Tracks on the Road*, 200. See also Hemenway, *Zora Neale Hurston*, chaps. 6–8, for an elaboration of Hurston's discovery of black folklore and Cudjoe Lewis.

24. Hurston, *Dust Tracks on the Road*, 200.

25. See Michael G. Cooke, *Afro-American Literature in the Twentieth Century: The Achievement of Intimacy* (New Haven: Yale University Press, 1984), chaps. 1 and 5.

26. Despite the increasing attention awarded to black literature in the halls of academe and the literary canons, the political and social implications of that literature are often obscured by literary exegesis. This overshadowing (which began in the late seventies and proceeded rapidly throughout the eighties) is, I would suggest, a political and social result of the expansion of the black middle class during the sixties and early seventies, coupled with the transformation of black nationalist concerns by this enlarged black middle class into a "neonationalism" and the absorption of black intellectuals into the university and thus out of the public space. On the cooptation of black intellectuals into the academy, I am extrapolating from the argument presented by Russell Jacoby, *The Last Intellectuals: American Culture in the Age of Academe* (New York: Basic Books, 1987). Although Jacoby is remiss in failing to consider black intellectuals (especially W. E. B. Du Bois), his analysis can certainly be extended to include their situation. See also Charles Johnson, *Being and Race*, for some perceptive comments on this issue. On the canon and the importance of black literature to it, see Henry Louis Gates's suggestive and insightful essay, "The Master's Pieces: On Canon Formation and the

African-American Tradition," in his *Loose Canons: Notes on the Culture Wars* (New York: Oxford University Press, 1992), 17–42.

27. Schuyler's concerns were not that far removed from those of Jesse Redmon Fauset, for example, who wrote out of the gentility of black middle class Philadelphia. See Rampersad, *The Life of Langston Hughes*, 1:131. See also Gates, "A Fragmented Man."

28. Quoted in Rampersad, *The Life of Langston Hughes*, 1:131.

29. Quoted in ibid.

30. James Baldwin astutely observed that black writers of this period, however grateful they may have been for the discovery of black folks by whites, nonetheless had to be careful of "strangers bearing gifts." The "gifts" could be dangerously compromising. Baldwin made these observations as part of a 1988 PBS documentary, "Langston Hughes: The Dream Keeper," produced by George Huston Baker. For evidence of the constrictions that went along with white patronage, see Rampersad, *The Life of Langston Hughes*, vol. 1, chaps. 7 and 8; Hemenway, *Zora Neale Hurston*, chaps. 7–10; and Lewis, *When Harlem Was in Vogue*, chap. 5. The autobiographies of the writers of this period also contain pertinent information on this matter. On the status of black publishing in the eighties and nineties, see "Blacks and the Book World: A PW Special Report," *Publisher's Weekly*, January 20, 1992.

31. See Kellner, *The Harlem Renaissance*, 51–52.

32. Starkey, "Jesse Fauset: An Interview," 218, 219. See also Addison Gayle, Jr., *The Way of the New World: The Black Novel in America* (Garden City, N.Y.: Anchor/Doubleday, 1975), 114–19.

33. Gayle, *The Way of the New World*, 119. The concern with passing—which at times led Fauset to create some unfortunate racial stereotypes—has continued to bedevil both black and white authors writing about African Americans. The issue would reemerge in the late eighties and nineties to haunt the enlarged black middle class as its youth sought to reject integration as merely a method of "whitening up" in favor of an identification with the "hip-hop" street culture of inner-city black youth. For a description of the "hip-hop" cultural nationalist position, see Greg Tate, "Cult-Nats Meet Freaky-Deke," *Voice Literary Supplement*, December 1986. A rebuttal of that position can be found in Stanley Crouch, *Notes of a Hanging Judge: Essays and Reviews, 1979–1989* (New York: Oxford University Press, 1990), especially pp. 210–11.

34. Gayle, *The Way of the New World*, 148, 144.

35. Quoted in Lewis, *When Harlem Was in Vogue*, 186; see pp. 180–82 for a discussion of the reaction of the black middle class to Van Vechten's novel. See also Kellner, *The Harlem Renaissance*, 367–68.

36. Jean Toomer is an exception. Although he brilliantly portrayed AfroAmerica along much the same lines as did the other writers, he self-consciously eschewed any racial identification. See Lewis, *When Harlem Was in Vogue*, 58–74.

37. Quoted in Rampersad, *The Life of Langston Hughes*, 1:39–40.

38. See Hurston, *Dust Tracks on the Road*, chap. 6; William J. Cooper, *Sojourner of Truth: The Biography of Claude McKay* (Baton Rouge: Louisiana State University Press, 1987), chap. 1.

39. Richard Wright, *American Hunger* (New York: Harper & Row, 1974). The book was originally part of Wright's autobiography *Black Boy* (New York: Harper & Row, 1942) but was instead published separately nearly thirty years later. In 1991 Arnold Rampersad brought the two together in the Library of America edition *Native Son and American Hunger*. For a detailed examination of Wright by someone who was close to him, see Margaret Alexander Walker, *Richard Wright: Daemonic Genius* (New York: Amistad/Warner Books, 1988).

40. Wright, *American Hunger*, 13.

41. Richard Wright, "How Bigger Was Born," in *Native Son*, reprinted with introduction and afterword (New York: Harper & Row, 1966), xxiv.

42. For a look at hip-hop culture, see Greg Tate, *Flyboy in the Buttermilk: Essays on Contemporary America* (New York: Simon & Schuster, 1992); Michele Wallace, *Black Popular Culture: A Project by Michelle Wallace*, ed. Gina Dent (New York and Seattle: Dia Center for the Arts and Bay Press, 1992). For a discussion of urban black crime in the postindustrial nineties, see Elizabeth Fox-Genovese, "Race and Crime," *The World and I*, September 1992, 558–72.

43. Richard Wright, *Uncle Tom's Children* (New York: Harper & Row, 1940).

44. Ibid., 184. Subsequent page citations to this work appear in the text.

45. Ralph Ellison, "Remembering Richard Wright," in *Going to the Territory* (New York: Random House, 1986), 212. See also Walker, *Richard Wright: Daemonic Genius*, for some cogent insights into Wright's career after he left the Party.

46. See especially Ralph Ellison, *Shadow and Act* (New York: Random House, 1956) and, of course, *Invisible Man* (New York: Random House, 1952). A fine assessment of Ellison's work can be found in Cooke, *Afro-American Literature in the Twentieth Century*, chap. 4.

47. See also Chester Himes, *Quality of Pain* (New York: Random House, 1975)—one of the finest examples of black autobiography.

48. James Baldwin, "Many Thousands Gone," in *The Price of the Ticket: Collected Non-Fiction, 1948–1985* (New York: Random House, 1986), 66. This

collection is the best place to study the development of Baldwin's prophetic message. Subsequent page references to essays in this volume appear in the text.

49. For critical assessments of Baldwin's work, see Julius Lester, "James Baldwin: Reflections of a Maverick," *New York Times Book Review*, May 27, 1984; Julius Lester, "Some Tickets Are Better: The Mixed Achievements of James Baldwin," *Dissent* 33, no. 2 (Spring 1986): 189–93.

50. See Clayborne Carson, *In Struggle: SNCC and the Black Awakening of the Sixties* (Cambridge, Mass.: Harvard University Press, 1982), chaps. 15, 16, 18. See also Allen Matusow, *The Unraveling of America: A History of Liberalism in the 1960s* (New York: Harper & Row, 1984), 350, 353; and Michael Thelwell, "Fish Are Jumping and the Cotton Is High: Notes from the Mississippi Delta," in Michael Thelwell, *Duties, Pleasures, and Conflicts: Essays in Struggle* (Amherst: University of Massachusetts Press, 1987), 74–87.

51. Carson, *In Struggle*, 1–5.

52. This was the tactic of the New Right during the Reagan-Bush years. The irony lies in the fact that Reagan and many of the conservatives in or out of high office were vigorously opposed to the civil rights movement and the idea of a "color-blind" society.

53. For an interesting summary and critique of the black aesthetic, see Cooke, *Afro-American Literature in the Twentieth Century*, chaps. 4 and 5; Johnson, *Being and Race* chap. 1; and David L. Smith, "The Black Arts Movement and Its Critics," *American Literary History* 3, no. 1 (Spring 1991): 93–110. On the SNCC and its influence, see Clayborne Carson, *In Struggle*.

The writers mentioned in the text have all been, in one way or another, on the cutting edge of black writing. See, for example, Alice Walker, *Meridian* (New York: Harcourt, Brace, Jovanovich, 1975); *The Third Life of Grange Copeland* (New York: Harcourt, Brace, Jovanovich, 1976); and *In My Mother's Garden* (New York: Harcourt, Brace, Jovanovish, 1984), a collection of essays. For June Jordan, see her *Civil Wars* (Boston: Beacon Press, 1976), as well as, for a sample of her poetry, *Some Changes* (New York: Dutton, 1970). Michael Thelwell has collected his essays and fiction from this period in *Duties, Pleasures, and Conflicts*. Julius Lester was equally prolific. For an example of his fiction, see *Do Lord Remember Me* (New York: Holt, Rinehart & Winston, 1985), and, for his nonfiction, *All Is Well* (New York: William Morrow, 1976); *Lovesong: On Becoming a Jew* (New York: Henry Holt, 1988); and *Falling Pieces of the Broken Sky* (New York: Arcade Press, 1990).

54. See Johnson, *Being and Race*, 26–29. See also Amiri Baraka, *Autobiography* (New York: William Morrow, 1987).

55. John A. Williams, *The Man Who Cried I Am* (New York: Bantam, 1965; repr. New York: Thunder's Mouth Press, 1990).

56. See Carson, *In Struggle*, especially chaps. 9 and 10; and Julius Lester, "The Current State of Black America," *New Politics* (June 1973): 4–13. The phrase "integrate into a burning house" can be found in James Baldwin's "The Fire Next Time," in *The Price of the Ticket*, and is often attributed to Malcolm X.

57. See Lewis, *When Harlem Was in Vogue*; and Moses, *Golden Age of Black Nationalism*. On Du Bois, see Gerald Horne, *In Red and Black: W. E. B. Du Bois and the Peace Movement* (Albany: SUNY Press, 1986), chaps. 1–5.

58. See Hemenway, *Zora Neale Hurston*. On the views of black males toward black women in the civil rights movement, see Michele Wallace, *Black Macho and the Myth of the Black Superwoman* (New York: William Morrow, 1978). See also her essay "Who Dat Say Who Dat: Zora Neale Hurston Then and Now," *Voice Literary Supplement* no. 64 (April 1988), 18–21, for an examination of feminist thought on Hurston.

59. Johnson, *Being and Race*, 12.

60. For more on these novels, see ibid., chap. 5.

61. For a survey of this controversy, see Mel Watkins, "Sexism, Racism, and Black Women Writers," *New York Times Book Review*, June 15, 1986.

62. For examples of how African Americans were represented in Hollywood film, see Thomas Cripps's extensive study *Slow Fade to Black* (New York: Oxford University Press, 1976); and Donald Bogle, *Toms, Coons, Mulattoes, Bucks, and Mammies* (New York: Viking Press, 1973). Cecil Brown, a black novelist and screenwriter, has written a novel about blacks in Hollywood, *Days without Weather* (New York: Farrar, Straus & Giroux, 1983). While this work is by no means flawless, Brown did possess an eerie prescience about what was to evolve regarding African Americans in the film industry. I will examine the challenges blacks have made to this medium in chapter 6.

63. See, for example, Houston A. Baker, Jr., *The Journey Back: Issues in Black Literature and Criticism* (Chicago: University of Chicago Press, 1982), as well as his *Modernism and the Harlem Renaissance*; Gates, *The Signifying Monkey*; Spillers, "A Hateful Passion, A Lost Love"; and Hazel V. Carby, *Reconstructing Womanhood: The Emergence of the Afro-American Woman Novelist* (New York: Oxford University Press, 1987).

64. Compare, for example, the title story, "Hue and Cry," with almost any of the vignettes in Naylor's book. Naylor produced a more didactic novel, *Linden Hills* (1986), which borrowed heavily from Dante's *Inferno* as it explored the black middle class. Her most recent book, *Mama Day* (1988), found Naylor trying to bridge African American storytelling with an academic sensibility, by drawing on the oral storytelling traditions of rural African Americans but within the canon of academic literature.

65. Charles Johnson has written excellent discussions of Clarence Major and Ishmael Reed; see *Being and Race*, 58–63, 64–67. A discussion of intimacy can be found in Cooke, *Afro-American Literature in the Twentieth Century*, chap. 7.

66. See Johnson, *Being and Race*, 102–3; Cooke, *Afro-American Literature in the Twentieth Century*, 141–42, 151. Morrison has continued to shower us with her literary gifts. In 1987 she wrote a Pulitzer Prize–winning novel, *Beloved*, that explored the devastating effects of slavery on African Americans. In 1992 Morrison demonstrated once again the blending of this new black literary aesthetic in her novel about the Harlem Renaissance, *Jazz*, and offered a provocative series of essays on the black presence in American literature that formed the William Massey Lectures at Harvard University. See Toni Morrison, *Playing in the Dark: Whiteness and Literary Imagination* (Cambridge, Mass.: Harvard University Press, 1992).

67. Charles Johnson, *The Oxherding Tale* (New York: Grove Press, 1982), 118–19. Subsequent page references appear in the text.

68. See Johnson, *Being and Race*, chap. 1. See also Charles Davis and Henry Louis Gates, Jr., *The Slave's Narrative* (New York: Oxford University Press, 1984), for analyses of slave narratives and their importance to American literature.

69. There is one interesting exception to my characterization of the tragic mulatto genre, namely, James Weldon Johnson's intricate novel of 1912 (republished in 1927), *Autobiography of An Ex-Coloured Man* (repr. New York: Vintage Press, 1990). This race-conscious novel was a masterful attempt not only to explain the black world to white Americans but also to issue a clear warning to the black middle class to take pride in and preserve their heritage, even as they struggle for inclusion into the mainstream of American society. Previously, the black take on the "tragic mulatto" had chiefly attempted to debunk white characterizations of mulattoes as hopelessly marginalized, even psychotic. Situating his mulatto character within a sociopolitical context, Johnson pushed the genre further, aiming to provide, by way of negative example, a means by which African Americans in the middle class could present a positive case for integrative cultural diversity.

70. *Middle Passage* (New York: Atheneum, 1990). Johnson won the 1991 National Book Award for this novel.

71. It should be noted that the same could be said for Native Americans and Latinos. Johnson's work, as well as that of Toni Morrison and others, makes clear the close relations of Native Americans and African Americans, a theme that can also be traced throughout black autobiographies. See, for example, Rampersad, *The Life of Langston Hughes*, vol. 1, chaps. 1 and 2; and Ralph Ellison, *Going to the Territory*.

72. The present discussion is based on reflections culled from Lester's two autobiographical works, *All Is Well* and *Lovesong: On Becoming a Jew*. Although the first work is both vastly underrated and often misunderstood, it is probably the best example of black autobiography of the period. *Lovesong* contains condensed versions of *All Is Well* but is more a sequel than an updating. Both works, however, contain a wealth of insights into the struggle and journey of an African American who has lived his life resisting societally imposed definitions of race, gender, and class.

73. Lester, *Lovesong*, 69. For examples of Lester's critique of the movement, see *Revolutionary Notes* (New York: Grove Press, 1969). Recent assessments of the movement by Lester can be found in his collection of essays, *Falling Pieces of the Broken Sky*, especially the section entitled "Race."

74. Julius Lester, "The Valley of the Shadow of Death," in Mel Watkins, ed., *Black Review 2* (New York: William Morrow, 1972), 109–36.

75. Lester, *Do Lord Remember Me*, 142. See also Julius Lester, "The Ram's Horn," *Massachusetts Review* 13 (Fall 1972), for a study of the effects of the early sit-in movement on southern middle-class blacks.

76. See Cornel West, "The Paradox of the Afro-American Rebellion," in Fredric Jameson et al., eds., *The 60's without Apology* (Minneapolis: University of Minnesota Press, 1984), 44–59.

CHAPTER 5: Sound and Image

1. William L. O'Neill, *Coming Apart: An Informal History of the 1960's* (New York: Times Mirror, 1971), chap. 8, is an excellent example of the historical treatment given this period.

2. For the history of black music and its connection to rock and roll, see Lawrence Levine, *Black Culture and Black Consciousness: Afro-American Folk Thought from Slavery to Freedom* (New York: Oxford University Press, 1977), chap. 4; Robert Palmer, *Deep Blues: A Musical and Cultural History of the Mississippi Delta* (New York: Penguin, 1981); Michael Bane, *White Boy Singin' the Blues: The Black Roots of White Rock* (New York: Penguin, 1982; repr. New York: Ivan Dee, 1992), 21–42; and Carl Boggs, "The Blues Tradition: From Poetic Revolt to Cultural Impasse," *Socialist Review* 34 (1975): 115–39.

3. On the blues, see Simon Frith, *Sound Effects: Youth, Leisure, and the Politics of Rock and Roll* (New York: Vintage, 1981), chap. 2; Levine, *Black Culture*, chap. 4; Boggs, "The Blues Tradition," 115–17.

4. Boggs, "The Blues Tradition," 117–18; see also Levine, *Black Culture*, chaps. 1–4. On sinful tunes, see Dena Epstein, *Sinful Tunes and Spirituals: Black Folk Music to the Civil War* (Urbana: University of Illinois Press, 1977).

5. See Robert C. Toll, *Blacking Up: The Minstrel Show in Nineteenth-*

Century America (New York: Oxford University Press, 1974), chaps. 1–3; Palmer, *Deep Blues*, 23–36; Levine, *Black Culture*, chaps. 1–4; Boggs, "The Blues Tradition," 117–18; and Bane, *White Boy Singin' the Blues*, chap. 1. On the role of the minstrel show in identity formation for whites, see David Roediger, *The Wages of Whiteness: Race and the Making of the American Working Class* (London and New York: Verso, 1991).

6. Boggs, "The Blues Tradition," 118. See also Imamu Amiri Baraka (Leroi Jones), *Blues People: The Negro Experience in White America and the Music That Developed from It* (New York: Grove Press, 1963), chaps. 2–7.

7. Quoted in Levine, *Black Culture*, 212.

8. Quoted in ibid., 243.

9. See Baraka, *Blues People*, chap. 8.

10. David Levering Lewis, *When Harlem Was in Vogue* (New York: Alfred A. Knopf, 1981), 5.

11. See Palmer, *Deep Blues*, 106; Boggs, "The Blues Tradition," 119.

12. See James O. Young, *Black Writers of the Thirties* (Baton Rouge: Louisiana State University Press, 1973), 147–48; and Lewis, *When Harlem Was in Vogue*, 173, on the disdain of the older black middle class.

13. See Bane, *White Boy Singin' the Blues*, 98–101; Baraka, *Blues People*, 218–20.

14. Baraka, *Blues People*, 169.

15. Frith, *Sound Effects*, 22–24.

16. See Bane, *White Boy Singin' the Blues*, 127–39. For a very fine analysis of the Presley phenomenon and the influence exerted by the blues, see Greil Marcus, *Mystery Train: Images of America in Rock 'n' Roll*, new ed. (New York: Penguin, 1982), 141–211.

17. On the early roots of the civil rights movement, see Harvard Sitkoff, *The Struggle for Black Equality, 1954–1992*, rev. ed. (New York: Hill and Wang, 1993), chap. 1; and Michael Namarato, ed., *Have We Overcome?* (Jackson: University Press of Mississippi, 1981). Two works indispensable to anyone studying rock history and its black roots are the lavishly illustrated text by Guy Peellaert and Nik Cohn, *Rock Dreams: Rock 'n' Roll for Your Eyes* (New York: Harmony, 1982), and Jon Pareles and Patricia Romanowski, eds., *The Rolling Stone Encyclopedia of Rock and Roll* (New York: Harmony, 1983). I am indebted to these texts for detailed facts and "memory refreshment." See also Bane, *White Boy Singin' the Blues*. Finally, for an excellent analysis of the sexual anguish and attempts at the repression of rock music in the 1950s and 1960s, see Steven Siedman, *Embattled Eros: Sexual Politics and Ethics in Contemporary America* (New York: Routledge, 1992), chaps. 1 and 2.

18. Lee Cooper, "Popular Music: An Untapped Resource for Teaching Contemporary Black Music," *Journal of Negro Education* 48, no. 1 (Winter

1979): 20–36. See also R. Serge Denisoff, *Solid Gold: The Popular Record Industry* (New York: Routledge, 1975), chap. 8.

19. An excellent biography of Pete Seeger is David Dunaway, *How Can I Keep from Singing?* (New York: Pantheon, 1982). Seeger, a true cultural hero, has consistently and continually sung the praises of the blues and of Afro-American folk music.

20. See Julius Lester, "The Freedom Singers," *Broadside*, no. 52 (November 20, 1964), 7. The names of the original singers were Cordell Reagon, Rutna Harris, Chuck Neglett, and Bernice Johnson. In 1964 Matthew and Marshall Jones, Emory Harris, and Rafael Bentham joined, after Cordell Reagon, Rutna Harris, and Bernice Johnson left. Rutna Harris and Bernice Johnson would later form a powerful women's folk music group, Sweet Honey in the Rock, whose concerts are still very well attended.

21. Lester, "Freedom Singers," 9. For the historical context surrounding the Freedom Singers, see Clayborne Carson's *In Struggle: SNCC and the Black Awakening in the Sixties* (Cambridge, Mass.: Harvard University Press, 1981).

22. In the mid-seventies this era and its music were immortalized in George Lucas's *American Grafitti* (Universal, 1974), a nostalgic—and commercially successful—film with a distinctly pre-Beatles soundtrack. For those wishing to study this period or any period in rock history, rock documentaries are a very rich source. For a fine listing, see Pareles and Romanowski, eds., *Rolling Stone Encyclopedia of Rock and Roll*, 188–89.

23. On Motown, see Bane, *White Boy Singin' the Blues*, 62–172. See also Peter Benjaminson, *The Story of Motown* (New York: Viking, 1976); and Nelson George, *Where Did Our Love Go? The Rise and Fall of Motown* (New York: Crown, 1987).

24. See Pareles and Romanowski, eds., *Rolling Stone Encyclopedia of Rock and Roll*, 32–35; Peellaert and Cohn, *Rock Dreams*. There are numerous biographies of the Beatles. See, for example, Peter Brown and Steven Gaines, *The Love You Make: An Insider's Story of the Beatles*, (New York: Simon & Schuster, 1983). The standard and, many say, the best treatment is Hunter Davies, *The Beatles* (New York: McGraw-Hill, 1978). Davies book, however, is unfortunately no longer in print.

25. See Brown and Gaines, *The Love You Make*, chaps. 1–3. The best interpretive biography of Jimi Hendrix is David Henderson, *Jimi Hendrix: Voodoo Child of the Aquarian Age* (Garden City, N.Y.: Doubleday, 1979), republished in a condensed and revised edition as *'Scuse Me While I Kiss the Sky: The Life of Jimi Hendrix* (New York: Bantam Books, 1983). I have used the original, more detailed version. For another recent interpretive analysis that situates Hendrix within the rock movement and black music, see Charles Shaar Mur-

ray, *Crosstown Traffic: Jimi Hendrix and the Rock 'n' Roll Revolution* (New York: St Martin's Press, 1989). This book is an excellent complement to Henderson's.

26. Julius Lester, *Search for the New Land* (New York: Dial Press, 1969), 113. See also Brown and Gaines, *The Love You Make*, chaps. 12 and 13.

27. See Carson, *In Struggle*, chaps. 6–8. See also Julius Lester, *All Is Well* (New York: William Morrow, 1976), for a sensitive and highly underrated insider's view of those turbulent times.

28. See Henderson, *Jimi Hendrix*, chap. 4.

29. On rock guitar and its links to the blues, see Palmer, *Deep Blues*, chaps. 1–4; Frith, *Sound Effects*, chap. 4; and Henderson, *Jimi Hendrix*, chaps. 1 and 2.

30. For more on the Monterey Pop Festival and these artists, see Henderson, *Jimi Hendrix*, chaps. 6–8; Bane, *White Boy Singin' the Blues*, chap. 5.

31. See Henderson, *Jimi Hendrix*, chap. 9 and coda; Julius Lester, "Jimi Hendrix: Going towards Heaven," *Evergreen Review*, November 1970.

32. Mary Wells of the Supremes, for example, performed with Rolling Stones and James Cotton with the Grateful Dead, and Bo Diddley was on the same bill as the Jefferson Airplane at the Fillmore Auditorium in San Francisco. I am grateful to Steve Soiffer for sharing this information with me.

33. See Todd Gitlin, *The Whole World Is Watching* (New York: Simon & Schuster, 1979), and *The Sixties: Years of Hope, Days of Rage* (New York: Bantam, 1987), chaps. 10–13. For the political significance of soul music, see Portia K. Maultsby, "Soul Music: Its Sociological and Political Significance in American Popular Culture," *Journal of Popular Culture* 17, no. 2 (Fall 1983): 51–61.

34. See Julius Lester, *Revolutionary Notes* (New York: Grove Press, 1970) for examples of trenchant criticism of the movement at that time. Excellent assessments of this ongoing self-criticism can be found in Abe Peck, *Uncovering the Sixties: The Life and Times of the Underground Press* (New York: Pantheon, 1985), and in Todd Gitlin, *The Sixties*.

35. On the "softness" and "hardness" of Afrocentricity, see the perceptive analysis by Robert Elliot Fox, "Afrocentrism and the X Factor," *Transition* 57, 17–25.

36. The most stinging indictment of the narcissistic self-absorption of the 1970s is Christopher Lasch's *The Culture of Narcissism: American Life in an Age of Diminishing Expectations* (New York: W. W. Norton, 1979).

37. An excellent introduction to reggae is James A. Winders, "Reggae, Rastafarian, and Revolution," *Journal of Popular Culture* 17, no. 1 (Summer 1983): 61–73.

38. Ibid., 69–71. On Marley, see especially Timothy White, *Catch a Fire: The Life of Bob Marley* (New York: Crown, 1983). In many ways equally useful is Jon Weiner's review of *Catch a Fire* in the *New York Times Book Review*, August 14, 1983. It is also worth noting that UB40 was an integrated group that did songs of sixties' groups and singers, both black and white, as, for example, on their album *Labour of Love II* (Virgin Records, 1989), a recording that did not get significant airplay in the United States until the early 1990s.

39. The rock critics referred to here were influenced by the civil rights movement and the counterculture. They include the late Lester Bangs, Steve Simmels, Jon Pareles, David Marsh, Greil Marcus, Stephen Holden, Robert Palmer, and Robert Christgau. Their writings can be found in major newspapers such as the *New York Times*, in record industry trade magazines and teen fanzines, and in journals such as *Rolling Stone* and the *Village Voice*.

40. See Denisoff, *Solid Gold*, chap. 5, on which much of the following discussion is based. See also Bane, *White Boy Singin' the Blues*, 90–103.

41. See Bane, *White Boy Singin' the Blues*, 226–40; see also Frith, *Sound Effects*, 61–181.

42. An excellent analysis of corporate rock is Bill Flanagan and Jock Baird, "The Failure of Corporate Rock," *Musician*, no. 50 (December 1982): 72–80; see especially pp. 73–77, on narrowcasting.

43. See ibid. See also "New Rock on a Red Hot Roll," *Time*, July 18, 1983; and "Britain Rocks America—Again," *Newsweek*, January 23, 1984. A full-scale study that synthesizes a wide range of material regarding the record industry's slump and resurrection is Robert Christgau, "Rock 'n' Roller Coaster: The Music Biz on a Joyride," *Village Voice*, February 7, 1984.

44. In "The Failure of Corporate Rock," Flanagan and Baird offered Warner Communications Records executive Karin Berg an opportunity to present a manager's view of the rock music industry ("The Live Music Antidote"). As Berg put it, "In the 60's, live music and the audience were the center of the industry. FM radio reflected the taste developed by America and what we heard at clubs and in concerts. . . . The record company took the initiative from the musicians" (75). Berg went on to lament the decline in live music, owing in part to the ambience of coffee houses, clubs, and halls like San Francisco's Fillmore, where young people went "for their own conversation." Berg also cited the raised drinking age in most states as one reason for the loss of an audience for new musical groups and called for nonalcoholic clubs that would feature new groups (presumably nurtured in corporate record incubators) designed to appeal to a "knowledgeable audience."

Apparently, Berg did not want to acknowledge the popularity of the "new wave" clubs that existed in Los Angeles, San Francisco, and numerous other cities or the fact that California had always had a higher drinking age (even in the sixties). Young people have always sought out music, whether live or on the radio; the inherently rebellious nature of rock and roll, and unfamiliar forms of Afro-American music, beckoned to the young then and now.

45. Steven Levy, "Inside MTV: The Selling Out of Rock & Roll," *Rolling Stone*, December 8, 1983. The present discussion relies heavily on Levy's insightful analysis.

46. "Black Cable Channel's Wild Ride," *New York Times*, June 1, 1992.

47. Quoted in Levy, "Inside MTV," 37.

48. There have been reams of press written about Prince and Madonna. Most of it for an adulatory and hyperbolic nature.

Even in the academic world the force of Madonna has caused a division among scholars that has often gone from the sublime to the silly. Some examples of the writing on these two artists can be found in Lynn Hirschberg, "The Misfit," *Vanity Fair* (April 1991), 158–168, 196–202 for Madonna; on Prince see Debby Miller, "Prince," *Rolling Stone*, April 23, 1983, 18–23, 73 and Kurt Loder, "Prince Reigns," *Rolling Stone*, August 30, 1984, 16–21, 46–47. An interesting survey and critique of academic analyses of Madonna can be found in Daniel Harris, "Make My Rainy Day," *Nation*, June 8, 1992, 790–3.

49. For an introduction to NWA, the album *Straight Outta Compton* (1988) is worth hearing. Public Enemy's best album is probably *Fear of a Black Planet* (1990), which gives the listener a good idea of the group's philosophy and politics. For an interesting commentary on West Coast rap groups and the messages in their songs, see Robin D. G. Kelley, "Straight from Underground," *Nation*, June 8, 1992. On the increased tensions between blacks and Jews in the eighties, see Jonathan Kauffman, *Broken Alliance: The Turbulent Times between Blacks and Jews in America* (New York: Scribner, 1988).

50. Julius Lester, "Race and Revolution," *Black Review*, No. 1 (New York: William Morrow and Company, 1971), 68–86.

51. Talking Heads, *The Name of This Band Is Talking Heads* (Sire Records, 1982) contains "Life during Wartime." "Swamp" can be found on their album *Speaking in Tongues* (Sire Records, 1983).

CHAPTER 6: Changing the Guard

1. See Christopher Lasch, *The Minimal Self: Psychic Survival in Troubled Times* (New York: W. W. Norton, 1984), and *The True and Only Heaven: Progress and Its Critics* (New York: W. W. Norton, 1991), chaps. 10 and 11, for an examination of this generation from a social and critical standpoint. See also Stuart Ewen, *All Consuming Images: The Politics of Style in Contemporary Culture* (New York: Basic Books, 1988).

2. Senator Edward Brooke (R) of Massachusetts left office in the mid-seventies; he was succeeded by Paul Tsongas. Carol Moseley-Braun (D.-Ill.) became the first black senator since Brooke and the first African American woman senator ever.

3. As I write, the debate about the Hill-Thomas controversy continues. Its political fallout, now that Thomas is a Supreme Court Justice, has already been felt in at least two areas: the issue of abortion—specifically, whether the Court will either undermine or completely overturn *Roe v. Wade* (1972)—and the 1992 elections, in which the anger of women over the appointment of Thomas and the behavior of senators on the Senate Judiciary Committee translated into more women being voted into political office. One particular outcome in that direction was the win of Carol Moseley-Braun of Chicago, a black woman, for the U.S. Senate seat of Al Dixon, a senior senator who supported Thomas. For commentaries on the Hill-Thomas affair, see the symposium "The Ongoing Struggle over Clarence Thomas," *Reconstruction* 1, no. 4 (1992): 58–77; and Courtney Leatherman, "Panel's Handling of Allegations against Thomas Brings Angry Response from Women in Academe," *Chronicle of Higher Education*, October 16, 1991. See also Toni Morrison, ed., *De-Racing Justice* (New York: Vintage, 1992), which contains extended critical analyses of the Hill-Thomas affair by African American intellectuals.

4. See "Blacks on the Rise in Business," *USA Today*, October 9, 1985; "Top 100 Black Businesses," *Black Enterprise*, May 1992; and *Black Issues in Higher Education*, March 5, 1989.

5. "Racial Divisions between Races Persist," *New York Times*, June 27, 1990. Although the white fear of straying into black neighborhoods is familiar, the knife cuts both ways. On the Howard Beach case of 1986, see Robert Weisbrot, *Freedom Bound: A History of America's Civil Rights Movement* (New York: W. W. Norton, 1990), 307. The August 1989 slaying of Yusef Hawkins in the Bensonhurst section of Brooklyn, widely covered in New York newspapers, was the basis for Spike Lee's movie, *Jungle Fever*.

6. For a sampling of the relevant census figures, see *USA Today*, January 18, 1988, and August 8, 1988; see also William P. O'Hare et al., eds., *African Americans in the Nineties* (Washington, D.C.: Population Reference Bureau, 1991).

7. See Cornel West, "Afro-America and Post-Modernism," *Zeta* 13, no. 4 (June 1988): 28.

8. Motion pictures, of course, had not always been so formulaic. In the beginning, the industry revealed a great deal of potential for innovation and creativity, even for the shaping of cultural attitudes. However, the combination of censorship, the desire for profits, and strong political pressure pulled

the reins in on the drive toward artistry. See Robert Sklar, *Movie-Made America* (New York: Harper & Row, 1975). That television presented the movies with a formidable rival is well known. See Erik Barnouw, *Tube of Plenty* (New York: Oxford University Press, 1973), for a fine history of that medium. For a fascinating dialectical approach to understanding television, see Elayne Rapping, *Through a Looking Glass: Non-Fiction Television* (Boston: South End Press, 1987). Much of my analysis has been influenced by her persuasive argument. On blacks in television, see Joanmarie Kalber, "Yes, There Are More Blacks on TV, But Mostly to Make People Laugh," *TV Guide*, August 13, 1988.

9. Oscar Micheaux was the preeminent black filmmaker of his day, and some of the racial themes he dealt with have been taken up by Spike Lee. For more on Micheaux, see Thomas Cripps, *Slow Fade to Black: The Negro in American Film, 1900–1942* (New York: Oxford University Press, 1977), chaps. 7 and 12. See also Cripps's *Making Movies Black: The Hollywood Message Movie from World War II to the Civil Rights Era* (New York: Oxford University Press, 1993), 146–47.

10. See Thomas Morgan, "The World Ahead," *New York Times Magazine*, October 25, 1985; and David Bradley, "Portrait of a Small Black Church," *New York Times Magazine*, June 30, 1985.

11. "Eyes on the Prize," Blackside Productions, 1986; the sequel appeared in 1989. On Dash, see Greg Tate, "Favorite Daughters: Julia Dash Films Gullah Country," *Village Voice*, April 12, 1988. Dash's film was released to the general public in 1991. See also the conversation of Julia Dash with Houston A. Baker, Jr., "Not without My Daughters," *Transition* 57, 150–66.

12. See Sut Jhally and Justin Lewis, *Enlightened Racism: The Cosby Show, Audiences, and the Myth of the American Dream* (Boulder, Colo.: Westview, 1992), who make arguments similar to mine.

13. Pryor's use of social commentary in his comedy routines was not original, of course. The tradition began more or less with Lenny Bruce, who is still acknowledged as the master of the form. Lily Tomlin, a friend of Pryor's, later became famous using a similar approach.

14. On Richard Pryor's comedy and his problems with Hollywood, as well as for a general overview, see the excellent article by Cecil Brown, "Blues for Blacks in Hollywood," *Mother Jones*, January 1981. Much more has been written since that time, including a sympathetic biography of Pryor by John Williams and son. A perceptive article about the recent rise of Afro-American comedians is Gerri Hershey, "The Black Pack," *Vanity Fair*, July 1988.

15. Murphy was interviewed on Oprah Winfrey's daytime talk show in 1987. It should be noted that for many years Winfrey operated in the tradition of the older black middle class ethic: her show was service-oriented and

tried to promote fairness, social justice, and racial harmony. Given the proliferation of talk shows in the late eighties, though, it was often necessary to
compromise principles in the interest of attaining ratings and advertising
revenue. Hence Oprah Winfrey, notwithstanding her admirable contributions in presenting positive images of AfroAmerica to the nation, "accommodated" to the system, at least to some extent, featuring her share of sensationalistic guests discussing their bizarre problems. As for Murphy's stance
on interracial marriage and dating, similar sentiments were expressed by
Spike Lee in interviews about his movie "Jungle Fever." See, for example,
"Interview: Henry Louis Gates, Jr., with Spike Lee," *Transition* 52 (1991):
125–35.

16. St. Clair Bourne, "Bright Moments," *Zeta* 14, no. 3 (March 1989): 40–
41.

17. The Nike commercial, captioned "This Is Spikes's House," was set in
an inner-city basketball lot that was designed in multiple colors, presumably
meant to represent cultural diversity. Likewise, the 501 jeans commercial was
given an ethnically diverse setting at San Francisco's Fisherman's Wharf. The
effect—much like that of the "United Colors of Benetton" ad campaign—
was to offer a vision of a multiethnic and multicultural America.

18. Lee's political proclivities were evident as well in the name of his production company: "Forty Acres and a Mule," a direct reference to the
reneged-upon Reconstruction promise of the Freedman's Bureau. As of this
writing Lee had recently completed a cinematic biography of Malcolm X,
which opened to critical acclaim on November 18, 1992. Although it was not a
runaway hit, its star, Denzel Washington, did garner an Oscar nomination
for Best Actor. Further, the film ensured that critical commentary on Malcolm X would continue. In fact, the controversy that surrounded the film
revealed the continuing tensions within the black middle class over the interpretation of Malcolm X and how he should be represented to AfroAmerica
and America at large. See Playthell Benjamin, "Bearing the Cross: Spike Lee
Films a Life of Malcolm X," *Emerge*, November 1991; see also "By Any
Reviews Necessary: A Symposium on 'Malcolm X,'" *Cineaste* 19, no 4: 5–24.

19. See Angela Mitchell, "Sex, Aids, and Responsible Behavior: How
Magic Johnson Put a New Focus on These Issues in Black America," *Emerge*,
March 1992.

20. On the issue of political correctness in the nineties, see Paul Berman,
ed., *Debating PC: The Debate over Political Correctness on College Campuses
Today* (New York: Bantam, 1992); and Patricia Aufderheide, ed., *Beyond PC:
Towards a Politics of Understanding* (St. Paul, Minn.: Graywolf Press, 1992).
On Afrocentricity, see Michael Eric Dyson, "Melanin Madness," *Emerge*,
February 1992. See also Henry Louis Gates, Jr., "African-American Studies in

the Twenty-first Century," in his *Loose Canons: Notes on the Culture Wars* (New York: Oxford University Press, 1992), 121–27.

21. For an interesting look at how African American middle-class professionals are approaching this task, see David J. Dent "The New Black Suburbs," *New York Times Magazine*, June 14, 1992.

22. *Ebony*, August 1985, a special issue devoted to "Black America in the Year 2000." The lack of concern about drug abuse and racial discrimination demonstrated the palpable effects of integration on the black middle class: drug abuse and overt racial discrimination apparently were perceived as problems facing the lower and underclass. Many of the respondents (68 percent) were also of the opinion that interracial marriages would increase. Compare, however, the results of this poll with the attitudes expressed by the black middle class residents of Prince Georges County, Maryland, in Dent, "The New Black Suburbs."

23. Rayford Logan, ed., *What the Negro Wants* (Chapel Hill: University of North Carolina Press, 1944); Gunnar Myrdal, *An American Dilemma: The Negro Problem and Modern Democracy*, 2 vols. (New York: Pantheon, 1972 [1944]). Page references to *What the Negro Wants* henceforth appear in the text.

24. To get the full effect of déjà vu with regard to the neoracist attitudes of the eighties, however, one really has to read the publisher's introduction by W. T. Couch. In an extended critique of Myrdal's massive study, Couch presents a southern moderate's polished and gentlemanly attempt to refute that study's call for integration on all levels. His main point is that cultural relativism is an error and that racism ("race prejudice") cannot be blamed for Afro-Americans' ills. His final statement perhaps best sums up his position: "Booker T. Washington came nearer than anyone else to stating the problem of the Negro in its true terms. . . . Nothing is more needed in the South today than rebirth of his ideas, restoration of the great leadership that he was giving" (xxii). See also Gerald Early, ed., *Lure and Loathing: Essays on Race, Identity, and the Ambivalence of Assimilation* (New York: Allan Lane, 1993), which, even though it deals specifically with Du Bois's double-consciousness theory, is an excellent updating of the Logan volume.

Selected Bibliography

Allen, Robert L. *Black Awakening in Capitalist America*. New York: Doubleday, 1972.

Anderson, Alan B., and George W. Pickering. *Confronting the Color Line: The Broken Promise of the Civil Rights Movement in Chicago*. Athens: University of Georgia Press, 1986.

Anderson, James D. *The Education of Black Folks in the South, 1860–1935*. Chapel Hill: University of North Carolina Press, 1989.

Appiah, Kwame Anthony. *In My Father's House: Africa in the Philosophy of Culture*. New York: Oxford University Press, 1992.

Asante, Molei Kete. *The Afrocentric Idea*. Philadelphia: Temple University Press, 1987.

Baker, Houston A. *Modernism and the Harlem Renaissance*. Chicago: University of Chicago Press, 1987.

———. *Afro-American Poetics: Revisions of Harlem and the Black Aesthetic*. Madison: University of Wisconsin Press, 1990.

Baldwin, James. *The Price of the Ticket: Collected Non-Fiction, 1948–1985*. New York: Random House, 1986.

Bane, Michael. *White Boy Singin' the Blues: The Black Roots of White Rock*. New York: Penguin Press, 1982; repr. New York: Ivan Dee, 1992.

Banner-Haley, Charles Pete T. *To Do Good and To Do Well: Middle Class Blacks and the Depression, Philadelphia, 1929–1941*. New York: Garland Publishing, 1993.

Baraka, Imamu Amiri (Leroi Jones). *Blues People: The Negro Experience in White America and the Music That Developed from It*. New York: Grove Press, 1963.

Barnouw, Erik. *Tube of Plenty*. New York: Oxford University Press, 1973.

Bell, Derrick. *And We Are Not Saved: The Elusive Quest for Racial Justice*. New York: Basic Books, 1987.

———. *Faces at the Bottom of the Well: The Permanence of Racism*. New York: Basic Books, 1992.

Bellah, Robert, et al. *Habits of the Heart: Individualism and Commitment in American Life*. Berkeley: University of California Press, 1985.

Berry, Faith. *Langston Hughes: Before and Beyond Harlem*. Westport, Conn.: Lawrence Hill, 1983.

Blassingame, John. *Black New Orleans*. Chicago: University of Chicago Press, 1972.

Bogle, Donald. *Toms, Coons, Mulattoes, Bucks, and Mammies*. New York: Viking Press, 1973.

Branch, Taylor. *Parting the Waters: America in the King Years, 1954–63*. New York: Simon & Schuster, 1988.

Brooks, Roy L. *Rethinking the American Race Problem*. Berkeley: University of California Press, 1990.

Buni, Andrew. *Robert L. Vann of the Pittsburgh Courier: Politics and Black Journalism*. Pittsburgh: University of Pittsburgh Press, 1974.

Carby, Hazel. *Reconstructing Womanhood: The Emergence of the Afro-American Woman Novelist*. New York: Oxford University Press, 1987.

Carson, Clayborne. *In Struggle: SNCC and the Black Awakening in the Sixties*. Cambridge, Mass.: Harvard University Press, 1981.

Carter, Stephen L. *Reflections of an Affirmative Action Baby*. New York: Basic Books, 1991.

Clecak, Peter. *America's Quest for the Ideal Self: Dissent and Fulfillment in the 60s and 70s*. New York: Oxford University Press, 1983.

Cooke, Michael G. *Afro-American Literature in the Twentieth Century: The Achievement of Intimacy*. New Haven: Yale University Press, 1984.

Cripps, Thomas. *Slow Fade to Black: The Negro in American Film, 1900–1942*. New York: Oxford University Press, 1977.

———. *Making Movies Black: The Hollywood Message Movie from World War II to the Civil Rights Era*. New York: Oxford University Press, 1993.

Crouch, Stanley. *Notes of a Hanging Judge: Essays and Reviews, 1979–1989*. New York: Oxford University Press, 1990.

Cruse, Harold. *The Crisis of the Negro Intellectual: An Historical Analysis of the Failure of Black Leadership*. New York: William Morrow, 1967; repr. 1984.

———. *Plural but Equal: Blacks and Minorities in America's Plural Society*. New York: William Morrow, 1987.

Davis, George, and Glegg Watson. *Black Life in Corporate America: Swimming in the Mainstream*. Garden City, N.Y.: Anchor/Doubleday, 1982.

Davis, Mike. *Prisoners of the American Dream: Politics and Economy in the History of the U.S. Working Class*. London and New York: Verso, 1986.

De Jongh, James. *Vicious Modernism: Black Harlem and the Literary Imagination*. New York: Cambridge University Press, 1990.

Denisoff, R. Serge. *Solid Gold: The Popular Record Industry*. New York: Routledge, 1975.

Dittmer, John. *Black Georgia in the Progressive Era, 1900–1920*. Urbana: University of Illinois Press, 1977.

Drake, St. Clair, and Horace Cayton. *Black Metropolis*. New York: Harcourt, Brace, 1945; rev. ed., 1962.

Du Bois, W. E. B. *Against Racism: Unpublished Essays, Papers, Addresses, 1887–1961, W. E. B. Du Bois*. Edited by Herbert Aptheker. Amherst: University of Massachusetts Press, 1985.

———. *Du Bois: Writings*. Edited by Nathan I. Huggins. New York: Viking Press, 1986.

Eagles, Charles, ed. *The Civil Rights Movement in America*. Jackson: University Press of Mississippi, 1986.

Early, Gerald, ed. *Lure and Loathing: Essays on Race, Identity, and the Ambivalence of Assimilation* . New York: Allan Lane, 1993.

Echols, Alice. *Daring to Be Bad: Radical Feminism in America, 1969–1975*. Minneapolis: University of Minnesota Press, 1989.

Elkins, Stanley. *Slavery: A Problem in American Institutional and Intellectual Life*. 3d ed., rev. Chicago: University of Chicago Press, 1976; orig. pub. 1959.

Ellison, Ralph. *Going to the Territory*. New York: Random House, 1986.

Epstein, Dena. *Sinful Tunes and Spirituals: Black Folk Music to the Civil War*. Urbana: University of Illinois Press, 1977.

Evans, Sara. *Personal Politics: The Roots of Women's Liberation in the Civil Rights Movement and the New Left*. New York: Alfred A. Knopf, 1979.

Ewen, Stuart. *All Consuming Images: The Politics of Style in Contemporary Culture*. New York: Basic Books, 1988.

Foner, Eric. *Reconstruction: America's Unfinished Revolution, 1863–1877*. New York: Harper & Row, 1988.

Fox-Genovese, Elizabeth. *Feminism without Illusions: A Critique of Individualism*. Chapel Hill: University of North Carolina Press, 1991.

Frazier, E. Franklin. *The Negro Family in the United States*. Chicago: University of Chicago Press, 1939; rev. and abr. ed., 1966.

———. *Black Bourgeoisie*. Glencoe, Ill.: Free Press, 1957.

———. *The Negro Family in America*. New York: Macmillan, 1957.

Frith, Simon. *Sound Effects: Youth, Leisure, and the Politics of Rock and Roll*. New York: Vintage, 1981.

Gates, Henry Louis, Jr. *Figures in Black: Words, Signs, and the Racial Self*. New York: Oxford University Press, 1987.

———. *The Signifying Monkey*. New York: Oxford University Press, 1988.

————. *Loose Canons: Notes on the Culture Wars*. New York: Oxford University Press, 1992.

Gatewood, Willard. *Aristocrats of Color: The Black Elite, 1880- 1990*. Bloomington: Indiana University Press, 1991.

Gayle, Addison, Jr. *The Way of the New World: The Black Novel in America*. Garden City, N.Y.: Anchor/Doubleday, 1975.

Genovese, Eugene D. *Roll, Jordan, Roll: The World the Slaves Made*. New York: Pantheon, 1974.

Giddings, Paula. *Where and When I Enter: The Impact of Black Women on Race and Sex*. New York: William Morrow, 1984.

Gilder, George. *Wealth and Poverty*. New York: Basic Books, 1981.

Gitlin, Todd. *The Whole World Is Watching*. New York: Simon & Schuster, 1979.

————. *The Sixties: Years of Hope, Days of Rage*. New York: Bantam, 1987.

Glazer, Nathan. *Disaffirmative Action*. New York: Free Press, 1974.

————. *Affirmative Discrimination*. New York: Basic Books, 1975; repr. 1987.

Graham, Hugh Davis. *The Civil Rights Era: Origins and Development of National Policy, 1960–1972*. New York: Oxford University Press, 1990.

Greene, Lorenzo. *Working with Carter G. Woodson, the Father of Black History: A Diary, 1928–1930*. Baton Rouge: Louisiana State University Press, 1989.

Gutman, Herbert. *The Black Family in Slavery and Freedom, 1725–1925*. New York: Pantheon, 1976.

Halpern, Stephen C., ed. *The Future of Our Liberties*. Westport, Conn.: Greenwood Press, 1982.

Hamby, Alonzo. *Liberalism and Its Challengers*. New York: Oxford University Press, 1984.

Harlan, Louis. *Booker T. Washington*, vol. 1, *The Making of a Black Leader, 1856–1901*; vol 2, *The Wizard of Tuskegee, 1901–1915*. New York: Oxford University Press, 1972 and 1983.

Harris, William H. *The Harder We Run: Black Workers since the Civil War*. New York: Oxford University Press, 1982.

Harrison, Alferdteen, ed., *Black Exodus: The Great Migration from the American South*. Jackson: University Press of Mississippi, 1991.

Hemenway, Robert. *Zora Neale Hurston: A Literary Biography*. Urbana: University of Illinois Press, 1981.

Henderson, David. *Jimi Hendrix: Voodoo Child of the Aquarian Age*. Garden City, N.Y.: Doubleday, 1978.

Henri, Florette. *Black Migration: Movement North, 1900–1920*. Garden City, N.Y.: Anchor/Doubleday 1976.

Henry, Charles P. *Culture and African American Politics*. Bloomington: Indiana University Press, 1990.

Hernton, Calvin C. *The Sexual Mountain and Black Women Writers*. Garden City, N.Y.: Doubleday, 1987.

Himes, Chester. *Quality of Pain*. New York: Random House, 1975.

hooks, bell. *Arn't I a Woman? Black Women and Feminism*. Boston: South End Press, 1981.

———. *Talking Back: Thinking Feminist, Thinking Black*. Boston: South End Press, 1989.

———. *Black Looks: Race and Representation*. Boston: South End Press, 1992.

Huggins, Nathan I. *Harlem Renaissance*. New York: William Morrow, 1972.

———. *Afro-American Studies: A Report to the Ford Foundation*. New York: Ford Foundation, Office of Reports, 1985.

Hurston, Zora Neale. *Dust Tracks on the Road: An Autobiography*. 2d ed. Edited by Robert Hemenway. Urbana: University of Illinois Press, 1984; orig. pub. 1942.

Jameson, Fredric, et al. *The 60's without Apology*. Minneapolis: University of Minneasota Press, 1984.

Jaynes, Gerald David. *Branches without Roots: Genesis of the Black Working Class in the American South, 1862–1882*. New York: Oxford University Press, 1986.

Jaynes, Gerald David, and Robin M. Williams, Jr., eds. *A Common Destiny: Blacks and American Society*. Washington, D.C.: National Academy Press, 1989.

Jhally, Sut, and Justin Lewis. *Enlightened Racism: The Cosby Show, Audiences, and the Myth of the American Dream*. Boulder, Colo.: Westview, 1992.

Johnson, Charles. *The Oxherding Tale*. New York: Grove Press, 1982.

———. *Being and Race: Black Writing since 1970*. Bloomington: Indiana University Press, 1988.

———. *Middle Passage*. New York: Antheneum, 1990.

Jordan, June. *Some Changes*. New York: Dutton, 1970.

———. *Civil Wars*. Boston: Beacon Press, 1976.

Kauffman, Jonathan. *Broken Alliance: The Turbulent Times between Blacks and Jews in America*. New York: Scribner, 1988.

Kaus, Mickey. *The End of Equality*. New York: Basic Books, 1992.

Kelley, Robin D. G. *Hammer and Hoe: Alabama Communists during the Great Depression*. Chapel Hill: University of North Carolina Press, 1990.

Kellner, Bruce. *The Harlem Renaissance: An Historical Dictionary for the Era*. New York: Metheun, 1987.

King, Martin Luther, Jr. *Stride toward Freedom: The Montgomery Story*. New York: Harper & Row, 1958.

———. *Where Do We Go from Here: Chaos or Community?* Boston: Beacon Press, 1968.

Kirby, John B. *Black Americans in the Roosevelt Era: Liberalism and Race*. Knoxville: University of Tennessee Press, 1980.

Landry, Bart. *The New Black Middle Class*. Berkeley: University of California Press, 1987.

Lasch, Christopher. *Haven in a Heartless World: The Family Besieged*. New York: Basic Books, 1977.

———. *The Culture Of Narcissism: American Life in an Age of Diminishing Expectations*. New York: W. W. Norton, 1979.

———. *The Minimal Self: Pyschic Survival in Troubled Times*. New York: W. W. Norton, 1984.

———. *The True and Only Heaven: Progress and Its Critics*. New York: W. W. Norton, 1991.

Lemann, Nicholas. *The Promised Land: The Great Black Migration and How It Changed America*. New York: Alfred A. Knopf, 1991.

Lester, Julius. *Revolutionary Notes*. New York: Grove Press, 1969.

———. *Search for the New Land*. New York: Dial Press, 1969.

———. *All Is Well*. New York: William Morrow, 1976.

———. *Do Lord Remember Me*. New York: Holt, Rinehart Winston, 1984.

———. *Lovesong: On Becoming a Jew*. New York: Henry Holt, 1988.

———. *Falling Pieces of the Broken Sky*. New York: Arcade Press, 1990.

———, ed. *The Seventh Son: The Thought and Writings of W. E. B. Du Bois*, vol. 1. New York: Random House, 1971.

Levine, Lawrence. *Black Culture and Black Consciousnesss: Afro-American Folk Thought from Slavery to Freedom*. New York: Oxford University Press, 1977.

Lewis, David Levering. *When Harlem Was in Vogue*. New York: Alfred A. Knopf, 1981.

Lincoln, Eric. *The Black Muslims in America*. Boston: Beacon Press, 1961.

Logan, Rayford W., ed. *What the Negro Wants*. Chapel Hill: University of North Carolina Press, 1944.

McFeely, William. *Frederick Douglass*. New York: W. W. Norton, 1991.

Mandle, Jay. *The Roots of Black Poverty: The Plantation Economy after the Civil War*. Durham, N.C.: Duke University Press, 1978.

———. *Not Slave, Not Free: The African American Economic Experience since the Civil War*. Durham, N.C.: Duke University Press, 1992.

Marable, Manning. *Blackwater: Historical Studies in Race, Class Consciousness, and Revolution*. Dayton, Ohio: Black Praxis Press, 1981.

———. *Black American Politics*. London and New York: Verso, 1985; rev. ed., 1987.

———. *From Rebellion to Revolution: Afro-American Politics from Civil Rights to Black Nationalism, 1954–1985*. Jackson: University Press of Mississippi, 1987; rev. ed., 1991.

Marable, Manning, et al., eds. *The Year Left 2: Towards Rainbow Socialism. Essays on Race, Ethnicity, Class, and Gender*. London and New York: Verso, 1987.

Marcus, Greil. *Mystery Train: Images of America in Rock 'n' Roll*. New ed. New York: Penguin, 1982.

Martin, E. Waldo. *The Mind of Frederick Douglass*. Chapel Hill: University of North Carolina Press, 1985.

Matusow, Allen. *The Unraveling of America: A History of Liberalism in the 1960s*. New York: Harper & Row, 1984.

Meier, August. *Negro Thought in America 1880–1915*. Ann Arbor, Mich.: University of Michigan Press, 1990; orig. pub. 1968.

Meier, August, and Elliot Rudwick. *Black History and the Historical Profession, 1915–1980*. Urbana: University of Illinois Press, 1986.

Morris, Aldon. *The Origins of the Civil Rights Movement*. New York: Free Press, 1984.

Morrison, Toni. *Playing in the Dark: Whiteness and the Literary Imagination*. Cambridge, Mass.: Harvard University Press, 1992.

———, ed. *De-Racing Justice*. New York: Vintage, 1992.

Moses, Wilson Jeremiah. *The Golden Age of Black Nationalism, 1850–1925*. New York: Oxford University Press, 1988; orig. pub. 1978.

———. *Alexander Crummell: A Study of Civilization and Discontent*. New York: Oxford University Press, 1989.

———. *Wings over Ethiopia: Studies in Afro-American Life and Letters*. Ames: Iowa State University Press, 1990.

Moynihan, Daniel P. *The Negro Family: The Case for National Action*. Washington, D.C.: Government Printing Office, 1965.

Murray, Charles Schaar. *Crosstown Traffic: Jimi Hendrix and the Rock 'n' Roll Revolution*. New York: St. Martin's Press, 1989.

Myrdal, Gunnar. *An American Dilemma: The Negro Problem and Modern Democracy*. 2 vols. New York: Pantheon, 1972; orig. pub. 1944.

Naison, Mark. *Communists in Harlem during the Depression*. New York: Grove Press, 1984.

Namarato, Michael, ed. *Have We Overcome?* Jackson: University Press of Mississippi, 1981.

Neiman, Donald G. *Promises to Keep: African Americans and the Constitutional Order, 1776 to the Present*. New York: Oxford University Press, 1991.

Novick, Peter. *That Noble Dream: The "Objectivity Question" and the American Historical Profession*. New York: Cambridge University Press, 1988.

O'Hare, William P., et al., eds. *African Americans in the Nineties*. Washington, D.C.: Population Reference Bureau, 1991.

O'Neill, William L. *Coming Apart: An Informal History of the 1960's*. New York: Times Mirror, 1971.

Painter, Nell Irvin. *Exodusters: Black Migration to Kansas after Reconstruction*. New York: Alfred A. Knopf, 1976.

Palmer, Robert. *Deep Blues: A Musical and Cultural History of the Mississippi Delta*. New York: Penguin, 1981.

Pareles, Jon, and Patricia Romanowski, eds. *The Rolling Stone Encyclopedia of Rock and Roll*. New York: Harmony, 1983.

Peck, Abe. *Uncovering the Sixties: The Life and Times of the Underground Press*. New York: Pantheon, 1985.

Peellaert, Guy, and Nik Cohn. *Rock Dreams: Rock 'n' Roll for Your Eyes*. New York: Harmony, 1982.

Pells, Richard. *The Liberal Mind in a Conservative Age: American Intellectuals in the 1940s and 1950s*. New York: Harper & Row, 1985.

Platt, Anthony M. *E. Franklin Frazier Reconsidered*. New Brunswick, N.J.: Rutgers University Press, 1991.

Raboteau, Albert J. *Slave Religion: The "Invisible Institution" in the Antebellum South*. New York: Oxford University Press, 1978.

Rampersad, Arnold. *The Art and Imagination of W. E. B. Du Bois*. New York: Schocken, 1990; orig. pub. 1976.

———. *The Life of Langston Hughes*, vol. 1, *1902–1941: I, Too, Sing America*; vol. 2, *1941–1967: I Dream a World*. New York: Oxford University Press, 1986 and 1988.

Rapping, Elayne. *Through a Looking Glass: Non-Fiction Television*. Boston: South End Press, 1987.

Record, Wilson. *The Negro and the Communist Party*. New York: Antheneum, 1971; orig. pub. 1956.

Reed, Adolph L. *The Jesse Jackson Phenomenon*. New York: Cambridge University Press, 1989.

Roediger, David. *The Wages of Whiteness: Race and the Making of the American Working Class*. London and New York: Verso, 1991.

Schuyler, George. *Black and Conservative*. New Rochelle, N.Y.: Arlington House Publishers, 1966; repr. 1971.

Seidman, Steven. *Embattled Eros: Sexual Politics and Ethics in Contemporary America*. New York: Routledge, 1992.

Siegel, Frederick F. *Troubled Journey: From Pearl Harbor to Ronald Reagan*. New York: Hill and Wang, 1984.

Sigelman, Lee, and Susan Welch. *Black Americans Views of Racial Inequality: The Dream Deferred*. New York: Cambridge University Press, 1991.

Sitkoff, Harvard. *A New Deal For Blacks: The Emergence of Civil Rights as a National Issue*, vol. 1, *The Depression Decade*. New York: Oxford University Press, 1978.

———. *The Struggle for Black Equality, 1954–1992*. Rev. ed. New York: Hill and Wang, 1993; orig. pub. 1981.

Sklar, Robert. *Movie-Made America*. New York: Harper & Row, 1975.

Sowell, Thomas. *Ethnic Minorities: A History*. New York: William Morrow, 1982.

———. *Civil Rights: Myth or Reality?* New York: William Morrow, 1983.

———. *Preferential Policies: An International Perspective*. New York: William Morrow, 1990.

Steele, Shelby. *The Content of Our Character: A New Vision of Race in America*. New York: St. Martin's Press, 1990.

Tate, Greg. *Flyboy in the Buttermilk: Essays on Contemporary America*. New York: Simon & Schuster, 1992.

Thelwell, Michael. *Duties, Pleasures, and Conflicts: Essays in Struggle*. Amherst: University of Massachusetts Press, 1987.

Toll, Robert C. *Blacking Up: The Minstrel Show in Nineteenth- Century America*. New York: Oxford University Press, 1974.

Toll, William. *The Resurgence of Race: Black Social theory from Reconstruction to the Pan-African Conferences*. Philadelphia: Temple University Press, 1979.

Trotter, Joe, ed. *The Great Migration in Historical Perspective: New Dimensions of Race, Class, and Gender*. Bloomington: Indiana University Press, 1991.

Udom, E. U. Essien. *Black Nationalism: A Search for Identity in America*. Chicago: University of Chicago Press, 1962.

Van Deburg, William L. *New Day in Babylon: The Black Power Movement and American Culture, 1965–1975*. Chicago: University of Chicago Press, 1992.

Walker, Alice. *Meridian*. New York: Harcourt, Brace, Jovanovich, 1975.

———. *The Third Life of Grange Copeland*. New York: Harcourt, Brace, Jovanovich, 1976.

———. *In My Mother's Garden*. New York: Harcourt, Brace, Jovanovich, 1984.

Walker, Margaret Alexander. *Richard Wright: Daemonic Genius*. New York: Amistad/Warner Books, 1988.

Wallace, Michele. *Black Macho and the Myth of the Superwoman*. New York: William Morrow, 1978; repr. London and New York: Verso, 1990.

———. *Black Popular Culture: A Project by Michele Wallace*. Edited by Gina Dent. New York and Seattle: Dia Center for the Arts and Bay Press, 1992.

Weisbrot, Robert. *Freedom Bound: A History of America's Civil Rights Movement*. New York: W. W. Norton, 1990.

Weiss, Nancy. *Whitney M. Young, Jr., and the Struggle for Civil Rights*. Princeton: Princeton University Press, 1989.

West, Cornel. *Prophesy Deliverance! An Afro-American Revolutionary Christianity*. Philadelphia: Westminster Press, 1982.

———. *Prophetic Fragments*. Grand Rapids, Mich., and Trenton, N.J.: Erdmanns Publishing Company and Africa World Press, 1988.

Williams, Juan. *Eyes on the Prize: America's Civil Rights Years 1954–1965*. New York: Viking Press, 1987.

Wilson, William Julius. *The Declining Significance of Race*. Chicago: University of Chicago Press, 1978.

———. *The Truly Disadvantaged: The Inner City, the Underclass, and Public Policy*. Chicago: University of Chicago Press, 1987.

Wintz, Cary D. *Black Culture and the Harlem Renaissance*. Houston: Rice University Press, 1988.

Wright, Richard. *Uncle Tom's Children*. New York: Harper & Row, 1940.

———. *Native Son*. New York: Harper & Row, 1940.

———. *Black Boy*. New York: Harper & Row, 1942.

———. *American Hunger*. New York: Harper & Row, 1974.

Woodson, Carter G. *The Mis-Education of the Negro*. Washington, 1933.

Young, James O. *Black Writers of the Thirties*. Baton Rouge: Louisiana State University Press, 1973.

INDEX